Research in Social Work series

Series Editors: **Anna Gupta**, Royal Holloway, University of London, UK and **John Gal**, Hebrew University of Jerusalem, Israel

---

Published together with the European Social Work Research Association (ESWRA), this series examines current, progressive and innovative research applications of familiar ideas and models in international social work research.

Also available in the series:

Adoption from Care
Edited by **Tarja Pösö, Marit Skivenes** and **June Thoburn**

Interprofessional Collaboration and Service User Participation
Edited by **Kirsi Juhila, Tanja Dall, Christopher Hall** and **Juliet Koprowska**

The Settlement House Movement Revisited
Edited by **John Gal, Stefan Köngeter** and **Sarah Vicary**

Social Work and the Making of Social Policy
Edited by **Ute Klammer, Simone Leiber** and **Sigrid Leitner**

Research and the Social Work Picture
By **Ian Shaw**

Find out more at:

policy.bristoluniversitypress.co.uk/
research-in-social-work

Research in Social Work series

Series Editors: **Anna Gupta**, Royal Holloway, University of London, UK and **John Gal**, Hebrew University of Jerusalem, Israel

---

Forthcoming in the series:

*Migration and Social Work:
Approaches, Visions and Challenges*
Edited by **Emilio J. Gómez-Ciriano**, **Elena Cabiati** and **Sofia Dedotsi**

*The Origins of Social Work:
Western Roots, International Futures*
By **Mark Henrickson**

Find out more at:

policy.bristoluniversitypress.co.uk/
research-in-social-work

Research in Social Work series

Series Editors: **Anna Gupta**, Royal Holloway, University of London, UK and **John Gal**, Hebrew University of Jerusalem, Israel

---

International Editorial Board:

Andrés Arias Astray, Complutense University of Madrid, Spain
Isobel Bainton, Policy Press, UK
Inge Bryderup, Aalborg University, Denmark
Tony Evans, Royal Holloway, University of London, UK
Hannele Forsberg, University of Tampere, Finland
John Gal, Hebrew University of Jerusalem, Israel
Anna Gupta, Royal Holloway, University of London, UK
Todd I. Herrenkohl, University of Michigan, US
Ephrat Huss, Ben-Gurion University of the Negev, Israel
Stefan Köngeter, Eastern Switzerland University of Applied Science (OST), Switzerland
Manohar Pawar, Charles Sturt University, Australia
Ian Shaw, National University of Singapore and University of York, UK
Alessandro Sicora, University of Trento, Italy
Darja Zaviršek, University of Ljubljana, Slovenia

Find out more at:

policy.bristoluniversitypress.co.uk/research-in-social-work

INVOLVING SERVICE USERS IN SOCIAL WORK EDUCATION, RESEARCH AND POLICY
A Comparative European Analysis

Edited by
Kristel Driessens and Vicky Lyssens-Danneboom

First published in Great Britain in 2023 by

Policy Press, an imprint of
Bristol University Press
University of Bristol
1-9 Old Park Hill
Bristol
BS2 8BB
UK
t: +44 (0)117 374 6645
e: bup-info@bristol.ac.uk

Details of international sales and distribution partners are available at
policy.bristoluniversitypress.co.uk

© Bristol University Press 2023

British Library Cataloguing in Publication Data
A catalogue record for this book is available from the British Library

ISBN 978-1-4473-5832-9 hardcover
ISBN 978-1-4473-5833-6 paperback
ISBN 978-1-4473-5834-3 ePub
ISBN 978-1-4473-5835-0 ePdf

The right of Kristel Driessens and Vicky Lyssens-Danneboom to be identified as editors of this work has been asserted by them in accordance with the Copyright, Designs and Patents Act 1988.

All rights reserved: no part of this publication may be reproduced, stored in a retrieval system, or transmitted in any form or by any means, electronic, mechanical, photocopying, recording, or otherwise without the prior permission of Bristol University Press.

Every reasonable effort has been made to obtain permission to reproduce copyrighted material. If, however, anyone knows of an oversight, please contact the publisher.

The statements and opinions contained within this publication are solely those of the editors and contributors and not of the University of Bristol or Bristol University Press. The University of Bristol and Bristol University Press disclaim responsibility for any injury to persons or property resulting from any material published in this publication.

Bristol University Press and Policy Press work to counter discrimination on grounds of gender, race, disability, age and sexuality.

Cover design: David Worth

Contents

List of figures and tables		ix
Notes on contributors		x
Acknowledgements		xix
1	Introduction *Kristel Driessens and Vicky Lyssens-Danneboom*	1

PART I Collaborative models in social work education

2	The gap-mending concept: theory and practice *Cecilia Heule, Marcus Knutagård and Arne Kristiansen*	11
3	Mending gaps in social work education in the UK *Helen Casey and Peter Beresford*	23
4	Service users as tandem partners in social work education *Kristel Driessens, Vicky Lyssens-Danneboom, Wendy Peeters, Cindy Van Geldorp, Piet Vandenhende, Hilde Bloemen, Caro Bridts, Sascha Van Gijzel and Henrike Kowalk*	35
5	Service users as supervisors in social work education: mending the gap of power relations *Mette Fløystad Kvammen and Tabitha Wright Nielsen*	49
6	Involving students with mental health experience in social work education *Hubert Kaszyński and Olga Maciejewska*	61
7	The Living Library in social work education *Robin Sen, Marianne Nylund, Ali Hayward, Rahul Pardasani, William Rivera and Michelle Kaila*	73
8	Creating a platform together for the voice of the service user: inspiration for organising an event together with service users *Ruth Strudwick, Suzanna Pickering and Joep Holten*	85
9	Reflections on inspiring conversations in social work education: the voices of Scottish experts by experience and Italian students *Susan Levy and Elena Cabiati with John Dow, Elinor Dowson, Keith Swankie and Gil Martin*	97
10	Joint workshops with students and service users in social work education: experiences from Esslingen, Germany *Thomas Heidenreich and Marion Laging*	109
11	Service users, students and staff: co-producing creative educational activities on a social work programme in the UK *Kieron Hatton, Kevin Holmes and Pete Shepherd*	117

PART II Collaborative models in research and policy

12 The co-researcher role in the tension between recognition, co-option and tokenism — 133
Ole Petter Askheim

13 Community of development: a model for inclusive learning, research and innovation — 145
Jean Pierre Wilken, Ellen Witteveen, Carla van Slagmaat, Sascha Van Gijzel, Jeroen Knevel, Toinette Loeffen and Els Overkamp

14 Dialogue, skills and trust: some lessons learned from co-writing with service users — 158
Sidsel Natland

15 Participatory pathways in social policymaking: between rhetoric and reality — 170
Peter Beresford and Heidi Degerickx

16 Experiential knowledge as a driver of change — 183
Har Tortike and Vicky Lyssens-Danneboom

PART III Reflective chapters

17 Experiences matter equally — 199
Henrike Kowalk and Jenny Wetterling

18 Ethical issues in the meaningful involvement of service users as co-researchers — 209
Hugh McLaughlin

19 Involving service users in social work education and research: is this structural social work? — 224
Kristel Driessens and Vicky Lyssens-Danneboom

Index — 238

List of figures and tables

Figures
2.1	Content of joint six weeks	14
11.1	A dynamic view of power	121

Tables
2.1	Example of roles given to actors in social work practice	16
4.1	Overview of methods of cooperation with service users in four institutions	43
10.1	List of service-user involvement seminars at Esslingen University	111
11.1	Service-user/carer involvement in creative activities at the University of Portsmouth	119

Notes on contributors

Ole Petter Askheim is Professor at the Faculty of Education and Social Work of Inland Norway University of Applied Sciences. His main research interests are user involvement, empowerment, co-production and disability studies.

Peter Beresford is Emeritus Professor at Brunel University London and the University of Essex, UK. He is Visiting Professor at the University of East Anglia and Edge Hill University. He has a long track record of working in the field of citizen participation as an educator, researcher, writer, service user and activist. His latest book is *Participatory Ideology: From exclusion to involvement* (Policy Press, 2021).

Hilde Bloemen is Lecturer in the Social Work educational programme at the University College Leuven-Limburg (UCLL) in Belgium. She is also a member of the research group Inclusive Society and involved in the project 'Exploring the work relationship of service users and their work-life balance'. She has conducted several other research projects on the topic of structural social work and is also a coach and trainer of service users.

Caro Bridts is a certified service user who works in non-profit organisations in the field of social cohesion and welfare. She is also involved in the Social Work curriculum of the University College Leuven-Limburg (UCLL) in Belgium, a member of the UCLL's research team Inclusive Society and is involved in the project 'Exploring the work relationship of service users and their work-life balance'.

Elena Cabiati is a social work researcher and Assistant Professor at the Catholic University of Milan, Italy. She teaches Methodology of Social Work and Intercultural Social Work in undergraduate, postgraduate and PhD programmes. She is a member of the Relational Social Work Research Centre. Her main research interests are: social work education, service-user involvement in social work education and research, intercultural social work and child protection. She is a registered social worker with fieldwork experience as a practitioner and middle-manager in child protection organisations.

Helen Casey is Lecturer with the Open University and International Coordinator with PowerUs. She is studying a PhD at Durham University. Helen's forthcoming doctoral thesis explores the impact of service-user and carer involvement in social work education. Her latest book is *The Routledge*

Handbook of Service User Involvement in Human Services Research and Education (Routledge, 2021).

Heidi Degerickx holds a PhD in Social Work and Social Welfare Studies. She worked for many years as an activist in close collaboration with self-advocates who experience poverty in the Flemish organisations where people in poverty take the floor (2000–2014). After obtaining her PhD at Ghent University (2014–2020), Belgium, she was appointed as a staff member on poverty policy at the Dutch speaking Women's Council of Belgium (2020) where she now works on the crossroads of poverty, gender and diversity.

John Dow initially worked in the Royal Air Force (RAF). After being medically discharged from flying, he held many other positions, including Senior Local Government Officer. John took early retirement due to medical issues which led to him being an in-patient for 18 weeks at a psychiatric hospital, and an out-patient for a further five years. His advocacy for the involvement and influence of those who require social services and their carers grew from his time associated with the psychiatric hospital. He was a co-founder and remains an active member of the Carers and Users Group, University of Dundee, UK.

Elinor Dowson has been an active member of the Carers and Users Group at the University of Dundee, UK, for over 10 years, a role that she finds meaningful and rewarding. Her involvement with the Carers and Users group stems from her being a family carer whose life changed when a close relative was diagnosed with a mental illness. Elinor is involved with the Scottish Recovery Network and is on the board of a mental health charity.

Kristel Driessens is Coordinator of Bind-Kracht (Strength of Ties), a collaboration of researchers, trainers/lecturers and experts by experience in poverty, with a mission to support and strengthen care providers and social workers. She is also Head of the Centre of Expertise for Strength-based Social Work at the Karel de Grote University of Applied Sciences, Belgium, where she promotes practice-based social work research. She is Associate Professor in the Master's of Social Work at the University of Antwerp, Belgium, where she teaches Society and Social Work and Social Interventions. Her passion is cooperative knowledge production with social professionals, volunteers and service users with a focus on the fight against poverty and the aim of inspiring educational programmes to work together with services users.

Kieron Hatton is Associate Lecturer in Social Work at Solent University, UK. Until 2019, he was Principal Lecturer in Social Work at Portsmouth University, UK, where he had been Head of Social Work for nine years. His main interests are contemporary social work, national and international social work, service-user involvement, participation/inclusion, social pedagogy, youth and community work and policy analysis. Kieron has published widely around these subjects.

Ali Hayward is a person with experience of disability social work services and former Development Lead for the involvement of people with experience of services in social work programmes at the Department of Sociological Studies of the University of Sheffield, UK.

Thomas Heidenreich is Professor and Vice Dean of the Faculty of Social Work, Health and Care at the University of Applied Sciences in Esslingen, Germany. His research interests are in cognitive-behavioural approaches to counselling and psychotherapy, mindfulness-based approaches, metaphors in counselling and therapy and prevention of substance abuse, and service-user involvement.

Cecilia Heule is a university teacher and a PhD candidate in the School of Social Work at Lund University, Sweden. She is one of the innovators of the Mobilisation course, which involves social work students and service users and was the start of PowerUs, which now has partners in 19 countries, with Cecilia as one of its coordinators.

Kevin Holmes is a consultant and disability activist who has developed innovative projects around service-user/carer inclusion and involvement in social work education. He was awarded an honorary fellowship by the University of Portsmouth, UK, for his contribution to social work education. He has primarily worked with the University of Portsmouth but also has links with other universities regionally and nationally. He specialises in using creative activities such as drama, film, dance, poetry and writing to enhance the student experience. He has presented at regional and national social work conferences.

Joep Holten is Lecturer and Researcher in the School of Social Work at the Amsterdam University of Applied Sciences, the Netherlands. His expertise lies in educational design and in creating courses in which students get involved with the world outside the university walls. For several courses he worked directly with experts by experience to create new ways for providing education. Recent projects include getting experts by experience involved in grading students' assignments and providing web lectures by experts by experience.

Notes on contributors

Michelle Kaila is a Bachelor of Social Services at Diaconia University of Applied Sciences, Finland, and a social counselor at MONIKU-service (Guidance for Multilingual Families) in the city of Espoo.

Hubert Kaszyński is Associate Professor, sociologist, clinical social worker, social work supervisor and Lecturer in Social Work in the Institute of Sociology at the Jagiellonian University in Krakow, Poland. He is involved in social therapy in the field of mental health. He is Vice-President of the Board of the Polish Association of Schools of Social Work, and President of the Institute of Social Therapy and Education–Association. His research focuses on social education methods for promoting mental health, as well as clinical social work, the theoretical foundation for which is the philosophy of dialogue and the personalistic paradigm in social work.

Jeroen Knevel holds a bachelor's degree in Social Work and a master's degree in Sociology and teaches at the School of Social Work of the Utrecht University of Applied Sciences, the Netherlands. He has a professional background in social work with people with intellectual disabilities. His research and teaching focus on human rights, social inclusion and people with intellectual disabilities.

Marcus Knutagärd is Associate Professor in the School of Social Work at Lund University, Sweden. His research interests include housing policy, homelessness and the importance of place for how social work is organised – its moral geography. Knutagård's research interests also concern social innovation from a welfare perspective, with a particular focus on service-user influence in practice research.

Henrike Kowalk has been using her lived experiences since 2010 in various social work practices and in educational and research programmes at the Amsterdam University of Applied Social Sciences, the Netherlands. Since 2017, her main focus is co-developing and lecturing in the Associate Degree for Experts by Experience. Apart from that, she is involved in projects organised by the municipality of Amsterdam regarding poverty policies and parent-child support teams. Currently, she is pursuing a master's degree in Comparative Cultural Analysis at the University of Amsterdam.

Arne Kristiansen is Associate Professor in the School of Social Work at Lund University, Sweden. His research interests include service-user involvement, substance abuse and homelessness. He has spent several years working as a social worker. He works closely with various service-user organisations, which he involves both in social work education and in research projects.

Mette Fløystad Kvammen is Associate Professor at the University of Agder, Norway. Her main areas of interest are empowerment, user perspective and experiential knowledge in social work education, as well as innovation in social work practice based on cooperation between service-user organisations, students and practitioners.

Marion Laging is Professor and Vice President of Education and Advanced Studies at the University of Applied Sciences in Esslingen, Germany. Her interests are international social work, comparative studies, service user-involvement and social work in the field of addiction.

Susan Levy is Senior Lecturer in Social Work in the School of Education and Social Work at the University of Dundee, UK. She is also Director of the Professional Doctorate Programmes in the Doctoral Academy. Her research focuses on disability, cultural and international social work and arts-based practice. She is Associate Editor of two journals, including the *European Journal of Social Work*.

Toinette Loeffen has a master's degree in Social Work. She is specialised in diversity and arts-based research. She works in the Participation, Care and Support Research Group (part of the Research Centre for Social Innovation) and the Institute for Social Work at the Utrecht University of Applied Sciences, the Netherlands.

Vicky Lyssens-Danneboom holds a PhD in Family Sociology and a bachelor's degree in Social Work. She works as Lecturer and Senior Researcher in the Centre of Expertise Strength-based Social Work at the Karel de Grote University of Applied Sciences, Belgium. Her expertise lies in qualitative research, client perspective, private relationships and user involvement.

Olga Maciejewska is a PhD candidate in the Institute of Sociology at the Jagiellonian University in Krakow, Poland. She is a graduate in social work, rehabilitation pedagogy and social policy. She is also Vice-President of the Institute of Social Therapy and Education – Association, and cooperates with the Polish Federation of Social Workers and Social Service Employees Unions as an advisor for education in the field of social work and cooperation with students in the field of social work. Her research interests and activities focus on promotion and protection of mental health, initiatives taken by patients, experience of trauma, the idea of strengthening the relational dimension of education and the support system. Olga is also interested in resocialisation and preventive social work.

Notes on contributors

Gil Martin is a graduate of the MSc Social Work programme at the University of Dundee, UK, and has been Lecturer in Social Work there since 2015. His focus has been around practice learning, expert-by-experience-led, rather than -involved, social work education, and considering the gap experienced between the practical and academic learning arenas. For 2017–2018 he was awarded 'Social Work Lecturer of the Year' by the Scottish Association of Social Work. He co-produced with expert by experience (EBE) Keith Swankie the letter-writing project discussed in Chapter 9 of this volume, which was awarded the Scottish Social Services Council 'Enlightened Approach to Practice Award' for 2018.

Hugh McLaughlin is Professor of Social Work at Manchester Metropolitan University, UK. His main areas of research are service-user involvement in social work education and research, critical professional practice and social work departments as learning organisations.

Sidsel Natland is Associate Professor in the Department of Social Work, Child Welfare and Social Policy at the Metropolitan University of Oslo, Norway. She holds a doctoral degree in cultural studies from the University of Bergen, Norway, where she researched violent girls. Since 2006 she has been teaching and conducting research in social work, with a special interest in social workers and the involvement of service users in research.

Tabitha Wright Nielsen is Senior Lecturer in the School of Social Work at Lund University, Sweden. Her research interests lie in social work, marginalisation, inclusion, empowerment, service-user involvement in social work education and innovation in social work.

Marianne Nylund is Senior Lecturer at the Diaconia University of Applied Sciences in Helsinki, Finland. Her research interests are community-based participatory research, community work, mutual support and volunteering.

Els Overkamp has a PhD in Social Sciences. She specialises in disability care and interprofessional collaboration. She works in the Participation, Care and Support Research Group (part of the Research Centre for Social Innovation) and the Institute for Social Work at the Utrecht University of Applied Sciences, the Netherlands.

Rahul Pardasani is a Bachelor of Social Services at the Diaconia University of Applied Sciences in Helsinki, Finland, and Talent Strategist at Yousician in Helsinki. His key interests are using ethical photography and storytelling as tools for community-based participatory research to promote positive social change.

Wendy Peeters is Lecturer at the Karel de Grote University of Applied Sciences of Antwerp, Belgium. Her expertise lies in training social work students in counselling and communication. For several years, she worked with experts by experience as tandem complementary trainers during the whole training course, Social Case Work.

Suzanna Pickering is Senior Lecturer in Social Work in the School of Social Sciences and Humanities at the University of Suffolk, UK. Her main areas of interest are inter-professional practice and learning, effective communication in social work, international social work and community development.

William Rivera is a Bachelor of Social Services at the Diaconia University of Applied Sciences in Helsinki, Finland, and a Master of Global Development and Management in Health Care at the Laurea University of Applied Sciences in Helsinki.

Robin Sen is Lecturer in Social Work in the School of Education and Social Work at the University of Dundee, UK, and Honorary Research Fellow in the Department of Sociological Studies at the University of Sheffield, UK. His research interests are children in the care system, family support, participatory research and community development.

Pete Shepherd has worked as a social worker in the statutory and voluntary sectors within the UK. Until recently, he was Senior Lecturer at the University of Portsmouth, UK. His main focus has been working with adults, but he was a key member of the academic team supporting service users to become involved in a range of activities within the programme of social work at the University of Portsmouth. He led on many creative activities and developed a range of new and innovative ways of assessing students.

Ruth Strudwick is Associate Professor and Subject Lead for Radiography and Interprofessional Learning in the School of Health and Sports Sciences at the University of Suffolk, UK. Her main areas of interest are professional cultures, interprofessional learning, service-user involvement and values-based practice.

Keith Swankie retired on ill health and became a member of the Carers and Users (CU) Group at the University of Dundee, UK. He is an active CU group member and his involvement led to his receiving the 'Winner for Non-Academic Teaching Award' in 2019, at the University of Dundee. He suffers with the life-limiting neurological disease progressive supranuclear palsy (PSP), and is an active campaigner for raising awareness of PSP. Keith has actively sourced funds from the Scottish government for research into

PSP. He enjoys sharing his experiences with future social work practitioners through his role at the University of Dundee.

Har Tortike was a cameraman and documentary filmmaker for 30 years before he started working as a freelancer in 2005 on projects in the Netherlands and Belgium based on experiential expertise as a source of social change. At first he worked with young people based on their experiences with child abuse; later this theme expanded to young people's rights. Since 2012, he has also been working with women of non-Western European descent on oppression and violence. His projects take various forms (forum theatre, video, publications, workshops), but they all aim at self-awareness and insight among participants and the public and actual change in the policy of civil society organisations, government institutions and (scientific) education.

Cindy Van Geldorp works as an EBE at the Network Against Poverty in Belgium, a network of associations wherein people in poverty take the floor. She is a peer supporter and is strongly involved in educational programmes about living in poverty. Earlier, she worked part time as an EBE at the Karel de Grote University of Applied Sciences where she co-teaches in tandem in various educational programmes. She is also involved in Bind-Kracht, and as a youngster she was a very active member in the Youth Movement of Recht Op, a poverty organisation in Antwerp, Belgium.

Sascha Van Gijzel has a master's degree in Social Work. She is a lecturer and researcher, specialised in working with experts by experience with mild intellectual disabilities. Sascha works in the Participation, Care and Support Research Group (part of the Research Centre for Social Innovation) and the Institute for Social Work at the Utrecht University of Applied Sciences, the Netherlands.

Carla van Slagmaat has a master's degree in Human and Organisational Behaviour. She is a senior lecturer, specialised in experiential knowledge. She is connected to the Participation, Care and Support Research Group (part of the Research Centre for Social Innovation) and the Institute for Social Work at the Utrecht University of Applied Sciences, the Netherlands.

Piet Vandenhende is a painter and fine artist. In his art he bears witness to a life in deep misery and to the way out of it, supported by social workers. With his creative projects he inspires students and people in vulnerable positions. He is an experience expert in Bind-Kracht (Antwerp, Belgium) and works part time in the Social Work Programme of the Leuven-Limburg University College (UCLL) and the Karel de Grote University of Applied Sciences in Antwerp.

Jenny Wetterling has been using her lived experiences since 2014 in various psychiatric and social work practices as well as in different user organisations in Sweden and internationally. She also participates in educational and research programmes at Lund University in Sweden. Since 2017, her main focus has been on developing psychiatric care that is in line with person-centred care, the different ways in which EBE can be used to improve care work and the education of staff members. She is also a registered nurse in pediatric care at Skanes University Hospital.

Jean Pierre Wilken has a PhD in Social Sciences. He is Professor of Social Work, leading the Participation, Care and Support Research Group (part of the Research Centre for Social Innovation) at the Utrecht University of Applied Sciences, the Netherlands. The research group develops knowledge for supporting persons in vulnerable positions, especially persons with disabilities, with a focus on participation and social inclusion. Jean Pierre and his colleagues have been involved in participatory action research and the community of development for many years.

Ellen Witteveen has a master's degree in Social Work. She is a senior researcher specialised in family care of people with acquired brain damage and dementia. She is connected to the Participation, Care and Support Research Group (part of the Research Centre for Social Innovation) and the Institute for Social Work at the Utrecht University of Applied Sciences, the Netherlands.

Acknowledgements

This book has a long history. Years of enthusiastic and powerful pioneering work at many locations in Europe preceded it. By writing this book, a group of researchers, lecturers and service users from all over Europe found each other and shared many experiences which we now want to share with our readers.

It goes without saying that behind every author there is usually a whole team of co-developers and supporters. Without their contributions, this book could never have been written. For our development work in Belgium, we would like to explicitly mention some supporters and ambassadors.

First and foremost, we are most grateful to the coaches of Bind-Kracht (the voluntary experts by experience) and the trainers, who have been working together for 16 years. A special word of thanks to Wim, Cindy, Piet, Melina, Monique, Roald, Marleen, Greet, Gonny, Walter, Veronique, Paul, Pascal, Martine, André, Mieke, Fauve, Anja, Eric, Kristien, Martin, Mamadou, Fatiha, Marcel, Joachim, Luc, Yola, Dinora, Aafje, Hilde, Diane, Mieblanche, Marnic, Lieve, Veerle, An, Beja, Carine, Annemie, Andy, Ellen, Heidi, our ever-enthusiastic master developer Koen Vansevenant and our academic support Tine Van Regenmortel.

A word of thanks also to the managers and teachers who jumped into this adventure: the general directors of the Karel de Grote University of Applied Sciences Veerle Hendrickx and Dirk Broos, the director of Welfare and Care Peter Brants, the heads of social work education Veerle Van Gestel and Rudy Verhoeven, and of social education care Katrien Verlinden and Mario Haine, who have anchored this educational model in their curricula. Also a heartfelt thank you to the heads of healthcare and education who supported the experiments in their curricula, and last but not least to all the teachers and researchers who have guided us.

Without additional funding we would not have been able to realise the numerous projects: we recognise Cera for the basic funding at the start, the Flemish government for the subsidy, the Karel de Grote University of Applied Sciences for the extra support through the Innovation Fund for the didactic developments and via the Valorisation Fund for this book project. and the European Social Fund that supported the international exchange and the creation of a database of cooperation models.

At the international forum, we are grateful to the European Social Work Research Association for the opportunity to develop a powerful network of researchers and professors led by a special interest group, 'Service Users Involvement in Education and Research'. Many members of this network have written a chapter in this book. We also thank PowerUs for involving us in their network. The collaboration with initiators Cecilia and Arne made it possible for us to start this book project. A special word of thanks also to all the participants of our working conference in Antwerp, and in particular to the large number of service users present. Their input enabled two peer authors to write a reflexive chapter on the meaning of participation from the viewpoint of the service users themselves.

Finally, we would also like to express our gratitude to the contributors for their invested time and commitment to this project and their willingness to share their experiences and inspire others. We are pleased to have been able to bring together a colourful mix of innovators: lecturers, researchers and service users who took up the challenge of getting to know each other and jointly writing a chapter about their comparable models of collaboration. And last but not least, we would also like to thank our publisher, Policy Press, who from the beginning believed in this particular project and continued to encourage us to write this book as non-native speakers.

1

Introduction

Kristel Driessens and Vicky Lyssens-Danneboom

Over the last three decades, governments in Europe and North America have increasingly emphasised and promoted user involvement in the planning, delivery and evaluation of social and health services (Omeni et al, 2014). Many factors drive the focus on user involvement, such as an increased focus on evidence-based practice and user-centred services, incentives offered by legislation, incentives from the user movement and professional development incentives (Waterson and Morris, 2005). The involvement of service users has become an important cornerstone of social practice and policy, but is also growing common in research and education, particularly in medical education, mental health nursing and social work (Rhodes, 2012). The rapid growth of the concept of user involvement in education shows in the emergence of many innovative collaborative practices across Europe and beyond, the scope and breadth of which differ across educational and national contexts. Whether sustained or developed on an ad hoc and experimental basis, all practices reflect a shift in professional theory and practice from passive to active models of working with vulnerable groups (Schön, 2015).

Although there is still a lot of work to be done with regard to evaluating the longer-term impact of user involvement on the practice of (social work) students (Chiapparini, 2016), it is beyond doubt that engaging service users in social work education contributes to professional learning and academic teaching. Because of their lived experiences, service users bring an eye-opening and clarifying perspective on what it means to live with disease, oppression or exclusion. They have a unique insight into what support is needed, which approaches work, and can provide valuable feedback on their personal experience with social services and professionals. Service users' rich experiences and real-world challenges offer major opportunities for equipping students with core skills and knowledge and preparing them for competent practice (Gutman et al, 2012; Dill et al, 2016). Besides improving the quality of social services and contributing to the professional development of future social professionals, user involvement is also considered a powerful means to empower vulnerable groups and end social exclusion and discrimination (Tanner et al, 2017; McKeever, 2021).

Despite its undisputable importance and its emergence as one of the most important new drivers within government policy in a number of countries, a structurally embedded involvement and participation of service users is still relatively uncommon in the European programmes of social work at the University (of Applied Sciences). As of writing here, the UK is the only country where service-user involvement is a mandatory part of the social work curriculum (Beresford and Croft, 2004; Anghel and Ramon, 2009; Askheim, 2011; Robinsons and Webber, 2013). This is mainly due to a number of organisational, legal and ethical issues and dilemmas surrounding service-user involvement, concerning, for instance, organisational space, a proper statute, fair compensation and monitoring, training and continuity. In order for the method of service-user participation to be disseminated to and integrated into more schools of social work, and in order for service users to make a real difference to social work training, research and practice, these shared practical and ethical challenges need addressing.

This book is the final part of a transnational research project that was subsidised by the European Social Fund (ESF). The research project has been conducted by the Karel de Grote University of Applied Sciences in Antwerp, Belgium, in cooperation with the School of Social Work of the Lund University, Sweden. The primary objective of the ESF project was to contribute to the further development and a wider dissemination of good models of cooperation with service users in social work education, research and policy throughout Europe.

Content of the book

The book collects many inspiring experiences of collaborative practices within education, research and policy throughout Europe. What is innovative and distinguishes this work from existing publications is its explicit, overarching transnational approach. Instead of presenting single local practices, this book contains co-written descriptions of similar collaborative models that have been implemented in different European countries. Contributors describe, across borders, how their collaborative models work, from which value framework they depart and what their added value is from a user, teacher and student perspective. In most cases, this approach has been successful.

Besides the range of collaborative models covered, the book offers some reflective chapters on ethical dilemmas, the perception of service users and the connection with structural social work. The origin and development of the cooperation models, the values-driven character of the cooperation, the ethical dilemmas as well as the organisational conditions for anchoring the described initiatives are reviewed. An important strength of the book lies in the inclusion of the unique views and voices of the service users. Service users have not only been asked about their experience but have been involved in the entire writing process and have written a reflective chapter on the meaning of participation. Their viewpoints, alongside those of academics and students, add further depth to the book.

Note on the use of terms

Together with the increasing involvement and participation of people with experiential knowledge, a range of terms to appoint these people has been developed. The term 'service user' is widely used across both health and social work to describe anyone using health and/or social work services, although 'patient', 'client' and 'carer' are also commonplace . More recently, alternative labels like 'experiential experts' or 'experts by experience' have gained popularity for their empowering focus on an individual's experiential knowledge base instead of summoning an image of a passive individual receiving services. In his article 'What's in a name: "client", "patient", "customer", "consumer", "expert by experience", "service user" – what's next?', Hugh McLaughlin (2009) critically considered the terms most commonly used and found each to be somewhat problematic. He suggests allowing those who use services to decide for themselves how they wish to be described, and stresses that, whichever label we adopt as social professionals, lecturers and researchers, we have to be well aware that the language we use is imbued with meaning and that terms can create a particular perception of an individual that may be positive and enriching or harmful and stigmatising.

For the purpose of the book, we, as editors, have systematically used the term 'service user', as over the last ten years it has become part of the vocabulary of social work and social care. Despite its mainstream acceptance in both practice and literature, we have deliberately chosen not to impose the term service user on our contributors for two main reasons. First, we did not wish to force them into a language or terminology with which they may not be entirely familiar or which they may not be supportive of within their own specific national or institutional context. Second, in the absence of a shared understanding of the groups and individuals identified by the term service user, we wanted to leave room for a rich variety of experiences and corresponding labels. However, in the interests of clarity, we did ask all authors to make the terminology adopted by them in their chapters explicit.

Structure of the book

The book is divided in three main parts. Parts 1 and 2 each describe several collaborative models in social work education, research and policy. Part 3 comprises three reflective chapters. All chapters have been written by lecturers, researchers and service users, some collaboratively, others individually. Each chapter will now be briefly introduced.

In Chapter 2, Cecilia Heule, Marcus Knutagård and Arne Kristiansen present the Mobilisation course, a gap-mending course developed at Lund University in Sweden in which social work students and service users study together. A central theme in this chapter is how community and trust can be arranged or choreographed between groups that might have prejudice towards each other. The chapter offers a number of strategies for gap-mending reflections.

Chapter 3 explores the context in the UK around the involvement of service users and carers for the improvement of social work education and how it has inspired international developments. Building on the previous chapter, Helen Casey and Peter Beresford provide a summary of how 'mend the gap' was introduced in the UK. Together the Lund and UK chapters demonstrate the strength of the approach and diverse contexts in which it has been applied.

In Chapter 4, Kristel Driessens, Vicky Lyssens-Danneboom, Wendy Peeters, Cindy Van Geldorp, Piet Vandenhende, Hilde Bloemen, Caro Bridts, Sascha Van Gijzel and Henrike Kowalk describe and analyse co-teaching in tandem in both Belgium and the Netherlands. The analysis focuses on values, objectives, programmes and actions, evaluation and organisational conditions.

In Chapter 5, Mette Fløystad Kvammen and Tabitha Wright Nielsen describe how service users are involved as supervisors in social work education in Sweden and Norway, and how they try to solve dilemmas and problems related to power, inequality and the creation of knowledge within the space of social work education.

In Chapter 6 Hubert Kaszyński and Olga Maciejewska present a Krakow training project to promote mental health. The project is based on the importance of direct contact with people experiencing deep emotional difficulties for overcoming the stigma associated with mental health problems and shaping professional attitudes of social workers.

Robin Sen, Marianne Nylund, Ali Hayward, Rahul Pardasani, William Rivera and Michelle Kaila describe in Chapter 7 two Human Library events in the United Kingdom and Finland. The Human Library method is used globally as an anti-oppressive tool to bring together representatives of different minorities in society who volunteer to share their life stories and experiences in order to help others overcome prejudice using active dialogue based on respect. The focus of the chapter is on how a Human Library event can be used in teaching social work.

Chapter 8 describes annual conferences that are run in partnership with service users in the United Kingdom and the Netherlands. Ruth Strudwick, Suzanne Pickering and Joep Holten give a description of both of the conferences and share their experiences of organising an event together with service users.

Introduction

For many years, experts by experience (EBE) have participated in the learning journeys of social work students at the University of Dundee, Scotland, and the Catholic University of Milan, Italy. Drawing on the voices of three EBE and three undergraduate students, Chapter 9 explores the experience and impact of user involvement on student learning, challenging perceptions of service users, and students at a personal level. Susan Levy and Elena Cabiati use the concept of 'inspiring conversations' as a conduit for guiding the future inclusion of tacit knowledge in social work education across Europe.

In Chapter 10, Thomas Heidenreich and Marion Laging discuss experiences from workshops that were conducted with service users and students in the B.A. course Social Work in Esslingen, Germany. Service-user groups included in the seminars were participants with mental disorders or criminal records as well as single parents. Typical workshop themes were 'What is good social work?' and 'Social work between help and coercion'.

Chapter 11 looks at the work of the Social Work Inclusion Group (SWIG) at the University of Portsmouth, UK. The most innovative work with which members of SWIG are engaged is based around co-producing creative artefacts with the social work students. This may involve film, dance, theatre or poetry and is based on the narratives of the service users and their accounts of their lived experiences. Kieron Hatton provides a theoretical framework built around social pedagogy, and presents individual accounts from service users, students and academic staff of their experience of this work.

In Chapter 12, Peter Ole Askheim closely examines the tensions and dilemmas that may arise when people with service-user experiences are involved in the research process. Based on the main challenges that appear, this chapter discusses actions to resolve tensions and dilemmas in a constructive way, so that cooperation can lead to a democratisation of knowledge production.

In Chapter 13, Jean Pierre Wilken and his colleagues from the Utrecht University of Applied Sciences in the Netherlands present the model of the community of development (CoD). In a CoD, professionals, service users, other stakeholders and researchers engage in a process of learning, action and reflection with the specific aim of improving a professional practice. The chapter describes the main methodological features and the results of an analysis of the effects of the model, referring to multiple CoDs in different domains of social work and healthcare.

Chapter 14 discusses the involvement of service users in one specific phase of the research process: text production. Sidsel Natland presents two cases where she, as a conventional researcher, cooperated closely with service users to produce texts disseminating results from a research project. The author critically examines the relations between the collaborating partners, barriers in the writing process regarding competencies and the time consumed, and also how to cope with users' expectations, including their willingness to take a distanced/critical approach to the data.

In Chapter 15, Peter Beresford and Heidi Degerickx engage in a critical investigation of the participation of marginalised groups in social policymaking processes. They focus on two historical cases: the disabled people's movement in the UK in the 1970s and the fourth world movement in the 1990s in Belgium. Both zoom in on how the concerned people themselves, in a political dialogue with many other societal stakeholders, challenged the pejorative rhetoric on their impairment or their poverty towards a rhetoric of participation, equality and respect from a human rights perspective.

In Chapter 16, Har Tortike and Vicky Lyssens-Danneboom present three types of projects: forum theatre, video projects and participation projects. Through forum theatre and video projects, the participants share their lived experiences with oppression. In participation projects, young people in youthcare have direct influence on the policy of institutions.

In Chapter 17, Henrike Kowalk and Jenny Wetterling explore, from their viewpoint as experts by experience, the factors that promote and hinder service-user involvement in education and research. This chapter is the result of their own work experiences and a meeting in Antwerp in 2018 where 15 service users with different background and nationalities contributed in a dialogue about service-user involvement in general and in education and research in particular.

In Chapter 18, Hugh McLaughlin focuses on the ethical issues concerning the involvement of service users as co-researchers and co-educators. He offers an examination of the limitations of the term service user, provides comments on degrees of participation and explores the ethical issues in the cooperation with service users. What is needed to realise such cooperation in a respectful and qualitative way?

To contribute to societal transformation and social justice, social work strives for partnerships to ensure that those whose voices are least heard are given opportunities to take their lives into their own hands. Collaboration with experts by experience not only aims to improve the quality of social work but also to jointly eliminate injustice and power inequalities in order to achieve a more equal society. In Chapter 19, Kristel Driessens and Vicky Lyssens-Danneboom look at how this collaboration makes the values underlying the social work profession more concrete.

We hope that the collaborative models discussed in this book can inspire you to work with experts by experience in your own educational or research practice. Our dream is that cooperation with experts by experience will become structurally anchored and a given in all European social work courses. Enjoy reading.

References

Anghel, R. and Ramon, S. (2009) 'Service users and carers' involvement in social work education: lessons from an English case study', *European Journal of Social Work*, 12(2): 185–99, DOI: 10.1080/13691450802567416.

Askheim, O.P. (2011) '"Meeting face to face creates new insights": recruiting persons with user experiences as students in an educational programme in social work', *Social Work Education*, 30, 1–13.

Beresford, P. and Croft, S. (2004) 'Service users and practitioners reunited: the key component for social work reform', *British Journal of Social Work*, 34: 53–68, DOI:10.1093/bjsw/bch005.

Chiapparini, E. (2016) *The Service User as a Partner in Social Work Projects and Education: Concept and Evaluations of Courses with a Gap-Mending Approach in Europe*, Berlin/Toronto: Barbara Budrich Publishers, p 144.

Dill, K., Montgomery, L., Davidson, G. and Duffy, L. (2016) 'Service-user involvement in social work education: the road less traveled', *Field Educator*, 6(2). Available from: https://pureadmin.qub.ac.uk/ws/portalfiles/portal/121421323/RoadLess16_137.pdf

Gutman, C., Kraiem, Y., Criden, W. and Yalon-Chamovitz, S. (2012) 'Deconstructing hierarchies: a pedagogical model with service user co-teachers', *Social Work Education*, 31(2): 202–14.

McKeever, B. (2021) 'The housing campaign: user involvement in action', in H. McLaughlin, P. Beresford, C. Cameron, H. Casey and J. Duffy (eds), *The Routledge Handbook of Service User Involvement in Human Services Research an Education*, London: Routledge, pp 85–93.

McLaughlin, H. (2009) 'What's in a name: client, patient, customer, consumer, service user, service user: what's next?', *British Journal of Social Work*, 19(6): 1101–17.

Omeni, E., Barnes, M., MacDonald, D., Crawford, M. and Rose, D. (2014) 'Service user involvement: impact and participation: a survey of service user and staff perspectives', *BMC Health Services Research*, 14: 491. Available from: https://doi.org/10.1186/s12913-014-0491-7

Rhodes, C. (2012) 'User involvement in health and social care education: a concept analysis', *Nurse Education Today*, 32(2): 185–9.

Robinson, K. and Webber, M. (2013) 'Models and effectiveness of service user and carer involvement in social work education: a literature review', *British Journal of Social Work*, 43: 925–44, DOI:10.1093/bjsw/bcs025.

Schön, U.-K. (2015) 'User involvement in social work and education: a matter of participation?', *Journal of Evidence-Informed Social Work*, DOI: 10.1080/15433714.2014.939382.

Tanner, D., Littlechild, R., Duffy, J. and Hayes, D. (2017). '"Making it real": evaluating the impact of service user and carer involvement in social work education', *British Journal of Social Work*, 47(2): 467–6.

Waterson, J. and Morris, K. (2005) 'Training in social work: exploring issues of involving users in teaching on social work degree courses', *Social Work Education*, 24(6): 653–75.

PART I

Collaborative models in social work education

2

The gap-mending concept: theory and practice

Cecilia Heule, Marcus Knutagård and Arne Kristiansen

Introduction

To reflect upon what causes gaps between people is a challenge that should involve social workers and service users in social work practice, education and research. Within the PowerUs network, gap-mending practices have been developed whereby more reciprocal relationships are aimed for between social work students, teachers and service users in joint development projects.[1] The principles of these practices are similar to those found in research about so-called strength-based social work, which emphasises the importance of enabling niches rather than placing an emphasis on categorising and diagnosing personal problems (Healy, 2014, p 166).

In this chapter we will write about a gap-mending course at Lund University in Sweden in which social work students and students from user organisations study together. The following chapter will explore how 'mend the gap' has been introduced in the UK. Together these chapters will demonstrate the strength of the approach and the diverse contexts in which it has been applied. In the Swedish example, marginalised and discriminated groups have been invited to study a 7.5-credit course together with social work students. The external students were recruited from different service-user organisations and have a background of drug abuse, mental health problems, homelessness, physical disabilities or a combination of these problems. Most of the external students can be considered to be far from the labour market. The work with the so-called Mobilisation course has continued, and the course ran for the 25th time this fall of 2019. In total, over five hundred social work students and 250 service-user students have participated in the course. The results of our research show that the participation in the course strengthens social work students as well as service-user students. Many of the service-user students continue on to further studies or work opportunities. Some of them are hired as guest teachers in other courses in the School of Social Work. Some continue to develop the project ideas that they have started with during their courses.

A central theme in understanding how gaps can be mended is how community and trust can be arranged or choreographed between groups that might have prejudice towards each other. We will discuss aspects that affect human interaction, such as roles, enabling niches, equal opportunities, co-production, institutional support and deconstruction/reconstruction. This chapter will offer a number of strategies for gap-mending reflections, based on our research, that we think also have relevance for co-productive practices that might differ from the Mobilisation course in Lund. However, we will use the practice in Lund as our example in this chapter.

Gap-mending principles

The concept of gap-mending was developed within the PowerUs network in a workshop in January 2012. People who have travelled on the underground in London have probably noticed the iconic phrase 'Mind the gap' that is to warn the passengers stepping between the train and the platform. However, within the network of PowerUs, we wanted to develop ways to decrease the distance between service users and professional social workers; in other words, to *mend* rather than *mind* a gap. Hence the concept of gap-mending was born and started to be used within our practices as a reflective tool in discussions about what mends and what creates gaps between different groups in society (Askheim et al, 2016; Heule et al, 2017).

There are other concepts that are related to gap-mending, such as co-production, community development, trust building and the decrease of prejudices between groups. Within research on how prejudices can be decreased by intergroup contact, it is well known that aspects like equality, cooperation, common goals and institutional support are essential for gap-mending results (Allport, 1954; Pettigrew and Tropp, 2011, pp 61–76). We will discuss those conditions in this chapter, together with other aspects that we have found relevant in planning for community building and gap-mending between so-called in-groups and out-groups.[2]

Background

The Mobilisation course at Lund University started as a joint project between the School of Social work and various service-user organisations. An important driving force in the development of the gap-mending strategies was the vision that people who have been using different social work interventions can be important recourses for developing social work practice. As a part of this, it was considered important to problematise and change dominating ideas of what roles and categories are valid and important in social work practice. We recognised that there were a lot of structural obstacles and hindrances that made equal and trustful relationships difficult between social workers, social work academics and service users.

Since 2005, teachers in Lund have made gap-mending adjustments in different areas of the course curriculum, and some of these areas will be more thoroughly discussed in this chapter. It is, however, important to give the reader some basic information about the history, development and structure of the course. We have been working with over 50 different service-user organisations throughout the years, run by former drug addicts, people with mental health problems, people with physical disabilities, people from ethnic minorities and people who have experiences of homelessness or a criminal background. Most of the students from service-user organisations have been severely marginalised in society for decades and have bad experiences from earlier education systems. But the variety of backgrounds among the service-user students also means that occasionally a student from a service-user organisation will have prior experience of university studies.

All students taking the course get 7.5 university credits for the six weeks of learning together. However, administratively they are admitted to three separate courses:

- Students from service-user organisations study on a basic university level and are admitted to a commissioned course which is externally funded. We call them commission students. By admitting them in a commissioned course, which is a model for courses normally given by the university to private or public workplaces, the teachers can admit students who wouldn't normally be able to study at a university level.
- Social work students study on an advanced level in the final semester of the social work program.
- Some students study the course on an advanced level as a part of their master's degree.

During the six weeks of co-production and joint learning, the students get the same theoretical frameworks and tasks. But in order to fulfil the demands of running a course on an advanced level in the curriculum system, the social work students have some weeks of preparational literature study with exams before the joint course. This means that the total length of the course for students on the advanced level is nine weeks. However, during this time there are few lectures or occasions to meet, as we don´t want a group to form before the joint course begins. The content of the joint six weeks is illustrated in Figure 2.1.

During the first day the students are divided into mixed groups and they do some tasks together that are designed to break the ice. In the following weeks, each student makes a personal presentation, on the topics: 1) 'Who am I', and 2) 'What do I think is important in social work practice'. This

Figure 2.1: Content of joint six weeks

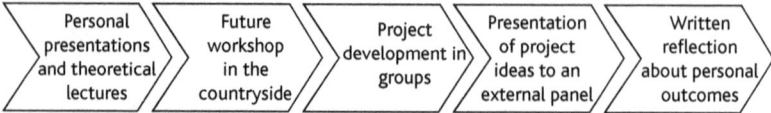

practice means a lot when it comes to building trust between students, as it is evident that no one is a category. Social work students can have several experiences of social problems, and commission students often have a very interesting history of contributing in social work within their organisations or with other skills. In this period there are also lectures held about social mobilisation, project development, power structures and principles of change in social work practice.

After about two weeks, all students take part in a two-day-long future workshop in a countryside hotel. The future workshop is a method for democratic and creative brainstorming about ideas to change and improve society (Jungk and Müllert, 1987). The workshop consists of three phases – a critique phase, a vision phase and a concretisation phase – which are playfully developed, and ends with a number of project ideas that the students themselves want to realise. The following two and a half weeks are spent back at the university developing the project ideas in mixed groups. The students test their ideas by contacting various stakeholders in practice. The projects are later presented orally and in written text (as a project application) to an external panel. The panel consists of persons with powerful positions in society, such as politicians, researchers, directors of social welfare or leaders within service-user organisations.

As a final task for the course, the students write reflections on what they have learned about working in a gap-mending way at the university. This material contains very rich narratives and is a basis for our joint-learning processes about gap-mending principles.

Roles and concepts

The concept of the service user and other related terms like 'service-user participation', 'service-user influence' and 'service-user perspective' have increased in importance during the last decades in social work education, research and practice (McLaughlin, 2009). But sometimes these concepts are not reflected upon, and other times some people might find these terms inappropriate. Who is a service user and what services are those people using? When using concepts like that of the service user, it is important to ask questions about, for instance, when service users *are* service users, and in relation to whom. What is it that the service users are supposed to have an influence over? The goal of service-user influence could be about affecting their own personal treatment and needs, but also about more structural or policy-oriented areas.

The roles we give people within our practices are of importance in framing the personal agency of participants. They affect the way people interpret their opportunities and frame their mutual action. If the boundary-setting between social workers and vulnerable groups is strongly emphasised, there is a risk that the roles will be characterised by opposite expectations, in which the client is expected to have a problem (being a receiver) and the professional is viewed as the one with knowledge and the solution (being the giver). However, some organisations consider the creation of alternative roles within their practices in order to reach gap-mending results. We illustrate this in the chart below.

People who come from service-user organisations and study at Lund University in the so-called Mobilisation course are not service users at the university. We call them commission students,[3] and as students they have a completely different agency and different expectations than they would as a service user. Most of the commission students have experiences of having been service users, but what becomes apparent during the course is that so do many of the social work students. We will further discuss the importance of equality of roles later in this chapter (see Table 2.1).

Enabling niches

Many social scientists have shown the importance of social niches, or more specifically, the importance of creating and sustaining enabling niches (Ryke et al, 2004; Rapp and Goscha, 2012). This is very much aligned with the four key conditions identified by Allport (1954). The prejudice that exists between groups can be reduced if the groups can interact with each other on equal terms, that is: 1) if they equal status during the interaction; 2) if the groups share common goals; 3) if the groups can work together in cooperation or in a co-productive manner; and finally, 4) if the interaction between the groups receives enough institutional support (Pettigrew and Tropp, 2011, p 61). We will elaborate on these conditions later in the chapter, but creating an enabling niche wherein the four conditions can take place is crucial. To create enabling niches, it is necessary to establish trust. The personal stories that are used at the beginning of the course are a key ingredient in the trust-building process.

For many marginalised groups there is a lack of enabling niches. Instead they might be caught up in entrapping niches. Even though it can be difficult to escape entrapping niches, they often consist of enabling elements (Ryke et al, 2004). We have identified the space offered during the Mobilisation course as an enabling niche that encourages the participants to bring forward their own resources and strengths. Without this space, the other conditions would be hard to fulfil.

Table 2.1: Example of roles given to actors in social work practice

Role/Relation	Example of organisation
Service user	Service User Council
Client	Social Services
Customer	Employment agencies, health insurance agencies
Patient	Psychiatry, psychotherapeutic treatment
Member	Club House Movement (Fountain House Movement)
Co-worker	Social enterprises like San Patrignano or Basta
Partner	Community development work
Neighbour	The Settlement Movement, like Hull House or Toynbee Hall
Student	Gap-mending courses, for instance at Lund University
Expert by experience	A concept of growing importance in the Netherlands and in Belgium

Equal status

In order for a gap-mending activity to be successful, it is essential that an environment of equal status is created for those engaged in it (Allport, 1954; Pettigrew and Tropp, 2011). This is of course a challenge in the Mobilisation course, where the group members represent two groups with different backgrounds and statuses. This applies not least to their positions in relation to university studies. While the students who take the Mobilisation course as part of the social work programme have a given position and status, the students who attend it as a commissioned course represent a group that usually does not get access to the university. The ambition of the programme – together with the students – is to problematise and exceed the unequal roles and power relations that exist in social work and which the students often carry with them into the Mobilisation course.

Over the years, we have developed an approach that creates conditions for building a platform with common goals for the course participants. Common goals are essential in order for groups to function and be able to cooperate (Pettigrew and Tropp, 2011). A fundamental part of this approach is that we try to respond to and treat all students in the same way regardless of whether they come to the Mobilisation course via the social work programme or do the course as commissioned education. We make the same demands on all students when it comes to, for example, attendance and participation in various activities. Therefore, we do not use terms such as 'service-user students' and 'social work students', but simply call them all students. This is facilitated by the fact that all students who complete the course receive 7,5 university credits. For those students who attend the course as part of the social work program, the credits are necessary for them to obtain their degree. For the students who attend the course as commissioned education, it means much to get proof that they have attended a university course. We are also careful, as soon as the course begins, to ensure that the students who attend the course as commissioned education receive key cards that give them the same access to university facilities as all other students; for example, to be able to enter the premises, borrow books and access the computer halls. We also mark the students' common status with different symbolic attributes by giving all students, at the beginning of the course, a bag, notepad and pens with the university logo. We also invite all students to participate in our networks on social media after the end of the course, and also invite them to alumni meetings, which we so far have arranged about ten times.

The Mobilisation course contains some elements in which the social work students have advantages insofar as they have a more practice performing academic work tasks, which may mean that the commission students will have less influence over the design of these tasks. This applies, for example, to writing project plans and different kinds of group work. In order to counteract this and create an equal interaction, we are always careful to encourage students to take part in relationship-building activities when they meet for group work, so that they do not only focus on the written work.

The personal presentations, which we spend a lot of time on during the first weeks of the course, are an important tool for problematising and exceeding various stereotypical roles that exist in social work. The personal presentations are also of great importance in creating an equal status regarding the power balance between the students, as they usually present the same challenge for all students. During the personal presentations, all students, and also the teachers, get about 15 minutes to talk about their background and why they have chosen to study social work. Each semester, students are surprised and touched by each other's presentations. We are told stories about experiences of vulnerability and of being subject to social efforts, as well as stories of happiness and success both for students who take the Mobilisation course as commission education and those who take it as part of the social work program. The personal presentations fulfil an important function in the relationship-building that takes place between the students, which is important for their cooperation and mutual development during the rest of the course. Based on Wenger (1998), the personal presentations can be regarded as stories in a communicative practice that creates a repertoire of common experiences, and which contributes to better cooperation and trust between the students.

Co-production

The development of methods for co-production started in the 1970s and is today an established research area (Brandsen et al, 2018). In the social sciences there are many studies that show a connection between the level of trust and how well societies and their services function (Ostrom, 1990; Putnam et al, 1992). Changing public services from a traditional management model to a co-productive one poses major challenges, not least because it requires other approaches that change the roles of both social workers and service users. The change involves going from seeing service users as recipients of service, or counterparties in decision-making processes, to seeing them as actors in co-production processes wherein dialogue and trust form an important basis. Trust is the basis for collaboration between social workers and service users, and allows them to be able to create solutions together.

The attempt to create a situation wherein students have fairly equal status with which to begin building trust is an important basis for the cooperation and the co-production that constitutes the foundation of the course after the first weeks. The Mobilisation course is based on cross-border cooperation. It has strived for a change in the common view of social work such that social work is seen to focus on community rather than on individual problems. The perspective shift occurs partly through the course's ideological and theoretical framing, but also more clearly through the joint project that is developed during the course. The theoretical framing of the Mobilisation course takes place both through structural theories, explaining how exclusion and inclusion works, and also through theories as to how social work can be conducted and understood. Another cornerstone in our pedagogy is the concept of learning by doing.

Institutional support

Serious attempts to mend gaps between service users and professionals in the education of social workers can, and will likely, challenge many of the traditional ways of academic culture and organisation. Teachers who have succeeded and maintained long-term service-user involvement in the education of social workers therefore often need backup from higher office, such as from an educational board or those running departments.

The importance of institutional support is recognised within the research on the effects of intergroup contact on prejudices (Pettigrew and Tropp, 2006, p 766). It is considered to be the most important factor in how different groups interact within established systems like academia. This entails the norms that is communicated within a system about what is considered important and what is legitimate. The Mobilisation course in Lund, since it started in 2005, has had the support of the leaders of the School of Social Work and its faculty. However, it has sometimes been difficult to finance the costs for the external students, and therefore the institutional support can be considered limited and should not be taken for granted.

Teachers who employ gap-mending initiatives in the education of social workers are almost always pioneers within their institutions in finding methods and strategies of inclusion and involvement of service users. It can feel quite like being the 'odd bird' within the academic system, which is why the network of PowerUs was initiated. The network consists of teachers and researchers in partnership with service users from 17 countries who exchanges experiences and conduct joint action together. Our experiences show that being a part of a growing international network can increase local institutional support for teachers who employ gap-mending initiatives.

Deconstruction and reconstruction

It is well known that binary pairs or dichotomies separated by clear boundaries can contribute to durable inequality (Tilly, 1999, p 96). According to this theory, one group is often exploited by the other. The relationship between social workers and their clients risks upholding such inequalities if the expectation is for the social worker to be the one with knowledge and recourse (a giver) and for the client to be the one with the problems, who lacks power and knowledge (a receiver). Once these relationship patterns get institutionalised, they can be difficult to change. One way to deconstruct the view of an institutionalised practice is by letting the narratives of the service users show alternative ways of understanding what works and what does not (Fook, 2002, p 89).

Processes of decategorisation and recategorisation have been the focus of experiments within intergroup contact research (Pettigrew, 1998; Gaertner and Davidio, 2000; Brown and Hewstone, 2005). Brewer and Miller (1984) found that group differences could come to be seen as less obvious according to different decategorisation processes. This could, for example, be done by increasing the diversity among the included out-group so that there would be fewer stereotypical similarities between the members of the out-group. Gaertner and David (2000) have developed a recategorisation model that involves creating a new inclusive group membership that includes both earlier in-group and out-group members.

The Mobilisation course in Lund has similarities with both models. As in the decategorisation model, the students represent a variety of backgrounds, and the narratives given in the personal presentations function in a decategorising way, as individual students are seen as much more complex individuals than the stereotypes of a social work student, ex-drug user or mental health patient suggest. Recategorisation has also been practiced since the start in 2005, as the different student groups are united in a new category: Mobilisation course students. While recategorisation strategies have provided a basic framework for more reciprocal relationships, the decategorising strategies have been essential in order to build trust and decrease prejudices between students in the Mobilisation course.

Conclusion

The Mobilisation course, which started as a pilot project to develop the service-user perspectives in social work education at Lund University, is today an established part of the education at the School of Social Work. The ambition is, together with the students, to problematise and exceed the unequal roles and power relations in social work. This is a core element of the gap-mending concept, and makes it possible for people and groups who previously did not meet on equal terms to meet, cooperate and co-create together.

As we mentioned earlier, more than eight hundred students have passed the Mobilisation course. Nearly three hundred of the students have their own experiences of social problems, and most of these are active in different service-user organisations. Many of them are today engaged as guest lecturers and supervisors at other courses in the social work programme in Lund. The Mobilisation course now works as an action-research-oriented platform for gap-mending-based networking, the development of innovative and alternative solutions to social problems and research on an emancipatory basis (Heule et al, 2017). Several of the project ideas developed during the Mobilisation course have been realised in different contexts in the community. Some new service-user organisations have been developed based on ideas developed during the Mobilisation course. One example is G7 in Helsingborg, which is a peer-support organisation for people who are or have been homeless. Many of our former students are active in development projects in various organisations and municipalities in Sweden. To give one example from a few years ago: when Malmö city ran a project for the development of service-user influence in the social services, a majority of those who represented service-user organisations in the project were people who passed the Mobilisation course.

Those of us who run the Mobilisation course are often asked to participate in different contexts that concern service-user influence and the development of alternative solutions to social problems. The Mobilisation course has been an important part of the development of the international PowerUs network, and has been a source of inspiration for the development of gap-mending activities in several countries in Europe.

We have also taken experiences and knowledge from the Mobilisation course with us into other research projects. One example is an action-research-oriented project on the social housing programme in Helsingborg city which ran between 2014 and 2017, and which was inspired by the gap-mending concept (Knutagård and Kristiansen, 2017). Currently, we are working on a three-year, EU-funded research project that includes a study of those who have been students at the Mobilisation course. Cecilia Heule's forthcoming doctoral thesis is based on the Mobilisation course.

Those of us who work with the Mobilisation course have seen it from the start in 2005 as an opportunity not only to conduct teaching and theoretically discuss, for example, categorisations and power relations, but also to study with our students what can happen when such phenomena are challenged in reality. We are not just *talking* about the importance of mutual relationships, gap-mending, co-production, mobilising and creating alternatives, we actually do it – the principle of learning by doing is embedded in our practice. We learn ourselves and develop as teachers, social workers, researchers and as persons. Many of our students have started initiatives inspired by actions within the course on both personal and professional levels.

Notes

[1] PowerUs is an international network of teachers, researchers and service-user representatives that develops methods and joint action about service-user participation. You can read more on www.powerus.eu

[2] In Gordon Allport's classical study *The Nature of Prejudice* (1954), the concept of ingroups and outgroups was first formulated. Members of an ingroup are recognised by a feeling of belonging, a 'we'. They develop common goals that are visible as codes, norms and views that binds them together.

[3] They are taking a commission course, and the social work students are taking a course that is embedded in the programme.

References

Allport, G. (1954) *The Nature of Prejudice*, Reading: Addison-Wesley.

Askheim, O-P., Beresford, P. and Heule, C. (2017) 'Mend the gap: strategies for user involvement in social work practice', *Journal of Social Work Education*, 36(2): 128–40 DOI: 10.1080/02615479.2016.1248930.

Brandsen, T., Steen, T. and Verschuere, B. (2018) *Co-Production and Co-Creation: Engaging Citizens in Public Services*, New York: Routledge.

Brewer, M.B. and Miller, N. (1984) 'Beyond the contact hypothesis: theoretical perspectives on desegregation', in N. Miller and M. Brewer (eds) *Groups in Contact: The Psychology of Desegregation*, New York: Academic Press.

Brown, R. and Hewstone, M. (2005) 'An integrative theory of intergroup contact', *Advances in Experimental Social Psychology*, 37: 255–343.

Fook, J. (2002) *Social Work: Critical theory and Practice*, London: SAGE Publications.

Gaertner, S. and Davidio, J. (2000) *Reducing Intergroup Bias: The Common Ingroup Identity Model*, Philadelphia: Psychology Press.

Healy, K. (2014) *Social Work Theories in Context: Creating Frameworks for Practice*, London: Palgrave McMillan.

Heule, C., Knutagård, M. and Kristiansen, A. (2017) 'Mending the gaps in social work education and research', *European Journal of Social Work*, 20(3): 396–408.

Jungk, R. and Müllert, N. (1987) *Future Workshops: How to Create Desirable Futures*, London: Institute for Social Interventions.

McLaughlin, H. (2009) *Service User Research in Health and Social Care*, London: SAGE publications.

Ostrom, E. (1990) *Governing Commons: The Evolution of Institutions for Collective Action*, Cambridge: Cambridge University Press.

Pettigrew, T. (1998) 'Intergroup contact theory', *Annual Review of Psychology*, 49: 64–85.

Pettigrew, T. and Tropp, L. (2006) 'A meta-analytic test of intergroup contact theory', *Journal of Personality and Social Psychology*, 90(5): 751–83.

Pettigrew, T. and Tropp, L. (2011) *When Groups Meet: The Dynamics of Intergroup Contact*, New York: Psychology Press.

Putnam, R., Leonardi, R. and Nanetti, R.Y. (1992) *Making Democracy Work: Civic Traditions in Modern Italy*, Princeton: Princeton University Press.

Rapp, C.A. and Goscha, R.J. (2012) *The Strengths Model: A Recovery-Oriented Approach to Mental Health Services*, 3rd edn, New York: Oxford University Press.

Ryke, E., Strydom, H. and Botha, K. (2004) 'The social niche: conceptualising the human environment', *International Journal of the Humanities*, 2(3): 1935–44.

Tilly, C. (1999) *Durable Inequality*, Berkeley: University of California Press.

Wenger, E. (1998) *Communities of Practice: Learning, Meaning, and Identity*, Cambridge: Cambridge University Press.

3

Mending gaps in social work education in the UK

Helen Casey and Peter Beresford

Introduction

The mandatory requirement for service-user and carer involvement in social work education with government funding to support this involvement for qualifying and post qualifying training, established an international precedent in 2002 (Branfield, 2009). Shaping Our Lives, a national service-user led organisation that has undertaken a wide range of research to promote the meaningful involvement of people in very diverse contexts, became a key partner in establishing the PowerUs network (see Chapter 2 – Heule, Knutagård and Arne Kristiansen) and initiating gap-mending practices in the UK. This chapter explores how PowerUs, in partnership with Shaping Our Lives, created a new direction for service users and carers to positively and critically impact social work education.

For a long time, the UK was the leader in service-user and carer involvement in professional social work education. Also, for a long time in the UK there seemed to be only one model for such involvement. More recently what we have learned is that, as is so often the case, it is only by combining the best of different international experience and learning that we are likely to develop the most effective approaches to this involvement. For this reason, the UK is a helpful, if sometimes uneven, case study of and starting point for understanding user involvement in professional learning and qualification.

There was talk of 'listening' to service users in UK social work from the 1970s onwards. The statutory reforms that took place and led to the creation of social services departments in 1971 made reference to participation: involving and including the perspectives of service users. The well-known text *The Client Speaks*, published in 1970 (Mayer and Timms, 1970), has often been taken to represent the real beginnings of such interest in user involvement, but in fact it was more concerned with using service users as a data source in research rather than listening to or involving them, and then it chose arbitrarily to leave out BAME (Black, Asian and Minority Ethnic) service users as 'immigrants' (Beresford and Croft, 1987).

It was really from the 1980s, with the emergence of the disabled people's, psychiatric system survivors' (the term 'survivors' is commonly used in the UK by people who have used psychiatry or mental health services) and other service-user movements, that pressure began to develop for user (and carer) involvement in social work education. User and survivor trainers, training packs and 'user training for the trainers' grew initially on an ad hoc basis and found their way into service systems, provision and educational institutions, providing learning for managers, practitioners, educators, researchers and students. This development was reinforced by the introduction of new legislation for social work with children and community care in the late 1980s and early 1990s which imposed new requirements for the involvement of service users and carers. It was not until 1994 that the first definitive publication taking stock of these developments was published by the then regulator of social work, the Central Council for Education and Training in Social Work (CCSTSW) (Beresford, 1994).

However, it was the new millennium that marked the crucial watershed in the development of UK service-user and carer involvement in social work. It was in 2001 that a new social work degree qualification was introduced in England. Through the leadership of Dame Denise Platt, who was committed to user involvement in social work and social care and was then head of social care services at the UK Department of Health, two key initiatives were taken. First, service-user and carer involvement was made a requirement in all aspects and all stages of social work degree programmes, and second, a budget to help pay for this was made available from central government to providers of such courses on an annual basis (Branfield, 2009).

These arrangements still hold, although Scotland no longer provides a central budget. The fact that there were requirements for such involvement has long been seen both domestically and internationally as a great strength of this UK system. A key aim for PowerUs colleagues at Lund University is to get the Swedish government to adopt the same approach and commitment to service-user involvement. While there have always been variations in the extent and determination with which these provisions have been implemented, there has been a consensus among students, policymakers, educators, practitioners, researchers, service users and carers that they have been a necessary and important development. Despite major cuts in funding for social work and social work education over the years, and the introduction of new approaches to such education, these provisions are still a much-valued and welcomed requirement.

However, while (as has been said) there has been some local variations in how these requirements have been implemented, for a long time there has essentially been one model employed to fulfil the requirements. Colleges have brought in service users and carers to help them fulfill the required involvement. This has ranged from users talking about their own experiences – an early way in which involvement was addressed, with its own strengths and limitations – to service users and carers providing teaching sessions, acting as educators, being recruited as educators and taking part in the selection and assessment of students and producing their own materials. Similarly, service users and carers have been actively involved in students' work placements. Some colleges have established their own user and carer groups to provide the basis for such involvement, others have turned to local user-led and other organisations. While some colleges in the UK have been more enthusiastic about such involvement than others, it cannot be dismissed as tokenistic. Colleges who fall short of required standards have to rectify the situation when they undergo review, just as with other key educational requirements. There has also been a continuing search to involve as diverse a range of service users and carers as possible (Beresford and Boxall, 2012).

This then has been the longstanding situation in the UK. However, in 2008, one of us (PB) had the positive opportunity to find out more about what was happening in this context in Swedish universities as a visiting professor at Lund University. With another local service user, I was able to visit and meet with staff, students, service users and carers working to make social work courses more participatory in a number of Swedish universities. This was a continuation of earlier contact I had with Lund University with a focus on participation and empowerment. It was also my first concerted opportunity to find out more about the emerging PowerUs approach to user and carer involvement first developed at Lund University. For us in the UK, this represented a fundamentally different approach to involvement, and while it was only part of the qualifying course, it did represent a sea change from the UK model, as in the Lund model students and service users would work together in roles planned to be equal to complete a module on empowerment, building trust and confidence in each other (Beresford et al, 2016).

As a social work lecturer with over ten years' experience of seeking to promote involvement and equality in social work education, I (HC) was beginning to question the processes for involvement, as were people with lived experiences who were contributing.

The value of involvement was undisputed, but the challenge to make involvement meaningful, not tokenistic, began to highlight many gaps. The Social Care Institute for Excellence (SCIE – a think tank established for social work/service-user and carer involvement research) had produced lots of guidance since 2002, and by 2008 was starting to question why seldom-heard voices were not participating in social work education (Robson et al, 2008). It had become common practice for universities to establish a reference group, which essentially meant that a core group of predominantly adult service users and carers contributed to university social work programmes. This was extremely valuable and important, but meant that diversity in the community was not adequately reflected in social work courses. It had been strongly argued that service user–led organisations that were diverse and community based would have been better placed to take a lead on involvement in educational settings (Beresford and Levin, 2007), however, common practice was for one person from the academic team to be in control. Further, research that sought to evaluate involvement activities found that evidence of impact was significantly lacking. (Beresford and Boxall, 2012; Wallcroft et al, 2012; Robinson and Webber, 2013).

When I first heard about 'mend the gap' – while attending a conference PowerUs workshop – what struck me most was the focus on outcomes for participants, which has been outlined in Chapter 2. The focus placed on equal participation and transformative learning was captured after the first programme at Lillehammer University, Norway, in an article by Ole Petter Askheim, one of the founders of PowerUs, 'Bringing People together face to face creates new insights' (Askheim, 2012).

This is what was needed most critically in social work education in the UK. Co-produced learning that would affect change and generate new knowledge was a clear gap in educational structures for involvement.

I had been in dialogue with young people in the care system who said things that research with young people had identified for years. We made a film based on their experiences and recommendations about what makes a good social worker, which confirmed what other studies had shown, that young people want social workers who listen to them, communicate empathy, who are reliable, take action on their behalf, respect confidences, see children and young people as whole persons and who don't overly associate children and young people with particular problems (Hill, 1999; Curtis, 2006; Morgan, 2006). The mend-the-gap approach presented a new way of engaging young people to mend gaps they identified, putting them in control, not professionals who would tell them what they needed, to change the dialogue.

I was fortunate to participate in a Shaping Our Lives visit to Lund University, Sweden. Drawing inspiration from the Mobilisation course at Lund, the first programme I introduced in the North of England was piloted in response to barriers identified by parents at a children's centre where social work students were on placement and excluded by parents from their support groups. The approach had been introduced at London Southbank University, where a new course entitled Advocacy, Partnership and Participation was established to explore how a co-participatory approach could promote equal and transformative learning leading (Beresford et al, 2016). In contrast to the approach taken at Lund, the programme introduced with parents in North East England was the first in the UK to be named Mend the Gap, and involved parents who were united by their negative experiences of having lost or been separated from their children by social workers and who agreed to pioneer this innovative approach. The aim of the first programme was to listen to parents' experiences and identify the gaps which created barriers between themselves and those in roles intended to support them. From the outset, parents said their interest in participating was stimulated by a focus on taking part in something that would lead to change, even though what this change would be was unclear. Characteristic of the approach was the far-reaching participation of the parents. It was a completely new experience for them to be able to set the agenda while usually they were only 'consulted' and received no feedback.

The programme's content was defined by parents identifying gaps as core themes around:

- communication
- professional values
- information sharing
- partnership working
- different roles
- rights

One parent summarised a key gap: "I'll never forget the way the social worker spoke to me, as if I wasn't even a human being, let alone a mother to my children. She made me feel this [fingers demonstrating extremely small] big" (Beresford et al, 2016, p 10). This unique empowering experience, putting parents in a lead role and prioritising their views, was the start of a groundbreaking programme, the outcome of which has created a legacy for other parents and changed the way that professionals can learn from those they are seeking to support, for example:

- Social workers from the local children-and-families team became involved with the programme and agreed areas for improvement, such as supervised contact arrangements.
- A creative writing group was established, resulting in published award-winning poetry for one parent.
- Parents contributed to teaching social work students in Universities and presenting at conferences.

Students who participated in this programme expressed feeling much more confident in their practice, building positive relationships with parents while maintaining focus on safeguarding children.

A more detailed account of this programme can be found in the first book about 'mend the gap' by Emmanuelle Chiapparini (2016, chapter 3). The success of the first programme paved the way for subsequent gap-mending programmes in a wide range of contexts, including for:

- children and young people in the child care system;
- children and young people with mental health problems;
- refugee and asylum seeker parents;
- unaccompanied asylum seeker youths; and
- disabled adults with mental health difficulties.

Each programme has provided unique perspectives, shared learning and measurable outcomes. However, all have centred around the core themes identified by parents in the first programme. These themes concerned pertinent gaps for students and practitioners to identify with. Most recently, the growing interest in what has become an innovative and accepted model for social work education in North East England has led to the involvement of qualified practitioners alongside social work students and has addressed a big gap in continuous professional development. By breaking away from the traditional classroom-based model, seldom-heard voices from the community are empowered to participate in social work education and practice.

This has been most strongly demonstrated when bringing people together from diverse cultures. Mending gaps with those who have no recourse to public funds, whose human rights are constantly eroded, has brought participants together as partners in learning and transformed educational methods in the North East of England, where a high proportion of refugees, asylum seekers and unaccompanied children are placed by central government. This need for a new and innovative approach to working with migrants was identified by Investing in People and Culture (IPC), a leading support organisation working with refugees and asylum seekers in the region.

By way of example, to demonstrate how inclusive the approach can be and how core principles underpin programmes and adapt to the chosen context, a gap-mending programme with single asylum seeker parents will be described in relation to key contrasts with the Lund Mobilisation programme.

Building positive relationships

The course at Lund starts with a residential weekend over which people get to know each other through walking as well as talking. The location of gap-mending programmes in North East England has tended to be in city centres, and a lack of funding has limited the possibilities for travel to the countryside. Instead, the principle of getting to know each other and building relationships has been applied in different ways. Single asylum seeker parents who were living in unsuitable accommodation preferred to travel to the local university (Teesside). We found other ways to get to know each other and build relationships and trust. Often this was with free time outside of dialogue, when biscuits, cake, informal conversation and laughter were shared.

Summary of activities

Over an eight-week period, participants met weekly, from 10am-2pm to fit in with childcare arrangements. The manager, three of the parents and I co-facilitated the programme. Teesside University provided a suitable venue where everyone could meet. Key gaps that had been identified prior to the programme informed the themes for dialogue.

Getting started

In the first session we shared our most important cultural traditions. Key learning points included:

- In Eritrea, International Women's Day (8 March) is very important. It is a national bank holiday which meaningfully recognises the equality that women have fought for. It is interesting that Eritrea is a third-world country yet there is greater recognition of equality for women than in Middlesbrough.
- The Ethiopian calendar is seven years behind the Western calendar. This is significant knowledge social workers need, especially when they are involved with assessing the age of young minors.
- Birthdays in some countries outside of the West are non-events. For example, in Eritrea, Sudan, Kurdistan and Ethiopia, birth dates are not marked. Someone will know their age according to the weather, season or another symbolic factor. It is the first question people are asked when they arrive in the UK. People are given a birthdate; often it is the 1st of January. Although the Home Office is required to allocate a birthdate in accordance with people's stated age, people often feel mistrusted.

Some examples of gaps identified, and the discussion points for how they could be mended, are outlined below.

Housing

Parents shared their experiences of unsatisfactory accommodation, families being forced to share, cultural clashes and tensions. Some parents described regular scenes when fights broke out due to insufficient space, especially in the kitchen, which children witnessed, explaining that police are called out regularly to deal with such disputes, but nothing happens and nothing changes. "No one intervenes and helps."

Discussion points for mending gaps

Social workers are best placed to fight, challenge and mend these gaps by referring to housing policy, which stipulates that 'people should receive fair treatment'. Clearly, when they are not, this should be reported and challenged. Social workers need to find the right information.

Female genital mutilation

FGM is practiced in a wide range of countries and regions, including those where participants were from: the Middle East, Gambia, Egypt, Kenya, Ethiopia, Eritrea, Somalia and Algeria. In such regions the practice is culturally acceptable and seen as the norm. People have strong views on the subject. Since the Female Genital Mutilation Act was introduced in 2003, the first prosecution in the UK was made in 2019.

Discussion points for mending gaps

It is important that social workers have knowledge and awareness of FGM and how girls and women can be protected. If someone is going away, social workers can support them by having an emergency plan in the event that they discover FGM is planned and they need to escape.

Parents said they feared asking social workers for help as they could take their children away. It was explained that the role of a social worker is to keep families together, support them and fight for their rights.

It was agreed that it is important to be open and honest with people, and that there is a lack of trust, an imbalance of power in communities.

Social workers need to make links with community leaders and organisations to work together.

Men need to be involved in discussions about banning this practice. Social workers need to be able to have these discussions with men as well as women.

It was noted that there is a lack of specific support services for men.

Education

Immigration status matters a lot, as in order for adults to meet the requirements for getting student loans, they must have the right status.

Asylum seekers are not usually eligible for either the 'home rate' for tuition fees or for student finance. However, there are some organisations that may be able to help, and some universities offer scholarships.

Different educational experiences were shared, including that in Eritrea, men and women must go to military college for three months. Everyone is trained and prepared to fight.

Discussion points for mending gaps

Anyone arriving in the UK should be given access to an English class as soon as possible. It is the starting point for people to integrate into the community.

Gaps in social policy mean it is impossible for asylum seekers to go to university or other higher education institutions, which limits people's life chances. People can wait many years to get their leave-to-remain/refugee status.

Social workers can be a good link between parents and schools. They can support parents by talking about their concerns about their children – their learning, behaviour or emotional well-being. Parents should not be afraid to talk about their concerns for fear of repercussion – against themselves or their children.

Safeguarding

The legal framework for safeguarding children was explained: The Children Act 1989 (updated 2004) underpins social work practice and sets out the duties and powers of the social worker and responsibilities of the local authority (Her Majesty's Government, 2004).

Some examples of where legislation applies are:

- protecting children from abuse – for example, physical, emotional or sexual abuse, as well as neglect;
- preventing harm to children's health or development, ensuring children grow up in a safe environment.

It was explained that all safeguarding cases go to court, where a judge decides about the safety of the children.

Discussion points for mending gaps

It is important that parents in the community are aware of safeguarding legislation to prevent problems such as leaving young children at home alone. An example was shared of a woman who went out to buy milk and returned to find social services and the police in her home. Her children were removed while her situation was investigated, as she had left them alone too young. In her own country this would have been culturally acceptable, but she did not know this was against the law in the UK.

Women expressed feeling that they have no choice, no rights and no work. There is lots of fighting in the hostels where they stay. Every time they complain they are seen as troublemakers. The police are called daily and do nothing. This raises lots of issues about safeguarding, as children are exposed to this. This highlights the importance of suitable accommodation and support.

Social Workers must adhere to professional guidelines, ethics and principles. Social workers can mend gaps by working in partnership with parents, and must explain the social work role – and have respect for families and their stresses, for instance by being non-judgmental, respecting diversity, ensuring clear communication (for instance by using an interpreter), building respectful relationships and not making assumptions.

The final stage of the programme is a celebration of learning and participation. This involves inviting friends and relatives of service users, students and academics, social workers and their managers. This event is similar to the celebratory event at Lund. Perhaps a key difference is that while 'mend the gap' is starting to be included in academic modules in the UK, it does not carry a level of credits for external students which they can use for further study, as is the case at Lund. This is an area for further development in the UK.

Outcomes

As with the Mobilisation course at Lund, outcomes are an important part of the projects. In Lund, the mobilisation courses usually end with particpants presenting proposals for future projects to an academic panel, but in the UK there is not this same focus. Instead, changes are identified by those who are in positions to implement them. The aims are similar: to ensure something transformational and sustainable comes out of the programme.

Outcomes of the programme with asylum seeker parents included;

- Parents have worked with the Home Office to inform future planning and support for asylum seekers' accommodation arrangements, which ultimately led to all parents being rehoused in single-family accommodation in the local area.
- A monthly 'drop in' has been established at the IPC community centre, co- facilitated by a social worker and project worker, for parents to attend to informally discuss their concerns and receive information and guidance on where to get further support. Social work students are also welcome to attend.
- Discussions are taking place to develop more 'mend the gap' programmes with asylum seekers and refugees, supported by Department of Education funding, within social work education.

Conclusion

Similar gaps and outcomes have been developed in other programmes, demonstrating how the gap-mending concept promotes experiential knowledge, equality and people's rights, with a growing evidence base to illustrate the difference this approach can make. As other universities take this approach forward, such as Northumbria, Birmingham, Wolverhampton, Staffordshire, Keele and Dundee Universities in the UK (and elsewhere internationally), there is mounting evidence for the effectiveness of this approach.

The shift away from traditional approaches and towards methods which focus on first-hand experiential learning and knowledge exchange promotes new and diverse insights which challenge existing educational structures.

This leaves a big question and challenge for universities who have not yet adopted this or a similar co-production approach. What difference are courses making when service users contribute to teaching and interviewing in limited ways? Perhaps when we start to question what difference we are making and realise we are making none, this makes us more resistant to change.

References

Askheim, O.P. (2012) 'Meeting face to face creates new insights: recruiting persons with user experiences as students in an educational programme in social work', *Social Work Education*, 31(5): 557–6.

Beresford, P. (1994) *Changing the Culture, Involving Service Users in Social Work Education*, London: Central Council of Education and Training in Social Work.

Beresford, P. and Boxall, K, (2012) 'Service users, social work education and knowledge for social work practice', *Social Work Education*, 31(2): 155–67.

Beresford, P. and Croft, S. (1987) 'Are we really listening?: the client speaks, by John Meyer and Noel Timms', in T. Philpot (ed), *On Second Thoughts: Reassessments of the Literature of Social Work*, London: Community Care/Reed Publishing, pp 50–5.

Beresford, P., Casey, H. and MacDonough, J. (2016) 'England: gap-mending: developing a new approach to user and carer involvement in social work education', in E. Chiappparini (ed), *The Service User as a Partner in Social Work Projects And Education*, Opladen: Barbara Budrich Publishers, pp 69–87.

Branfield, F. (2009) 'Developing user involvement in social work education', London: Social Care Institute for Excellence. Available from: https://www.scie.org.uk/publications/reports/report29.asp

Branfield, F., Beresford, P. and Levin, E. (2007) 'Position paper 7: common aims: a strategy to support service user involvement in social work education', London: Social Care Institute for Excellence. Available from: https://www.scie.org.uk/publications/positionpapers/pp07.asp

Chiapparini, E. (2016) *The Service User as a Partner in Social Work Projects and Education: Concepts and Evaluations of Courses with a Gap-Mending Approach in Europe*, Opladen, Berlin and Toronto: Verlag Barbara Budrich.

Curtis, D. (2006) *Options for Excellence: Improving and Developing Social Care, Children and Young People's Consultations on Their Experience of Social Care*, London: National Children's Bureau.

Her Majesty's Government (2004) *Children Act 2004*, London: Her Majesty's Stationery Office. Available from: http://www.legislation.gov.uk/ukpga/2004/31

Hill, M. (1999) 'What's the problem? Who can help? The perspectives of children and young people on their well-being and on helping professionals', *Journal of Social Work Practice*, 13(2): 135–45.

Mayer, J.E. and Timms, N. (1970) *The Client Speaks: Working Class Impressions of Casework*, London: Routledge and Kegan Paul.

Morgan, R. (2006) *About Social Workers: A Children's View Report*, Newcastle upon Tyne: Commission for Social Care Inspection.

Robinson, K. and Webber, M. (2013) 'Models and effectiveness of service user and carer involvement in social work education: a literature review', *British Journal of Social Work*, 43(5): 925–44.

Robson, P., Sampson, A., Dime, N., Hernandez, L. and Litherland, R. (2008) 'Position paper 10: seldom heard – developing inclusive participation in social care', London: Social Care Institute for Excellence. Available from: https://www.scie.org.uk/publications/positionpapers/pp10.asp

Wallcroft, J., Fleischmann, P. and Schofield, P. (2012) *The Involvement of Service Users and Carers in Social Work Education: A Practice Benchmarking Study*, London: Social Care Institute for Excellence.

4

Service users as tandem partners in social work education

Kristel Driessens, Vicky Lyssens-Danneboom, Wendy Peeters, Cindy Van Geldorp, Piet Vandenhende, Hilde Bloemen, Caro Bridts, Sascha Van Gijzel and Henrike Kowalk

Introduction

In this chapter, we describe and analyse a collaborative practice in social work education that is applied in a similar way in different European educational institutions, namely co-teaching in tandem. For the purpose of the chapter, we focus solely on the Flemish (Belgium) and Dutch (the Netherlands) context, since both have many characteristics in common. Typically, the involvement of service users has started with the involvement of people with experiences of poverty and social exclusion. Flanders is internationally known for its participatory anti-poverty policy. Through a scientifically informed, structural vision of poverty integrated in policy thinking, we focus on 'vulnerable people in society' who have multi-dimensional problems but also many strengths. With the recognition and subsidisation of associations wherein people in poverty cooperate to influence policy and practice (Dierckx and Francq, 2010) and of the non-profit organisation De Link – which since 1999 has developed the methodology and a training programme for 'experts by experience in poverty and social exclusion' (Spiesschaert, 2005) – Flanders, with the act on the fight against poverty (Decreet betreffende de armoedebestrijding, 2003), has enabled people in poverty to participate in anti-poverty policy and practices (Driessens and Goris, 2016). De Link stimulated 'working in tandem with an educated expert by experience' in various settings. Bind-Kracht, anchored at the Karel de Grote University of Applied Sciences and Arts, developed training programmes in qualitative social work, in which people in poverty are recruited by the associations together with researchers and lecturers. Both organisations inspired lecturers from universities of applied sciences in the Netherlands to implement this method of working in tandem in their own educational programmes (Bouwes and Philips, 2016).

An influencing factor was that, since 2009, there have been some fundamental changes in the Dutch social system: the decentralisation of responsibilities for various components of care and support from the central government to municipalities went hand in hand with fierce cutbacks; the introduction of 'New Style Welfare', as a result of which the role of social workers shifted from that of 'problem solvers' to that of facilitators; and the new Participation Act. With this transition, the Dutch government wanted to move away from the welfare state to a participation society. Values that are important in this society are participation, empowerment and self-reliance and responsibility. For social workers/social work organisations, this meant reaching out, being generalists, showing initiative and working in integrated, multidisciplinary neighbourhood teams. There were similar trends in welfare policy, including: an evolution towards community care; the direction of the client over his help, we see in Flanders. Following this development and transformation there has been a growing interest in the expertise and experience of service users in co-producing care and support in practice and at a policy level. In social work, the recognition of experience-based knowledge (EBK), alongside evidence-based and practice-based knowledge, is spreading.

In this context, working in tandem with experts by experience in social work education is developing in the Low Lands of Europe. In this chapter we describe and analyse the development of long-term projects in four universities of applied sciences in Belgium and the Netherlands, with a specific focus on their values, objectives, programmes and actions, the evaluation, their organisational conditions and their conclusions.

From poverty, the gaps theory and experts by experience to empowerment in an educational practice

Since the *General Report on Poverty* (see chapter 15 of Beresford and Degerickx), commissioned by the King Baudouin Foundation in 1994, poverty has remained on the political agenda in Belgium. The Belgian anti-poverty policy is based on a common and scientifically founded definition of poverty. Since 2001, the National Action Plan for Social Inclusion (NAPIncl) has defined poverty, as scientifically elaborated by professor emeritus Jan Vranken, as 'a network of forms of social exclusion that extends over different areas of individual and collective existence. It separates the poor from the generally accepted modes of existence in society, creating a gap that poor people cannot bridge on their own' (Dierckx et al, 2010). This definition has also been used in the Flemish Poverty Decree and the federal plans for the fight against poverty since 2008. The fact that people in poverty cannot bridge the gap without assistance – a gap that obviously does not only exist in terms of financial deprivation – is generally accepted as one of the structural characteristics of poverty. The more effective and structural road leads to a society that is organised in such a way that the gaps are closed or reduced so that people in poverty can bridge them on their own (Driessens and Goris, 2016).

Bottom-up, from experiential knowledge, De Link developed their theory of gaps. They distinguished five gaps: the structural and participation gaps, the feeling gap, and the knowledge and skills aptitude gaps. People in poverty are in all areas of life separated from the rest of society by a deep divide. Due to the structural and participation gaps, people in poverty are deprived of all basic rights and lose control over their own lives and over social decision-making. Poverty brings with it an enormously hurt feeling from within and an unfulfilled sense of belonging. Under the influence of poverty, basic knowledge and basic skills needed in order to survive in society are not acquired. Moreover, the strength and resilience of people in poverty are often not even seen or recognised (Casman et al, 2010). The structural mechanisms of exclusion are responsible for people staying deprived of these basic rights and for their losing their grip on their own lives and on social decision-making processes.

The missing link involves the mutual ignorance of people living in poverty on the one hand and policymakers and social professionals on the other. It concerns ignorance of each other's living situations, each other's feelings and expectations, each other's values and norms and each other's thinking patterns and solution/survival strategies. It also concerns their not being aware of the fact that they are not familiar with all these aspects of each other's worlds. This missing link is partly responsible for the fact that exclusion persists.

Experts by experience in poverty and social exclusion can, through dialogue, indicate the missing link and the perception of poverty. Expertise by experience, or experiential expertise, is the concept that we use in Flanders and the Netherlands, because it is broader than the term 'service users' (see McLaughlin, 2009). Most experts by experience can talk about their experiences as users/clients of various social services, but we see them as actors with vulnerabilities and strengths, with special experiential knowledge. Experiential expertise is seen as being the result of the fact that one has reflected on certain personal experiences, in this case with social services and matters such as recovery, poverty, mental health problems and so on (Vanspauwen et al, 2020).

An expert by experience has acquired certain knowledge and skills in order to collect and translate own and other's personal experiences for students and professionals (Sedney and Kowalk, 2018). In their work, they focus on the fundamental difference in position between an excluded person, who is forced to live in exclusion in the long term, and social professionals or policymakers who are not familiar with the harsh reality of living in exclusion, and particularly not with the feeling of shame and humiliation caused by the fact that the excluded have no control over their own lives. They emphasise the need to change perspectives on ways of life or 'deviant' behaviour. Bringing in their knowledge gained from the lived experience of social and healthcare systems and their experience of coping with exclusion, mental distress and poverty, and being able to communicate about this logic, is clarifying for understanding the reactions of people in poverty. This experiential knowledge should be regarded as an alternative and equal knowledge to the academic body of knowledge.

With this strength-oriented approach, working in tandem with an expert by experience is in line with the empowerment paradigm, integrated in the global definition of social work (IFSW, 2014). By acting as a role model, facilitating and stimulating recurring dialogues, and modelling working together in relational equality and reciprocity, lecturers transform theoretical frameworks into concrete action through a positive, strength-based attitude. The partnership strengthens different sources of knowledge. The experiential expert needs the lecturer's professional knowledge to remove obstacles and create a discretionary and welcoming space to use and share his/her knowledge, for example in the classroom. The lecturer needs the expert's knowledge to make what she or he teaches credible and valuable. Through the participation of experts by experience, lecturers can touch the essence of the social profession and work more meaningfully (see also Beresford and Boxall, 2012). Understanding what vulnerability means and developing the capacity for human empathy or connection is a core competency of social workers. By teaching and training alongside a lecturer, the expert by experience introduces openness and courage to discuss and share life experiences in an atmosphere of equality, respect and reciprocity. Within this context, human-to-human encounter emerges, and participants let go of their prejudice or stigma. In this way, individuals and groups become interconnected and aware of each other and the circumstances they are dealing with. These insights make the structural mechanisms of exclusion visible instead of pointing to individual responsibility. In this way, experts by experience become colleagues, fully fledged partners in the creation and delivery of classes.

The four cases in short

Collaboration in tandem at the Karel de Grote University of Applied Sciences and Arts

In 2013, the Social Work and Socio-educational Care Departments of the Karel de Grote University of Applied Sciences and Arts and Bind-Kracht started a project to convert the educational model of cooperating with experts by experience in training programs into the bachelor's program. It was funded by the innovation fund of the university college, and facilitated the recruitment of an expert by experience in addition to the team of volunteers already in place.

In this experiment, a lecturer assisted by an expert by experience provided an entire module in tandem. This was done with the conviction that the development of a deeper, more advanced dialogue would provide additional understanding of and insight into the client perspective, while at the same time contributing to the development of a respectful attitude towards service users. Two programme components were selected. In social work, the project was carried out in the third-year training course in Social Case Work, which was taught in groups of approximately 15 students. In socio-educational care work, it was conducted in the second-year substantive course in Family-Centred Practice in Youth Care, which is taught in groups of approximately 32 students (Driessens et al, 2016). The project was supported by Bind-Kracht (translated as Strengths of Ties), a collaborative partnership of experts by experience and academic researchers (Driessens and Van Regenmortel, 2006).

Several Bind-Kracht trainers and experts with years of experience in providing educational programmes for professional service providers participated in the project. After two years and a positive evaluation, the project was awarded the Excellent Education Prize Frank Swaelen by the University of Applied Sciences. We continued the project with a European Social Fund transnational project grant, with which we were able to anchor the collaboration in social and social educational work and extend it to teacher training and healthcare. As a result of this project, through international collaboration we developed a database of collaborative models in education, as well as this book (Driessens et al, 2019). Over the course of seven academic years, 27 lecturers, 15 service users and 1900 students were involved in the project.

University of Applied Sciences Louvain-Limburg

In Louvain-Limburg, lecturers have been involved in De Link's training programme from the very beginning. They occasionally invite experts for a course or guidance. Since 2016, working with experiential knowledge is imbedded in the social work curriculum, and recently also in the curriculum of social educational work and teacher training. In social educational work, mainly skills are trained, for the purpose of working on building trust in relationships. In social work, the aim of the involvement of experiential experts is the co-creation of a curriculum and course contents. Lecturers and expert(s) share knowledge, practices and life experiences side by side, as a tandem. Communication is practiced through role playing, and insight into poverty and social exclusion is gained through a theme week in which experts by experience are involved. When people bring their own knowledge and experience into the process, awareness will increase. In this process of awareness, dialogue and mutual respect are essential. The involvement of experiential knowledge is necessary for the implementation of critical thinking and critical practice (Adams et al, 2002).

In social work, in the first year, all students commit themselves to an organisation. By working as volunteers they come into contact with others and learn how to connect with people in vulnerable situations. They also meet experts in the lectures on Basic Social Work and in Social Work in a Global Perspective. The following year, the students work in small groups and each of them have a number of conversations with an expert by experience. They support them in the analysis of a theme and, finally, the students become aware of the personal and structural mechanisms of exclusion. In the final year, students are able to participate in a gap-mending project in which they work together with community-service users. The training in the curriculum of social work is carried out in small groups with lively interaction.

UCLL opts for the employment of experience experts. They have hired two experts for part-time jobs. The experts are no longer service users, clients or patients but colleagues with experiential knowledge. Being colleagues and working as a tandem are part of a paradigm shift in the organisation. By structurally integrating the experience of poverty and social exclusion, social work education enables future social workers to be aware of a number of gaps that separate them from the users of services and to have the courage to be vulnerable and to dare to invest in relationships.

Amsterdam University of Applied Science

At the Faculty of Applied Social Sciences and Law at the Amsterdam University of Applied Science (AUAS) around 2000, a handful of lecturers began to invite experts by experience into their programmes, and over time more lecturers joined this movement on their own account. They wanted the students to hear people's personal experiences first hand and to teach in a way that would make them better social workers. The emphasis was on equal recognition of service users as human beings, despite differences, and stimulating a critical attitude towards policies in organisations.

In 2009, the research group Outreach Work and Innovation hired an expert by experience, giving experiential expertise an official position within the research institute. This was a personal commitment to a service user based on the conviction that service users can relate much better what problems they encounter in society and how they experience the help of social workers. Changes in politics and the field inspired the Outreach Work and Innovation research group to strive for a proper structural integration of experts by experience in the various study programmes. In 2012 they hired a second expert by experience, as being the only expert by experience in the team proved to be difficult for the first hire.

The number of AUAS staff members who supported the structural involvement of experts by experience grew, and the long and persistent investment of AUAS staff members resulted in a structural involvement of experiential experts in the curricula of the Departments of Social Pedagogic Work (SPH), Social Work and Community Services (MWD) and Social Legal Services (SJD), as well as in the Department of Education and Development, which organised courses and practical training for social workers. There was a team of experiential experts, who were active on a voluntary basis as guest speakers in the first, second and fourth years. They shared their personal experiences and were involved in role playing, entering the field with students and in assessments. Around 2016–17 they were involved in more than 160 courses a year.

The two employed experts by experience were also involved in: trainings/workshops for regular care/social professionals outside the AUAS; area-specific and recovery-oriented research; development questions concerning the curriculum; and organisation and developments regarding the cooperation with experts by experience in education and in the field. In these tasks they were active co-producers in education and research, and they also advised faculty members (Driessen et al, 2013). In 2014, a vision document about the involvement of experts by experience at the AUAS was written in an attempt to arrive at an unambiguous unified vision and effort. Although this document has been positively received, it never led to an organisational vision regarding the involvement of experts by experience (Kowalk, 2015). Due to changes in staff with different priorities, the above achievements have been diminished since 2017, and now the integration of experts by experience lies again in the hands of individual lecturers who find it meaningful and important. The two experts by experience are currently involved in developing and educational tasks at the Associate Degree for Experts by Experience and in lecturing in social work courses.

Utrecht University of Applied Sciences

The Institute of Social Work is developing ways to utilise EBK as a third source of knowledge in its educational programme. One way is by working together with peer experts as co-teachers. Within the tandem project, the EBK of the co-teacher is seen as an important addition to academic and professional knowledge. It is not only an addition but also strengthens the knowledge, mostly academic and professional, of the regular lecturers.

In the period 2017–19, the university participated in the Erasmus+ Project 'Inclusive Campus Life'. The goal of the project was to make the campus a more inclusive place. Both the research group Participation, Care and Support and the Bachelor of Social Work programme were involved. The co-teachers participate in workshops, lectures and consultation on research questions during the four years of the programme. They work with small groups of students (normally 15 to 20 students) and reach nearly two hundred students in total. They teach about living with an intellectual disability and stigmatisation, socially valued roles, empowerment, personal future planning and communication and networking. Within the workshops, stereotyped images of people with intellectual disabilities are challenged, and we try to contribute to a positive image. In the second year, we organise dialogues about 'good' social work practice between experts by experience and students. In the third year we programmed an elective course with a dialogue about ethical dilemmas in student practice. In the fourth year we train communication skills and practice them with experts by experience. There is an elective gap-mending course in which students of social work and people with mild intellectual disabilities work together in teams on a social challenge. Students in this course are guided by a tandem of a lecturer and a co-teacher. The courses in the fourth year are parts of a minor aimed at inclusion-oriented collaboration with people with a disability.

The co-teachers have experiences with mild intellectual disabilities. They are employed by the National Interest Organisation by and for people with intellectual disabilities (LFB) who is a partner in this project. The LFB is an advocacy organisation for, and led by, people with intellectual disabilities, and operates at both the national and regional level. The co-teachers come from the Training and Education Department, which offers people with intellectual disabilities an opportunity to develop their peer expertise through the educational programme STRONG!

Overview of involvement in a diversity of teaching methods

In summary, we can list the projects of cooperation in tandem with experts by experience in the four involved Universities of Applied Sciences in the Low Lands as follows (see Table 4.1).

Results and added value

In all settings, web surveys, digital questionnaires, focus groups and in-depth interviews showed that the students were extremely positive about the input provided by the experts by experience. The experts' openness, honest contributions, experiences and new perspective have enhanced the realism of the course, brought the theoretical insights to life and provided captivating examples. The students were introduced to 'people living in another world', and were giving the opportunity to feel the effects that exclusion can have and to see how social services can lead to negative reinforcement or positive change. Sometimes it is confrontational, but students admit that they have

Table 4.1: Overview of methods of cooperation with service users in four institutions

	Amsterdam	Utrecht	Leuven	Antwerp
	Social work, social legal services, education and development department	Social work, ecological pedagogy	Social work, social educational care and teacher training	Social work, socio-educational care work, healthcare and education
1	Sharing experiences/ personal stories Studying counselling	Workshop imaging and destigmatisation	Social issues, meet experts, insight into social gaps	Sharing experiences/ personal stories in theoretical courses (social work – poverty)
2	Sharing experiences/ personal stories methodology, diversity cycle	Incidental dialogues about 'good' social work practice	Discussion/support in group assignment, awareness of mechanism of exclusion – training skills: building a trust relationship	Substantive course in 'family-centred practice in youth care'
3		Dialogue about ethical dilemmas of students practice (elective)	Gap-mending projects with community service users (elective)	Training counselling, communication skills, connecting to clients, working on trustful relationship Supervision Primary care in healthcare
4	Minors mental health services educational care worker', 'outreach work and innovation' and 'domestic and sexual violence'	Training communication skills, gap-mending course (elective)		

Source: Lyssens-Danneboom et al, 2019

to adjust their prejudices and gain more insight into peer expertise and see service users as people with possibilities.

The experts by experience felt that they were treated with respect, in addition to receiving recognition and appreciation. A few quotes (Heule and Kristiansen, 2017):

> Education is an ideal place to provide students with respect and insight into the heavy life on the verge of society and the difficult path of reintegration.

I want to tell students how important it is that they are willing to listen, to be understanding and patient. These skills will enable them to make a difference and allow newcomers and people with roots in migration to really come home.

I stand for for dialogue. No monologue but a conversation in reciprocity. Though students' prejudices sometimes make me mad, they do give rise to some interesting, learning confrontations. Entering into dialogue with care, that's what I want to do.

Lecturers found the experience and dialogues very valuable. 'Students and care professionals learn a lot of things from experiential experts that I cannot teach them.' They were satisfied with student attendance, the authentic dialogues and the stimulating learning moments. All parties involved were convinced of the benefits of this type of collaboration and are committed to continuing it.

Organisational conditions and obstacles in the evolution towards sustainable involvement

The ability to convert collaboration with experts by experience into a qualitative pedagogical method is subject to various conditions.

Lecturers and experts by experience require extra time for preparation and debriefing. For tandem teaching, it is important that both actors are well attuned to each other, are sufficiently familiar with each other and can trust each other. Those involved have to develop a person-oriented and task-oriented cooperation (Sedney and Kowalk, 2018).

The degree of ownership in the design of the lessons, insight into objectives and context and a clear division of roles and tasks enables a well-coordinated interaction. Lecturers who are new to this cooperation often function as a bridge builders between the experts and the students. When the relationship between the expert and the lecturer is more developed and there is more confidence, there is more initiative on the part of the experts. In addition to the tasks and roles that have been prepared, it is an important skill of the social work lecturer to observe the possibilities for using the peer expertise. Sometimes it is more important for the learning process to support students and experts in dialogues on a topic than to get everything in the programme done. One obstacle to achieving a level of quality, professionalisation or development is the lack of continuity due to an absence of structural funding for the implementation of tandem-cooperation. Preparation and support concerning the tandem-cooperation takes more time, so it is also important to facilitate this support or coaching. Another challenge is to find the right peer expert for the course. A good substantive match seems to be a critical factor for meaningful participation and involvement. One solution is to work with a pool of experts with experience on various themes and topics. The disadvantage of meeting a diversity of experts is that there is less room to develop a relationship with the co-lecturer, which is also a critical success factor for the tandem concept. In these cases we look for a balance in this regard.

All projects work together with organisations that train, recruit and supervise experts by experiences. In this way, lecturers are assured of a qualitative match and the experiential experts can talk to the students about the current situation in the field. The experiential experts have a network in which to share their experiences and learn from others. Some organisations also train and support tandems (Sedney et al, 2016).

Experts by experience at the four universities of applied sciences are involved as employees or on a voluntary basis, some with a voluntary contract. Volunteers receive vouchers or a voluntary allowance, which they may combine with their benefits if they stay below a certain maximum annual volunteer allowance. Several university colleges report budget cuts for guest speakers, which means that it becomes more difficult for experts to participate in the full course. There is also a shortage of resources for the employment of experts by experience.

Experts by experience usually work on temporary projects, and when they are not working on a full-time basis, risk falling victim to the poverty gap, as a result of their monthly income is lower due to cuts in their benefits and the loss of additional support measures for low-income families. In education, employment is linked to diploma requirements, with salaries scaled according to qualifications and not according to job descriptions. Management and HR need to be creative in their efforts to pay fair wages that are not detrimental to those involved.

Conclusion

The results of cooperation projects in tandem with experts by experience in Dutch-speaking social work education indicate that all parties involved perceive the experience as positive. Gaining extra insight into different life experiences; feeling the limitations of one's own frame of reference; reflecting on one's own first impressions; communicating and acting; developing a respectful, positive attitude; and daring to enter into a dialogue with the client – these are all valuable learning outcomes related to the involvement of experts by experience in social work education. Nevertheless, the various projects have indicated that this collaboration is fragile. It requires lecturers to adopt a more facilitating role, while experts by experience are expected to have a certain degree of stability in their lives in addition to openness, communication skills, diplomacy and resilience. Organisational support is also of fundamental importance in terms of training, coaching and support for the experts and the lecturers.

The extra time the tandems need to invest in relationship building, preparation, delivery and debriefing requires additional resources, as does the practical organisation of such collaboration. Even if such resources are available, the balance is tenuous: confrontations, necessary survival strategies and clashes between contrasting life experiences are very likely in any real collaboration. Collaboration transcends the professional, brings ethical dilemmas to the surface and touches the essence of the profession that we are training students to enter. Despite the care and reframing it demands, the benefits of these educational innovations deserve further investment and implementation on a structural basis.

References

Adams, R., Dominelli, L. and Payne, M. (2002) *Critical Practice in Social Work*, London: Palgrave Macmillan.

Beresford, P. and Boxall, K. (2012) 'Service users, social work education and knowledge for social work practice', *Social Work Education: The International Journal*, 31(2): 155–67.

Bouwes, T. and Philips, A. (2016) 'Nothing about us without us'. Ervaringsdeskundigen in het onderwijs. Recorded interview. Hogeschool Amsterdam. Available from: https://www.hva.nl/akmi/gedeelde-content/nieuws/nieuwsberichten/2016/06/nothing-about-us-without-us.html

Casman, M.T., Vranken, J., Dierckx, D., Deflandre, D. and Campaert, G. (2010) *Experts by Experience in Poverty and in Social Exclusion Innovation Players in the Belgian Federal Public Services*, Antwerp: Apeldoorn Garant.

Dierckx, D. and Francq, B. (2010) 'Engaging the poor in policy making', in D. Dierckx, N. Van Herck and J. Vranken, *Poverty in Belgium*, Leuven: Acco.

Dierckx, D., Herck, N. and Vranken, J. (2010) *Poverty in Belgium*, Leuven: Acco.

Driessen, E., Holten, J., Huber, M., Passavanti, E., Sedney, P. and Vado Soto, X. (2013) *Begrippenkader Ervaringsdeskundigheid en aanverwante begrippen*. Hogeschool van Amsterdam, Kenniscentrum Maatschappij en Recht, lectoraat Outreachend Werken en Innoveren. Amsterdam.

Driessens, K. and Goris, J. (2016). 'Anti-poverty policy in Belgium: an integrated approach'. Comments paper: *Belgium* in EU peer review: *Social Protection and Social Inclusion Programme* in Social Community Teams against Poverty, the Netherlands. Available from: http://ec.europa.eu/social/BloBServlet?docId=15064&langId=en

Driessens, K. and Van Regenmortel, T. (2006a) *Bind-Kracht in Armoede: Leefwereld en hulpverlening*, Leuven: Lannoo campus.

Driessens, K. and Van Regenmortel, T. (2006b) *Force du Lien contre la pauvreté: Sphère de vie et relation d'aide*, Leuven: Lannoo campus.

Driessens, K., McLaughlin, H. and van Doorn, L. (2016) 'The meaningful involvement of service users in social work education: examples from Belgium and the Netherlands', *Social Work Education*, 35(7): 739–51.

Driessens, K., Lyssens-Danneboom V., Peeters, W., Vansevenant, K., Van Geldorp, C. and Vandenhende, P. (2019) *Samenwerken in tandem met ervaringsdeskundigen: methodiekboek voor databank modellen van samenwerking met ervaringsdeskundigen*, Antwerp: ESF Vlaanderen & Karel de Grote Hogeschool, p 65. Available from: https://www.kdg.be/sites/default/files/rapport-ed_tandempartner_v2.pdf

Heule, C. and Kristiansen, A. (2017) 'Experiences matter'. Photo exhibition of PowerUs. Financed by ESF-project 'Mending the Gap'. Paris: Conference of European Association of Schools of Social Work (EASSW) 27-29/6/2017.

IFSW (2014) 'Global definition of social work', IFSW. Available from: https://www.ifsw.org/what-is-social-work/global-definition-of-social-work/

Kowalk, H. (2015) *The Other Perspective: The Story of an Experiential Expert at the Amsterdam University of Applied Sciences*, Amsterdam: Amsterdam Research Institute for Societal Innovation. Available from: https://www.amsterdamuas.com/binaries/content/assets/subsites/kc-mr/lectoraat-oi/the-other-perspective-edit-2017.pdf

Lyssens-Danneboom, V., Van Gijzel,S. and Driessens, K. (2019) 'Challenges connected to working in tandem in social work education', paper presented at *ESWRA Preconference SIG Service Users Involvement*, 10 April, Katholic University of Leuven.

McLaughlin, H. (2009) 'What's in a name: client, patient, customer, consumer, service user, service user: what's next?', *British Journal of Social Work*, 19(6): 1101–17.

Sedney, P. and Kowalk, H. (2018) 'Leren voor en door tandemsamenwerking', in M. Boer, S. Karbouniaris and M. De Wit (eds), *Van levenservaring naar ervaringsdeskundigheid*. Oud-Turnhout/'s Hertogenbosch: Gompel & Svacina, pp 175–85.

Sedney, P. Remmelink, L. en Passavanti, E. i.s.m. Herman en Lidie (2016) 'Tandems van ervaringsdeskundigen en docenten zoeken, herkennen en overbruggen kloven tijdens het tandemontwikkeltraject', *Participatie en Herstel*, September: 32–6. Available from: https://www.hva.nl/binaries/content/assets/subsites/kc-mr/lectoraat-oi/artikel-herstel-en-participatie_tandemsamenwerking-tot.pdf

Spiesschaert, F. (2005) *Ervaringsdeskundige in armoede en sociale uitsluiting: een inleiding tot de methodiek*, Leuven: Acco.

Vanspauwen, N., Deceuster, C., Lyssens-Danneboom, V. and Van der Elst, D. (2020) *Diversiteit in de inzet en ontwikkeling van ervaringskennis Een Verkennend Onderzoek in Vlaanderen en Brussel*, Brussel: De Link & Expertisecentrum Krachtgericht Sociaal Werk Karel de Grote Hogeschool. Available from: https://www.delinkarmoede.be/sites/default/files/publications/diversiteit_in_de_inzet_en_ontwikkeling_van_ervaringskennis_in_vlaanderen_en_brussel_rapport_maart_2020.pdf

5

Service users as supervisors in social work education: mending the gap of power relations

Mette Fløystad Kvammen and Tabitha Wright Nielsen

Introduction

This chapter presents two projects in which service users are involved as supervisors of students in social work training at the University of Lund, Sweden, and the University of Agder, Norway. The chapter describes how both institutions relate to and try to solve dilemmas and problems connected to power, inequality and the creation of knowledge within the context of social work education.

Power and inequality in social work

Within social work education it is increasingly recognised that service users should play an active role in the development of education and knowledge (IASSW – AIETS, 2014). However, the many experiences of engaging and involving service users in education have also revealed several dilemmas and problems that need to be addressed. These dilemmas are mainly related to the fact that social work is an area defined by power and inequality in power, which affects social relations and the production of knowledge within that area.

Although the idea of service-user involvement in social work and social work education can be traced to different political and ideological discourses (Rae, 2012; Beresford, 2016), it is deeply rooted in a participatory and democratic discourse. Anti-oppressive practice and the willingness to change unequally distributed power are central to the involvement of service users in social work education as well as in practice and research (McLaughlin, 2009a, 2009b; Beresford, 2016; Beresford and Carr, 2012). The dynamics of power and inequality and their consequences thus become explicitly expressed key points, and we keep a critical focus on the identification of dilemmas and the different kinds of problems related to involving service users in social work education.

We find it useful to take a structural perspective on relations of power and their impact on social work, practice and education. We are here inspired by Bourdieu, who pictures inequality in relations of power as inequality in social positions distributed within a social field. These relations of power are, in Bourdieu's terminology, a result of struggles over worshiped goods or capital (Bourdieu, 1984). Bourdieu's concept of field is useful for helping us understand, reflect on and analyse these struggles and their outcomes. The increasing demand for user involvement in social work education has brought new agents into the field. Both user organisations and service users are invited into the field of social work education. The capital they bring in is experience and knowledge about the services. Bourdieu's theory provides a framework for understanding the struggles in the field of social work education between agents in the field and for new agents, such as service users, looking to gain access to the field.

Involving service users in social work education – dilemmas and problems

A common theme of debate revolves around power, questioning if service-user involvement in education really changes existing power relations within the field of social work (Rae, 2012) or rather risks preserving and reproducing these relations.

McLaughlin (2009b) questions the reductionism inherent to the term 'service user'. The reduction of human identity to one single relation marks a lower status in a hierarchical society. McLaughlin furthermore questions the inherent neglecting of people who do not even have access to or use the service they are entitled to out of fear of stigmatisation. Thereby, the terminology risks becoming exclusionary (McLaughlin, 2009b, p 15).

Heule et al (2017) problematise the risk of service users becoming objects instead of agents in the creation of knowledge through how they are introduced to students. Meetings between social work students and service users often take place during the students' practical placements period, with the students in the role of social workers and the service users as their clients. Or social service users are occasionally invited 'to tell their stories' to students in large classrooms. The structure of these kinds of meetings marks the differences in power and status between students and service users, which not only affects the relations between social work students and their future clients but also the students' knowledge and understanding of social problems. As such, these meetings rather mark the gap of power relations between service users and social work students instead of mending it (Heule et al, 2017).

Another dilemma within the field of social work concerns the specific kind of knowledge service users possess and share with students: the risk of individualisation of experiences (Green and Wilks, 2009) and the professionalisation of service users (Andreassen, 2009) are some of the dilemmas and questions which are debated when service users become a part of the field of education. A final dilemma related to the professionalisation of user involvement concerns benefit systems. How are service users to be compensated for their work in education (Turner and Beresford, 2005)? Should they be?

These are some of the dilemmas which have been taken into consideration at the School of Social Work in Lund University and the University of Agder. Both educational institutions have a long tradition of working with service users. This involvement is based on the conviction that the role of service users must change from being that an object of research to become that of active agents in the development of social work knowledge (Heule et al, 2017). This means an involvement of service users which recognises that the knowledge they hold is as important as the academic knowledge presented by social work lecturers and the practical knowledge of the professional social workers supervising the students during their practical placement.

Involvement of service users at the School of Social Work at Lund University

At the School of Social Work in Lund there is a tradition of involving service users in education. Kristiansen et al (2009) argue that the involvement of service users in education has several motives. It relates to a perspective on evidence-based social work practice as consisting of three types of knowledge: research, professional expertise and the perspective of the user (Sackett et al, 1997). It is based on the conviction that 'the voices and experiences of clients and service users are an essential source of knowledge in social work' (Kristiansen et al, 2009, p 2). This belief relates to the recognition of the dichotomy and unequal relationship of power, which is a premise affecting the relationship between the service user and the professionals. Finally, the involvement of service users and service-user organisations in education is not only about teaching students about the complexity of social work but also about how people who have been dependent on and exposed to social work can change their lives (Kristiansen et al, 2009).

Service users are involved in social work education in Lund in different ways. Among others, they are involved in the first semester when representatives of service-user organisations give lectures to students about their organisations and their own lives. In the fifth semester, when students do their internships, they must address the service-user perspective by investigating and analyzing service users' points of view on the organisation where they do their internship. The Mobilisation course in the seventh semester is one wherein social work students and service users study together.

This course, which is described in more detail in Chapter 2, enables students from service-user organisations to study and work together with social work students. By collaborating on creating social innovation projects, social work students and service users gain a common knowledge of social work and its conditions and possibilities, and the course is an example of creating knowledge about social work together. The course is based on theories of power, inclusion, exclusion and social mobilisation, and seeks to integrate different types of knowledge (Heule et al, 2017). The Mobilisation course is an example of the joint creation of knowledge about social work. Finally, in the last course, Professional Social Work, which is mandatory for students, service users work as supervisors for the students.

Service users are also involved in other ways at the School of Social Work. The Service User Council is a council in which researchers, teachers and students from the School of Social Work, as well as representatives of the various service-user organisations in the Skåne region, discuss issues related to the education and practice of social work. The Service User Council started in 2011 and meets once a semester. Finally, a group of students from the Mobilisation course started producing a podcast in spring 2019, *Kunskapsluckan* (The Door to Knowledge). The aim is to create a dialogue with service users and to open the door to new knowledge about their experiences that may prove useful to students. So far, *Kunskapsluckan* has produced 14 podcasts.[1]

Case 1: The School of Social Work at Lund University – the Professional Social Work course

Professional social work is a mandatory course (15 ECTS) in the last semester of social work education. During the course, students have to write an individual assignment, that is, an intervention plan based on a fictional case describing a specific social problem. In the intervention plan, students must independently identify the problems, suggest solutions and show how to help the client in the best way.

The intervention plan must meet the specific requirements described in the curriculum plan of the course. For example, the intervention plan should rest on an evidence-based practice in social work, which means that research, professional expertise and the user's perspective must form the basis for the development of the assignment. In doing so, students should make use of all sources of knowledge – social research, theories, experiences from practice, service users' perspectives, legislation and regulations and so on. The intervention plan should also be based on ethical standards, which include being aware of an ethical approach to the service user's perspective. Supervision by the service users is intended to support and strengthen the work of students with this specific perspective. Work involving the intervention plan has similarities with problem-based learning. Green and Wilks (2009, p 191) define this as follows: 'Students are presented with a situation or problem. This is then defined and clarified through a process of reflection. Resources are sought and theory applied to the problem. In bringing these resources to the problem, students try out different strategies to manage it.'

Since the beginning of the course in 2008, service users have been involved as supervisors for students taking the Professional Social Work course. Each semester, ten service users on average have been engaged in supervising students who write their intervention plans before they graduate as social workers. The service-user supervision is mandated and organised once during the course. It takes place in groups. Every semester there are 20 groups, each consisting of seven to ten students and two service-user supervisors. The groups spend three to four hours discussing the students' proposals for intervention plans. The service-user supervisors work three days in a row, supervising three different groups.

The service-user supervisors are recruited from among service users who have completed the Mobilisation course at the School of Social Work. The knowledge and the experience that service-user students gain from studying together with social work students constitutes a solid knowledge base for working as a supervisor. The service-user supervisors are employed on average 25 hours per semester. This includes supervising as well as preparing and evaluating meetings. The supervisors are paid according to the rates of the collective agreement of the university. Furthermore, their transport costs are reimbursed.

The service-user perspective is incorporated in different ways during social work education at Lund University. It is part of evidence-based social work and is necessary for presenting the complexity of social work to the students. in the Professional Social Work course, we are working to recognise this perspective on equal terms with other kinds of social work knowledge.

Service-user involvement in social work education at the University of Agder

The involvement of service users in social work education at the University of Agder has developed from individual service users being invited to take part in lectures based on ad hoc initiatives to cooperation with the department on an organisational level. Service-user organisations are now partners with social workers when educational issues and research are discussed. This cooperation has resulted, for instance, in a course in which social workers from different institutions work together with service users to develop services through small projects.

In 2019, the department hired a person with experience as a service user in a 20 per cent FTE position to work together with the lecturers. The students meet her in their first semester, both in lectures and groups, where she uses her own experiences to highlight the importance of user participation. In the second semester, the students meet service users as part of a programme on sexual abuse, the title of which is 'Dare to Ask ...'. The programme is planned together with the two service users involved, and has been part of social work education in the second semester for the last five years.

In the fifth semester of the social work programme, the students do their internships, and during the internships the students are supervised by service users in addition to a social worker from the given workplace. This is the project presented as case two below.

Case 2: Social work education at the University of Agder – supervision in practical placement

At the University of Agder in Norway, the social work students are supervised during their internships by people with user experience in the field of social work. This supervision started in 2011, as a result of cooperation between two user organisations and the University of Agder. The aim of this specific cooperation was to systematise and eventually prepare a specific curriculum in which service users recruited from two user organisations (ROM-Agder and A-LARM), together with students and staff of the Social Work Department, were involved in both the design and implementation of the programme.

The representatives of the two service-user organisations played an important role in the planning process of this project, ensuring that the supervisors with experience received training with lecturers from the university before meeting the students. They also stressed the importance of the supervisors with experience being able to meet each other in between the meetings with the students, and their having room for sharing their supervising experiences. The remuneration of the supervisors was also a topic of discussion during the planning process. The supervisors are remunerated at the same level as university teachers, and each supervisor with experience is employed on average 45 hours per semester.

The supervisors with experiences have three meetings with the students during their practical placements. These meetings are mandatory for the students, and each group meeting lasts for two hours. Each group consists of seven to eight students and two supervisors with experience, one from each user organisation. Teachers from the university do not participate in the groups.

Cooperation with the user organisations is a crucial element in this project. The user organisations take part in both the selection of and follow-up with the supervisors with experiences. To become a supervisor, service users must apply for an hourly position. Applicants are interviewed by the coordinators of ROM-Agder and A-LARM. They decide who will be employed. The emphasis in the interviews is on the applicants' history, whether it is processed adequately, and their motivation for this kind of work. The supervisors with experiences work in pairs consisting of a new and an experienced supervisor, and represent experiences from different services.

Dilemmas

Using the mindset of Bourdieu, social work education can be seen as a specific field that reflects conditions of structural inequality in social work and in society in general. This inequality is expressed in the aforementioned dilemmas: the risks of individualisation of experiences and professionalisation of service users. Due to structural inequality, the dilemmas cannot be solved, but we feel that there is an obligation to be aware of these dilemmas and to act to them. In what follows, we will discuss the dilemmas we experienced in our projects in Lund and Agder.

The risk of individualisation of experiences

The need to involve service users in social work education is about creating a knowledge of social work that incorporates the perspectives and experiences of those in need of social services. In social work education, service users are often introduced to students as individuals who tell their personal stories. This entails a risk of individualisation of experiences, which could be counterproductive to the goal of creating a common knowledge based on co-production (Askheim et al, 2016). The personal testimony model is a powerful and often-used way of imparting the experience of service users to students. Green and Wilks (2009) problematise the use of the personal testimony model in social work education. On the one hand, this so-called biographical narrative offers an authenticity that helps students to understand the problems that have led individuals to come into contact with social services (Green and Wilks, 2009, p 193). On the other hand, this personal testimony model, incorporating service users' experiences, risks creating a distance and 'otherness' between people with experiences of social services and the rest of society, making their knowledge seem valid only as it relates to these specific experiences (Green and Wilks, 2009). Due to its specificity, it is not exchangeable in a field of knowledge. Green and Wilks (2009) problematise that, as a storyteller, you are not part of the process of acting and creating knowledge from the story. You tell your story, and the story will be interpreted and used afterwards by the professors and the students in the classroom.

In Agder and Lund, the ambition has been to involve service users in a way that takes their participation beyond their roles as biographical storytellers. In the Professional Social Work course in Lund, the dilemma of individualisation is addressed in at least three ways. Firstly, the requirement that the supervisors complete the Mobilisation course creates a common platform of knowledge that brings the individual experience of being a service user to the level of a collective knowledge and experience. Secondly, during the course we emphasise that the competencies and knowledge shared by the supervisors with the students relate primarily to their position and experience of being service users in relation to the social welfare system. The supervisors carry with them a personal story and experience which, obviously, will and should affect how the subjects in question are approached. But being a service user is also a position and a role that creates certain kinds of relations, restraints and possibilities, which we will all more or less encounter in our lives. Finally, being a supervisor involves dialogue and discussion, and thereby playing an active part in the student's creation of knowledge.

At the University of Agder, service users are involved in all aspects of the supervision, implementation and planning processes. The involved representatives of the service-user organisations are responsible for advertising, interviewing and selecting applicants for the job as supervisors with experience. Service users wishing to apply for the position do not have to be members of either of the two user organisations, but the coordinators are always members of the organisations. The service-user organisations, supervisors with experience and teachers jointly prepare the content and course of the supervision. They discuss how to present experiences to the students and how to supervise and make them reflect on their own experience during their practical placements. Both the experiences of the supervisors as users of social services and the experiences of the students from their practical placements and from their own lives are central to the supervision. The idea is that students, when supervised by people with user experiences, get to reflect on the supervisors' experience and knowledge of the situations that the students bring up for discussion. The students' reflection notes clearly show that the supervisors' input offers the students the opportunity to view the situations from a new perspective, conjuring self-reflection and creating new knowledge. The students describe an open dialogue within the groups which challenges them to discuss difficult topics based on their practical placement experiences.

When involving service users in social work education, our intention has been to recognise service users as equal partners. The term 'equal partners' testifies to good intentions, but structural and cultural frameworks limit equality, and these structures are difficult to change. Askheim et al (2016) describe co-production as a way of working with these structures. But they say that co-production should be at a transformative level, and write: 'The transformative level of co-production requires a relocation of power and control, through the development of new user-led mechanisms of planning, delivery management and governance' (Askheim et al, 2016).

Professionalisation of service users

The idea of service-user supervision is rooted in the premise that service users should be agents instead of objects in the development of social work knowledge. Based on her literature review of service-user involvement in social work, Ulla-Karin Schøn (2016) concludes that service-user involvement is often developed on an ad hoc and inconsistent basis. This could be counterproductive to the aim of avoiding the individualisation of experiential knowledge and of users becoming agents within the field of social work education. One way to transform the role of service users from objects to active agents is by providing them a base of knowledge and institutional recognition, enabling them to speak and act from a position that is acknowledged by other agents within the field of social work education. To realise such institutional recognition and anchoring of service users' knowledge and experience, the educational programme in which service users are involved must be a part of the ordinary curriculum, as pointed out by Beresford and Croft (2004). This could be seen in relation to the work of Tone Alm Andreassen (2018), who describes how measures and models of service-user involvement have enabled service users to be presented in new positions where they are reconfigured from being seen as individuals in need of expert knowledge to being seen as possessors of knowledge.

In Lund, the Mobilisation course is the foundation of user involvement, creating a common base of knowledge among the service-user supervisors. In Agder, the project in which service users supervise students during their internships is firmly rooted in both the two service-user organisations and the university's educational programme.

In addition, in both institutions, supervision by service users is included in the curriculum and plans. Moreover, for service users to be acknowledged as active agents in the field of social work education, it is necessary to compensate for the supervisors' involvement on equal terms with other agents who provide performance for the University (of Applied Science). In both Lund and Agder, service users are paid according to the institution's collective agreement. They are paid for the preparation and the hours used for supervision. The way in which we have chosen to involve service users in Lund and Agder, with employment, training, payment and supervision of the service users, may raise the question of whether we are creating a professionalisation of service users and thereby missing out on the voice of the most excluded groups of service users in social work education.

Two frequently asked questions are who the service-user supervisors represent and whether their professionalisation hinders the authenticity of their service user experience. Although reflexivity and knowledge development, both inherent to becoming a service-user supervisor, could indeed change the knowledge and perspective of the service user, it is questionable whether this makes his or her experience less authentic.

In our opinion, problematising the quality of service-user representativeness degrades and undermines the legitimacy of the knowledge that service users have in the field of social work education. As Alm Adreassen states: 'Labelling the representatives as "professionals" signals that they do not embody sufficient representativeness' (Andreassen et al, 2014, p 336). But questioning professionalism and representativeness also places service users in a trap that is difficult to escape.

Both in Lund and in Agder, we have provided a platform within the field of social work education from which service users can act out their agency in relation to all the other agents who are part of the field of social work education.

Conclusion

The involvement of service users in social work education in Lund and Agder expands the knowledge base of social work and brings in important perspectives, not only for the students and teachers but also for the service users who work as supervisors. However, due to the inequality and relations of power which are an inevitable part of social work, it is not possible to involve service users in social work education without addressing substantial dilemmas. Thus, in this chapter, we have looked at how issues of power and inequality create dilemmas in knowledge creation that need to be considered when service users enter the field of social work education.

In this chapter we have chosen to focus on three dilemmas. The dilemma of the reductionism inherent in the concept of the service user, which narrows what is valued as worthy capital in the field of social work and social work education. The dilemma of the individualisation of experience, which means that service users' experiences are not recognised as valid and thereby exchangeable in the field of social work knowledge. And the dilemma of the professionalisation of service users, which means that their knowledge as valid and genuine service user knowledge can be questioned.

Due to the inequality of power, which structures positions and relationships in the field of social work, these dilemmas cannot be resolved. But by recognising them, it is possible to work with them and change some of the conditions that affect relations of power. At the School of Social Work at Lund University and in the University of Agder, we have focused on the organisational frameworks, equal working conditions and the inclusion of the service user's knowledge in the curriculum. In doing so, we've tried to contribute to the recognition of service users' knowledge as being equivalent to or as important as the academic knowledge presented by teachers in social work education or by the professional social workers who supervise the students.

Note
1   https://www.facebook.com/kunskapsluckanpodd/

References

Andreassen, T.A. (2009) 'The consumerism of "voice" in Norwegian health policy and its dynamics in the transformation of health services', *Public Money & Management*, 29: 117–22.

Andreassen, T.A., Breit, E. and Legard, S. (2014) 'The making of "professional amateurs": professionalizing the voluntary work of service user representatives', *Acta Sociologica*, 57(4): 325–40.

Andreassen, T.A. (2018) 'Service user involvement and repositioning of healthcare professionals: a framework for examining implications of different forms of involvement', *Nordic Welfare Research*, 1(3). Available from: https://www.idunn.no/nordisk_valfardsforskning/2018/01/service_user_involvement_and_repositioning_of_healthcare_pr

Askheim, O.P., Beresford, P. and Heule, C. (2016) 'Mend the gap: strategies for user involvement in social work education', *Social Work Education: The International Journal*, 36(2): 128–40.

Beresford, P. (2012) 'The theory and philosophy behind user involvement' in P. Beresford and S. Carr (eds), *Social Care, Service Users and User Involvement*, London: Jessica Kingsley Publishers.

Beresford, P. (2016) *All Our Welfare: Towards Participatory Social Policy*, Bristol: Policy Press.

Beresford, P. and Croft, S. (2004) 'Service users and practitioners reunited: the key component for social work reform', *British Journal of Social Work*, 34: 53–68.

Bourdieu, P. (1984) *Distinction: A Social Critique of the Judgment of Taste*, Cambridge, MA: Harvard University Press.

Green, L. and Wilks, T. (2009) 'Involving service users in a problem based model of teaching and learning', *Social Work Education*, 28(2): 190–203.

Heule, C., Knutagård, M. and Kristiansen, A. (2017) 'Mending the gaps in social work education and research: two examples from a Swedish context', *European Journal of Social Work*, 20(3): 396–408, DOI: 10.1080/13691457.2017.1283589.

IASSW – AIETS (2014) 'Definition of international social work', IASSW – AIETS. Available from: https://www.iassw-aiets.org/global-definition-of-social-work-review-of-the-global-definition/

Kristiansen, A., Lahti Edmark, H. and Svensson, K. (2009) *Inclusion of a Third (Indispensable?) Perspective in Social Work Education*, working paper vol. 2009, no. 4, Lunds Universitet, Socialhögskolan.

McLaughlin, H. (2009a) *Service User Research in Health and Social Care*, London: Sage.

McLaughlin, H.(2009b) 'What's in a name: "client", "patient", "customer", "consumer", "expert by experience", "service user" – what's next?', *The British Journal of Social Work*, 39(6): 1101–17. Available from: https://doi.org/10.1093/bjsw/bcm155

Rae, R.J. (2012) *Trust, Power and the New Professionalism: A Case Study of Service User and Carer Involvement in the Selection of Social Work*, Huddersfield: University of Huddersfield.

Sackett, D.L., Straus, S.E., Richardson, S., Rosenberg, W. and Haynes, R.B. (1997) *Evidence-Based Medicine: How to Practice and Use EBM*, New York: Churchill Livingstone.

Schön, U.-K. (2016) 'User involvement in social work and education: a matter of participation?', *Journal of Evidence-Informed Social Work*, 13(1): 21–33, DOI: 10.1080/15433714.2014.939382.

Turner, M. and Beresford, P. (2005) *Contributing on Equal Terms: Service User Involvement and the Benefits System*, London: Social Care Institute for Excellence.

6

Involving students with mental health experience in social work education

Hubert Kaszyński and Olga Maciejewska

Introduction

For many years we have been pointing out that a promising method of teaching about mental health is to provide interested parties (especially students and social therapists in general) with first-hand knowledge about mental illness (Kaszyński, 1999). It is therefore essential to have direct contact with individuals with mental illnesses in order to understand them and modify our stereotyped view of deep emotional problems (Couture and Penn, 2003). This approach, which we call 'social education', requires above all a willingness to submit to the authority of those who are predominantly the focus of our educational interactions and themselves subject to authority. As a result, this approach makes us advocates of empowerment. If the objective of our educational activity is to answer the question of how to support people in their development and motivate them to change, then an essential condition becomes our ability to perceive and experience the external world from the subjective perspective of those who become partners in the educational relationship.

First, we present the history of shaping the concept of service-user involvement at the Institute of Sociology of the Jagiellonian University in Krakow, Poland. We emphasise that its indisputable strength is the involvement and cooperation of various actors – academic teachers, people with experience of the diseases, students, social welfare practitioners and therapists. It is necessary to highlight at this point the particular importance of the participation of students with experience of emotional difficulties in the educational process.

History of cooperating with service users

The activities described in this chapter are undertaken by a team of lecturers professionally associated with the Institute of Sociology of the Jagiellonian University and social practitioners involved in various activities for people with mental health problems. From the very beginning, the project was based on close cooperation between both groups.

The first attempts to include the individual experiences of mentally ill people in educational practice were made in 1996–2005 as part of a project called the Educational Group. During co-teaching classes at the Occupational Therapy Centre of the Association for Psychiatry and Community Care (a non-governmental organisation) in Krakow, user-participants shared their lengthy experiences of 'illness, treatment and rehabilitation' with students of social work, occupational therapy, nursing and other professions. Dialogical work in the Educational Group, which consisted of therapists and service users, provided students and those interested in the issues discussed with a certain emotional reinforcement but also made for a testing challenge for the service users: meeting other people, talking openly about themselves and being in the centre of attention. However, the dialogical work also carried a major threat. During classes, the service users could experience themselves as subjects of renewed stigmatisation. After many hours of co-teaching, it became clear that the only possible safeguard against repeated injury for the service users was to build an empathetic relationship between the two people jointly leading the course. We also stress that the essence of social education is its relational, dyadic nature, and that the gauge of its success is the declaration by those who lead and participate in it that the objectives of mutual understanding and of overcoming the barrier of difference have been achieved.

The Educational Group's initiatives adhered to the tradition of the clinical work of Antoni Kępiński, who always stressed the cognitive value of direct contact with people with illnesses. Individuals with such experiences were, and still are, asked for their story of their inner world, dominated by a complex message that is often not understood and extremely hard to articulate. And yet, what interests students is their lengthy experience of difficulty with mental health, searching together for the meaning of suffering, the struggle for health and ways of coping in daily life. Gradually, both the subject matter and the form of teaching are changing – learning about clinical symptoms is being replaced by a subjective approach to understanding the illness.

We made two assumptions in our work with the Educational Group. The first about the mutual benefit that students and members of the Educational Group should take from the courses, and the second about referring to the strengths of the service-user during classes: the focus should be on building their strengths rather than analysing their weaknesses, and on their health despite the diagnosis rather than on the illness.

The development process of the Educational Group was positively determined by the openness of the students and a dyad of educators, consisting of a lecturer and a person with experience, training those who wished, as part of their university courses or professional training, to obtain knowledge about mental illnesses directly from people who have experienced an emotional crisis. These first educational experiences led to gradual changes in the teaching style:

- from people with experience solely presenting on forms of treatment and psychiatric rehabilitation to discussions about the value of participation of mentally ill people in social life;
- from discussions in which the therapist spoke about the service users in their absence to conversations in which the therapist spoke alongside service users;
- from conclusions being made by the therapist to conclusions being developed together with the service users.

Between 2006 and 2008, the work of the Educational Group was continued within the framework of the Partnership for Development – Cogito Krakow Initiative for Social Economy, funded by the EQUAL Community Initiative of the European Social Fund, which developed the social education method and tested its usefulness in teaching. A particularly important modification was the change of the teaching location from a rehabilitation centre to the premises of higher education institutions in Krakow. Classes were consistently led by people who combined two fundamental competencies: being both support and help practitioners as well as lecturers. In this period, the first short book in Poland edited by mentally ill people was composed, consisting only of their articles. This particular publication contributed to making it possible for healthy individuals to meet people in the process of recovering their mental health or who have already done so. We emphasised the commendable work of the authors, as this was evidence of a unique form of removing the social stigma associated with people susceptible to damage. What we meant by this was to show recognition and respect for the knowledge and understanding that comes from experience, and which allows people to be seen as possessing their own views and voices and not as an object of the knowledge of others (Janik and Wroński, 2008).

The next stage in the development of the method was to link social education with the operation of the Open the Doors Association in Krakow (one of the first organisations in Poland operating in the field of support and assistance for mentally ill people), whose broad aim is to fight the stigmatisation of mentally ill people. Working closely with the members of the association, in 2008–11 the possibility of conducting social education exclusively in the student environment was developed. A particular manifestation of this work was the association's training grant[1] they got for their project, 'Through Education to Acceptance', which consisted of members of the association presenting on the value of work in the healing process to groups of students. The knowledge was transferred to the students in close cooperation between service users and professional lecturers – in line with the idea of working in a dyad. More than 150 students participated in the training. The vast majority (96 per cent) stated that the messages they took from the training were useful, while 91 per cent of those surveyed declared that the training had given them a better understanding of the everyday problems of mentally ill people. At the same time, they stressed the honesty, authenticity and directness of what the people leading the classes had to say. Most of them appreciated the value of direct contact with people who had experienced psychological crises, and regarded this as the most important experience they could take away from the meeting (Kaszyński, 2013).

Among the effects of several years of intensive collaboration with the Open the Doors Association was the introduction of regular, open workshops titled 'Let's Talk about Mental Illness'. These were held over the course of three years (2010–12) at the Institute of Psychology of the Jagiellonian University in conjunction with the university's Psychology Students Research Society and the Institute of Sociology (Rynda, 2010). The workshops, led by recovering individuals, gave participants not only an emotional insight into the nature of mental illness but also an experience of how the concepts of respect, patience, dialogue and the ability to listen have a personal meaning and are important and accessible therapeutic possibilities. 'Let's Talk' consists principally of meetings of students, practitioners, lecturers and individuals particularly interested in the issues discussed and those with diverse professional and personal experiences for whom the problem of recovering from mental illness is a life challenge, frequently a passion, but also a research question, degree subject, practical activity or part of their everyday educational work.

Another unique social education initiative in Poland, which the Institute of Sociology of the Jagiellonian University had the opportunity to launch, came in 2010 with training for the Inter-university Psychological Assistance Centre, operating among other sites at Kraków University of Economics (Kaszyński et al, 2019). A significant change here was the involvement in the social education process of students of Krakow's higher education institutions who had experienced mental health disorders and were willing – as students – to share their experience. The series of workshops, open to everybody from Krakow University of Economics, was aimed at two groups of participants: university academic and administrative staff as well as students. The classes were prepared and led in collaboration with students of several universities in the city who suffered from mental illnesses or so-called 'collective mental disorders'. The series of meetings addressed experiences of psychosis, mood disorder (depression) and depression and anxiety disorders. In 2014 we introduced training covering the problem of anorexia, while in 2015, in response to the need highlighted by staff of the disability services offices at the various universities, the issue of students with Asperger syndrome was incorporated. The subject matter of the meetings mostly focused on specific emotional problems experienced, the possibility of reconciling psychiatric treatment with the demands of academic life, discrimination encountered from university staff and other students and methods for supporting mentally ill students.

As a result of these initiatives, but also because of the consistent promotion of mental health in the academic community, in 2012 a group of students, social therapists and academic staff decided to form a civic organisation named the Institute of Social Therapy and Education – Association, which took charge of the substantive content of the training held in Krakow's universities, including the Jagiellonian University, the Pontifical University of John Paul II, the University of Economics and recently also AGH University of Science and Technology.[2]

An important objective of the association is to prepare – on the basis of training course evaluations – a support model ensuring a significant increase in the opportunities for students with mental disorders to obtain a university degree and also to find and keep a job. Its second aim is to develop courses to promote mental health adapted to young people's needs. In 2013, association members conducted pilot workshops entitled 'Promotion of Young People's Mental Health' at the Holy Family of Nazareth Catholic High School in Krakow. Their main aim was to provide school pupils with basic knowledge on mental health. The lesson plan was divided into three meetings. During the first, the participants analysed autobiographical histories written by young people dealing with a mental health crises.[3] In the second, they worked with a person who told them the story of his/her recovery. The third addressed the possibility of changing the stereotypical perception of their mentally ill contemporaries.

The last form of educational work introduced in 2013 was a series of cyclical seminars which we called 'Seminars Focused on a Person'.[4] The crux of these seminars was dialogue between people, which, as Hannah Arendt emphasised, differs from ordinary conversation or even discussion in that it is entirely imbued with the satisfaction stemming from another person and their words. During the seminars, 'wounded stories' transform the physical act of speaking into an ethical act, which is especially important to the learning process of people intending to work with others.

The context of the project implementation

In this part of the article we present the results of a long-term participatory action research study carried out at the Institute of Sociology of the Jagiellonian University on the possibilities of participation of mentally ill people in the training of social workers (Kaszyński, 2013; Kaszyński and Maciejewska, 2016; Kaszyński et al, 2019).

The aim of the research was to continuously identify and critically analyse the key substantive and formal aspects of the training of social workers involving the participation of service users (including students with experiences of mental healthcare), enabling the formation of open (non-oppressive) spaces for dialogue that contribute to reducing the stigma associated with mental health but which can also be used in programs of social work education.

The service users were individually invited to the activities by a project team consisting of lecturers and people with experience of mental health problems as either:

- representatives of NGOs and self-help groups working in mental health protection;
- people with no affiliation but who are involved in sharing their experience with others through publications, lectures, exhibitions and other forms of artistic expression; or
- social work students with experience of mental health problems who expressed a desire to take part in the project during the courses. Invitations were of an informal nature.

The first phase consisted of conducting optional workshops (which were part of social work studies at the Institute of Sociology of Jagiellonian University) involving a group of social work students with the aim of recognising the complexity of mental health issues from a phenomenological perspective and overcoming stigmatising ideas about the incurability and degradative (non-developmental) consequences of mental disorders. Our practice shows that it is not the illness itself but rather the recovery aspect on which both the service users and social workers tend to focus. The basis of both educational activities and work with students on mental health issues should be an attempt to answer the question of what health actually means after the unique developmental crisis of an illness. The working method adopted in the project was based on the study of essays written by service users and on individual meetings with those who use the traditional services of psychiatric medicine or rehabilitation.

In the second phase, students who revealed their own experiences during the introductory workshops were: prepared by lecturers for educational activities and teaching with the permanent possibility of consulting service users with teaching experience; and included in conducting classes for social work students as part of optional courses. The particular educational method applied and evaluated in the project involved classes being run by a dyad (consisting of an academic staff member and an experienced person).

This approach was characterised by three main challenges (though these were not the only challenges) relating to:

1. the continuous monitoring and reduction of authority of lecturers resulting from the linguistic domination of the professionals, which limited or nullified the validity of their experiential knowledge;
2. the willingness and ability to learn the language of the service users, which is an important indicator of their acceptance;
3. the willingness of professionals to credit the vernacular language of people with experience as a fast and accurate form of communication (rather than, as professionals often do, seeing it as a paraphasis of professional language).

It proved possible to compensate for these linguistic threats in the project by subjecting educational actions to regular individual and group reflection with the participation of the service users.

From the very beginning of the project implementation, we have attached great importance to its evaluation, which was based on three pillars:

1. Service users were involved in the research team in accordance with the assumptions of the participatory action research – the basis was a cooperation agreement supported by unstructured interviews with students, educators and participants in project and research activities focusing on the substantive and formal aspects of the educational work through a systematic survey of the trainees at the start and end of the course.
2. We discussed the specific educational actions in which the service users regularly take part in the common group discussions and recorded the conclusions. Particularly important topics of group reflection were all identifiable ethical- and therapy-related dilemmas concerning the participation of service users in educational work.
3. The following data-collection techniques, adapted to the needs of the evaluation, were used: interviews in free form and questionnaires carried out with the training participants – the students; recordings of the individual educational meetings; preparation of a film to promote social work training with the participation of service users; and writing publications in which knowledge in this field is popularised.

Involving students with experience in mental healthcare – recommendations for practice

Social education, which we sometimes refer to as an 'open space for education' or a 'space for reflection', is an approach to learning which we base on four general premises. First, the possibility of meeting and dialogue between people with similar social status (for instance, one student could meet another student; a lecturer with some emotional problems was able to talk to another teacher – perhaps in a different life situation) or – what we consider particularly important – the capacity for openness towards the other despite differences in status. Second, the creation of safe conditions for the exchange of ideas, that is, in which one is as free as possible from the threat of being judged negatively by others and by oneself. Third, the development of an atmosphere of cooperation and shared responsibility between the participants in education for the process of mutual transfer of knowledge and the creation of a safe emotional space. And lastly, the initiation of workshops in which participation is entirely voluntary.

We also emphasise the importance of more detailed assumptions for educational practice: in social education, it is important to take into account the 'principle of minimal difference', which means that the workshops should be designed and implemented in such a way that initial ideas about people with mental illnesses will not markedly differ from the image formed as a result of the training and direct encounters with service users. This is to avoid interpretations according to which the person with an illness who jointly leads the meeting is seen as 'merely' an exception that proves the rule.

Healthy dialogue in a meeting requires that it is moderated in such a way that not only the service user refers to his or her own experiences. The gauge of a good meeting is that it includes all participants in the discussion. The creation of a space of trust allows for the sharing of responsibility for the dialogue, the discerning of the possibility of avoiding emotional reductionism towards mentally ill people and also reflection on the possibility of responding to the needs present in the face of the other.

Some remarks and reflections to clarify our vision:

- With regard to the fundamentals of social education, we would like to share a simple reflection that is often not fully appreciated: the traditional spaces for educational encounters with persons with mental illness (for example, psychiatric hospitals, occupational therapy centres or other mental health protection institutions) fundamentally define the future relationship as being one of 'healthy person versus sick person'. In this model, one party needs help and the other is obliged to provide it; one has more power and knowledge, and the other must be dependent. This fact inevitably restricts the opportunities for the person leading the training to share his or her own experiences and opinions – due to the huge difference in status resulting from social attitudes, stigma and differences in the division and distribution of power. This process of division and stigmatisation is particularly reinforced in the institutional context. This

makes it practically impossible, or at least incredibly difficult, to adjust the relationship and the ideas of the parties about each other. That is why social education must take place outside these institutions. Our practice involves meetings generally at universities or in galleries or public administration offices, that is, outside the context of stigmatising notions of psychiatric treatment. Due to the proximity of the educational site for the participants, the experience of mental illness is no longer unprecedented and absent in everyday life and the immediate social environment.
- In addition to this remark on the importance of the spatial context in which education takes place, we stress the need to take into account a specific psychological context. By this we mean the moderator's concern to prevent the conversation from placing the service user in the role of a person with an illness, thus passing on his or her frustrations, criticism and demands to the listeners, who in turn adopt a defensive position. In order to avoid such a narrative of 'wronged plaintiff' versus 'accused defendant', the story of the service user must be presented in a form that reveals the truth of the individual experience.
- A personalised narrative is a specific way to facilitate dialogue which not only levels the traditional 'slanted' healthy person/ill person relationship but also helps to construct a space of shared emotional experience. At this point, it is worth using the idea that although everyone has their own life experience, it is part of the world common to all people.

The importance of including students in social education

In this part, we highlight some fundamental conclusions that we have drawn from the implementation of the project. They all relate to the issue of involving students with experience of mental illness in the complex process of teaching and the professional preparation of social therapists.

In the course of our educational practice, students participating in the training often admitted that these meetings gave them an insight into the world of people with illnesses. By listening to personal histories of those dealing with illness and the psychiatric therapy system, they learn to understand how such an individual may feel and what care he or she needs. The meetings show them the needs and capabilities of service users, as well as the suffering they may endure – not as 'clients', 'patients' or 'invalids', but as people.

Service users are perceived as people who are worth discovering and learning from. Training participants also point out the strengths of people with illnesses, including their reflectivity, critical faculties and wisdom.

The participants declare that the experience of meeting and talking with service users has changed their one-dimensional perspective on people with illnesses; often for the first time, they realise not only that such individuals are able to lead independent lives but also that these lives can be a source of satisfaction, characterised by searching for and finding meaning.

The service users leading the classes stressed the significance of contact with the participants in the training. When the feeling of uncertainty about how they would be received gives way to satisfaction, with deep interest and openness, this helps them to recover and strengthen their sense of influence on reality.

We highlight the particular importance of the participation of students with experience of emotional difficulties in the training process of social workers, alongside the traditional model of 'training visits' by mental health service users. The effectiveness and greatest value of the student-involvement approach lies in the fact that it is valuable for students to experience that the boundary between health and disease is not clear cut.

Conclusion

When applying social education, one cannot ignore the internal barriers created in the academic community:

- the status of knowledge arising from experience, which is unclear and often questioned (or even openly attacked);
- the demand for empirically proven effectiveness of service-user participation in the academic world, which tends to ignore the axiological justifications of this particular teaching method;
- and the doubts we share about the extent to which wounded stories can be institutionalised without removing their values of authenticity, which is a prerequisite for empathetic learning.

A fundamental condition for building a healthy society is the shift from mechanical interaction to personal cooperation with people with illnesses. In this respect, social education is particularly useful. It is important to leave behind the archaic but in practice still-applied assumption that professionals are better able to organise and carry out care for people with illnesses than they are themselves. The answer to the question why is clear: a system based on all kinds of coercion produces a seemingly irrational aversion and even resistance on the part of patients to recovery, the details and objectives of which have not been discussed with them. It can always be said that three-quarters of patients do not follow doctors' orders with regard to drug therapy.

However, this question can also be put in quite different terms: the majority of doctors do not take account of patients' needs and expectations, and therefore prescribe medication incorrectly, leading to resistance in these patients. How can we combat these obstructive social relations that perpetuate mutual hostility and mistrust and turn a person into an instrument for others to use? The answer could lie in educational work on increasing social sensitivity, which develops our ability to empathetically understand individual human fortunes through a willingness to learn from each other.

Inclusion is a sign of recognition, which, in turn, is fundamental in order to be able to talk about social change, a change in the educational system and a change in the place of experienced people in the field of education. Social education emphasises the importance of the empowerment concept for the mentally ill and their immediate environment. It is an experimental approach, allowing contact with sick people and learning from them in an open, non-threatening situation, which complements the traditional model of teaching based on the knowledge of specialists. From the perspective of social education, so-called academic knowledge is seen not as the only valid kind of knowledge but as a small piece of a much larger puzzle.

Notes

[1] The grant was announced by the Cooperation Fund, titled: 'Promotion of Social Economy on the Basis of the Experiences of the EQUAL Community Initiative Programme'.
[2] The website of the Institute of Social Therapy and Education – Association can be found at: http://ities.pl/
[3] The guest of the first seminar, 'Recovered Joy', in 2013 was Aleksandra Kożuszek, the author of a book by the same title (*Radość odzyskana*, see: http://ities.pl/relacja-z-seminarium-skoncentrowanego-na-osobie-szukajcie-mnie-wsrod-szalencow/); Krystian Głuszko, author of *Szukaj mnie wśród szaleńców* (Look for me among the lunatics), meanwhile, accepted an invitation to the second seminar in 2015 (see: http://ities.pl/relacja-z-seminarium-skoncentrowanego-na-osobie-szukajcie-mnie-wsrod-szalencow/)
[4] Kociołek, R. (2013) Książka jako historia zdrowienia. Znaczenie dla autora doświadczonego zaburzeniami zdrowia psychicznego, znaczenie dla czytelnika, unpublished dissertation, Uniwersytet Pedagogiczny w Krakowie, Kraków. The author presents the possibility of employing selected texts by people with mental illnesses in bibliotherapeutic work with young people.

References

Couture, S.M. and Penn, D.L. (2003) 'Interpersonal contact and the stigma of mental illness: a review of the literature', *Journal of Mental Health*, 3(12): 291–305.

Janik, J. and Wroński, K. (2008) *Stowarzyszenie 'Otwórzcie Drzwi': O barierach w zatrudnianiuipracy – perspektywa beneficjentów*, Krakow: Stowarzyszenie 'Otwórzcie Drzwi'.

Kaszyński H. (1999) 'The role of the patient as a psychiatric teacher', in *Schizophrenia and Borderline Disorders: A Challenge for Science and Society – Abstracts* at the 12th Congress of the World Association for Dynamic Psychiatry WADP, Schizophrenie und Borderline-Storung, 17–21 March, Berlin.

Kaszyński, H. (2013) *Praca socjalna z osobami chorującymi psychicznie*, Krakow: Wydawnictwo Uniwersytetu Jagiellońskiego.

Kaszyński, H., Maciejewska, O. (2016) 'Praca socjalna z osobami z zaburzeniami psychicznymi. Rekomendacje dla kształcenia w "nowej" specjalizacji', *Zeszyty Pracy Socjalnej*, 4(21): 161–76.

Kaszyński, H., Ornacka, K. and Maciejewska, O. (2019) 'Open spaces for dialogue promoting mental health as a social work education methodology', *Social Work Education*, 38(1): 103–18.

Kociołek, R. (2013) Książka jako historia zdrowienia. Znaczenie dla autora doświadczonego zaburzeniami zdrowia psychicznego, znaczenie dla czytelnika, unpublished dissertation, Uniwersytet Pedagogiczny w Krakowie, Kraków.

Liberadzka, A. (2008) 'Sprawozdanie z Projektu zatytułowanego "Przez edukację do akceptacji"', in H. Kaszyński (ed), *Edukacja społeczna jako metoda przeciwdziałania stereotypizacji osób chorujących psychicznie na rynku pracy. Raport, Krakowska Inicjatywa na Rzecz Gospodarki Społecznej – COGITO*, Krakow: Krakowska Inicjatywa na Rzecz Gospodarki Społecznej, pp 55–69.

Rynda, M. (2010) 'Kilka refleksji na temat spotkań "Porozmawiajmy o chorobie psychicznej"', in I. Białek, H. Kaszyński and H.M. Lupa (eds), *Moja wędrówka: Refleksje studentów i wykładowców UJ o chorobie psychicznej i studiowaniu*, Krakow: Biuro ds. Osób Niepełnosprawnych UJ, pp 170–175

7

The Living Library in social work education

Robin Sen, Marianne Nylund, Ali Hayward, Rahul Pardasani, William Rivera and Michelle Kaila

Introduction

A Human Library or Living Library is a metaphorical version of an actual library where, in place of actual books, Living Books, people with experience using social work services, directly or as carers to those receiving services, narrate a chapter from their experiences to a small group of social work student 'readers'. Two approaches are presented from two universities, one from the United Kingdom and the other from Finland. In the University of Sheffield (UK), people with experiences of social work services, teachers and students have developed living libraries as a regular feature of the syllabus for a qualifying master's degree programme in social work since 2014. In the Diaconia University of Applied Sciences (Diak, Finland), bachelor-level students in social services initiated and organised a Human Library event as part of their project studies. In this article, the terms Living Library and Human Library are used interchangeably.

Background to the Human Library/Living Library

The Human Library method has been employed globally as an anti-oppressive tool to bring together representatives of different minorities in society who volunteer to share their life stories and experiences in order to help others overcome prejudice using active dialogue based on respect (Pardasani and Rivera, 2017). The development of the Human Library has offered a new way of bringing the experience of people who have used social work services into the classroom. According to the Council of Europe web pages (Council of Europe, n.d.), 'the first ever living library (*Menneske Biblioteket* in Danish) was organised in Denmark in 2000 at the Roskilde Festival. The original idea had been developed by a Danish youth NGO called "Stop the Violence" (Foreningen Stop Volden) as part of the activities they offered to festival goers' (Human Library, n.d.).

Vision, values goals

The Living Library seeks to challenge oppression. Everyday oppression occurs when individual actions, the application of discriminatory laws or the operation of social structures impairs a person's ability to engage in civic society fully. This might include deprivation of an individual's right to make a fair living, to partake in different facets of social life or to enact certain of their human rights. Additionally, oppression can include particular ways of imposing belief systems, values, legal frameworks and lifestyles on others, through passive or violent mediums. Such imposition can undermine particular communities' abilities to enact their civic and human rights. These examples illustrate 'outer oppression', but oppression can also be internalised when marginalised communities favour, and operate under, the hegemonic principles of wider society in a way which reproduces inequalities and reinforces their disempowerment. Internal oppression can entail self-hatred practices, auto-censorship, ignominy and the forsaking of individuals or cultural groups (Baines, 2011).

Theoretical background

The Human Library has developed into an international movement seeking to use the concept as a tool to break down barriers between people (Little et al, 2011). The founders of the Human Library drew on social psychological theory (Allport, 1954) to theorise their purpose: a lived encounter with someone from a different background is a mechanism for promoting understanding and getting beyond stereotypes. Developers of the Living Library in social work education have drawn on wider social theoretical and philosophical concepts to deepen its conceptualisation. Schütz's (1967) development of the 'lifeworld' as a qualitative sociological concept from phenomenology is relevant: Living Library exchanges are shaped around those parts of Living Books' everyday thoughts, feelings and life experiences which they choose to share. However, there is an idealist tradition within phenomenological thought that conceives of the mind as separate to the body. Sen et al (2016) therefore sought to draw on the work of Merleau-Ponty (2013) and Levinas (1969) to theorise the face-to-face, embodied, character of the Living Library exchanges. Living Books and readers experience and learn from each other as 'embodied subjects'; the focus is on the corporeally situated subjectivities of each.

Arnstein's highly cited model of citizen participation (1969) might be used to critique the participatory claims of the Living Library. Despite its laudable aims, might the short-lived character of a Living Library exchange, within far larger social work education curricula, actually represent a form of tokenistic involvement with 'no muscle, hence no assurance of changing the status quo; (Arnstein, 1969, p 217)? This challenge is a necessary reminder that any involvement of people with experience of services within 'professional' curricula risks forms of tokenism. There are no guarantees that the experiences a Living Book narrates in the Library will inform students' future practice in the way Living Books might hope. However, our experiences of organising living libraries suggest this critique underplays the impact which the conduct of the Living Library, and student reflection on the Library exchanges, can have on students' practices beyond the Library (see Sen et al, 2016). Indeed, Arnstein (1969) herself acknowledged that her framework of involvement is a simplification of how genuine participation in partnerships may be conceived, experienced and achieved. As detailed in Sen et al (2016), Sheffield social work students' own discourse, several months after living libraries, illustrates how these encounters can be deeply meaningful to students, staying with them and thereby influencing the ways they engage in, and conceive of, practice. The Living Library at Diak was undertaken through a participatory approach in which the human books were always involved at every stage of its implementation. Several days after the event, the organisers got in touch with the most vulnerable human books in order to check up on their welfare and to check that their the disclosure of their stories in the Living Library had not caused them any distress. None of them reported being negatively psychologically affected.

The model of partnership within the Living Library is conceived to be reciprocally consultative, collaborative and connective. The goal of this partnership is to engender dialogue in a discursive forum whereby all are given both the freedom and the obligation to talk openly about their differential experiences, fears and hopes for social work. Through this process, opportunities are created for all to consider how improvements that meet all stakeholders' interests may be achieved. As Arnstein (1969, p 217) argues, the underlying issues for participation are broadly similar across a range of contexts, namely: '"nobodies" ... are trying to become "somebodies" with enough power to make the target institutions responsive to their views, aspirations, and needs.'

Pedagogical background

The Living Library method can be used as an anti-oppressive tool to bring together people from different groups in society. The approach can also be used as a tool to help social work students identify their own unconscious biases, reflect on individual blind spots and develop competence to become better professionals working with people from different social and cultural backgrounds. The Human Library has also been developed for use in nursing education (Kendall-Raynor, 2009) and high/secondary school education (Orosz et al, 2016). The Human Library became part of the Council of Europe's programme in 2003, and the impetus behind its inclusion was the acknowledgment that human rights cannot be defended and promoted by legal documents and laws alone (Council of Europe, n.d.). Consequently, the Human Library model is seen as valuable in youth work, global education and human rights education (Allianssi, 2020; Council of Europe, n.d.).

The Living Library model requires student readers to make sense of the embodied otherness of Living Books; in so doing, they need to engage in thinking through how the everyday experiences narrated by Living Books fit in with, differ from or challenge their own experiences and understandings. This conceptualisation of the live encounters in the Living Library is consistent with the three 'deep learning' traits outlined by Marton and Säljö (1997). Students in deep learning are described as engaging with the knowledge they are presented with by abstracting meaning/making sense of content, understanding reality in a different way and developing as a person. To achieve deep learning by engaging with the knowledge people with experience of services provide in the classroom, students must start to make sense of the narratives they hear and explore how these cohere with or challenge their own experiences of social work. Through this they extend their understandings of how social work might be delivered and how they might individually practice their professional craft. The Living Library format is designed to facilitate such deep critical engagement.

The second paradigm we draw on here relates to human geographical understandings of space and place: Who can access a given space, and what identities and status they are accorded within it, is both reflective and generative of wider social stratification (Valentine, 2007). Part of the aim of the Living Library is to help better connect the learning that people with experience of services bring to the academic part of social work courses with student practice in social work organisations during placement periods. Underpinning this has been a conscious choice to locate the living libraries in the university space, emphasising it as one that is open to people with experience of social work services. This is both due to the expertise their experience brings to the academy and because they are members of the local community in which the university is situated.

The Living Library at the University of Sheffield

In October 2014, the first Living Library took place in the MA social work programme at Sheffield University. By the end of the 2019 summer semester, the Living Library had been used as a medium on 13 occasions and had become an embedded tool in the teaching syllabus. While the involvement of people with experience in social work courses in England is mandated, there is no prescription as to what form this should take, therefore it is a choice the MA programme tutors have made to utilise the Living Library as a tool for student learning. Six of the living libraries that have been run have been generic, which means that they included a range of people with wide experiences of different kinds of social work services. Seven have been specialist, which means that they focused on the life experiences of particular people with experience of services; for example, people from the LGTBQIA communities, asylum seekers and refugees and people with learning disabilities, autism or both.

The Living Library provides a platform from which the Living Books have power and control over their input and how they wish to deliver it. It is important to note that Living Books also have choice of whether or not to be involved in the first place. This may seem a strange thing to highlight, but a lack of choice is inherent in the daily lives of many people with experience of services. The recruitment happens in different ways. In some instances, people with experience of services have been approached who have worked with the MA social work programme before. In some, Living Books have heard about the living libraries from others and have contacted the programme to volunteer. In other instances, the programme tutors have specifically approached people or organisations and discussed the possibility of their, or people they work with, volunteering as Living Books. This last approach involves substantial preparation. For example, for the first specialist LGTBQIA Living Library, the organisers approached a local organisation working with young LGTBQIA people. They discussed the Library with a development worker at the organisation, and attended a drop-in for the young people where the Living Library was discussed and where the organisers role played how a Living Library exchange might develop. Young people from the drop-in then decided if they wished to take part or not. Those who did were supported by the organisation's workers at the Living Library in question.

The course tutors offer support for anything Living Books may need in order to take part, but ultimately they choose what they want their Living Book to be about, which part of their story they want to share, the title of their Living Book chapter and their book cover. The naming of something is an important symbol of ownership. At Sheffield, as is consistent with one of the founding principles of the Human Library, Living Books have not been paid for their attendance. This principle is rooted in the idea that living libraries are based around the free, reciprocal exchange of knowledge between 'books' and 'readers'. We do, however, pay for all transport costs of Living Books, ensure plentiful refreshments are available and pay for the costs of any supporters a Living Book needs to attend. In a few cases, we have also been able to reciprocate Living Book' contributions at the Living Library by facilitating their access to university library collections after they requested such access.

Once volunteers have indicated they wish to be Living Books, course tutors meet with them to write the text of their book cover. These are typically shared with students before a Library. The book cover has two functions: First, it gives the student readers a taste of the books available at the Library so they can gain an overview of the titles on offer and express preferences for which books they might prefer to read. Second, and most importantly, it helps the Living Book to think about what they do and do not wish to share during a Living Library exchange.

A real example is given in here in Box 7.1 (used with permission, but the name has been changed to preserve anonymity):

Box 7.1

Name: Mary
Reason for services: Cerebral palsy and associated conditions
Book Title: Invitation to My Party?
Short Book Description: Soon to be 16 years old, Mary knows what it's like to have professionals in her life. From neurologists to speech therapists, physiotherapists to social workers, and plenty more besides, she's had appointments with them all. Some of her earliest friendship memories include the people she's worked with, only later to realise they weren't actually her friends and wouldn't be coming to her birthday party. Mary's story looks at a childhood understanding and feelings towards needing services.

The Living Library model challenges traditional teaching and learning roles. Tutors, the traditional social work teachers, are only there as librarians – organisers of the event, timekeepers and supports to Living Books or students, if needed. The Living Book has the scope within the reading time to speak about more or less anything they choose, including control over how to answer readers' questions.

The structure of each of our living libraries has broadly remained the same:

1. A brief introduction and opening of the Living Library, from one of the Librarians (social work tutors) (five minutes).
2. Session 1 – the Living Book's first reading followed by questions from the readers and discussion (30 minutes).
3. Refreshment break (ten minutes).
4. Session 2 – the Living Book's second reading followed by questions from the readers and discussion (30 minutes).
5. Readers write their Living Book reviews in groups – Living Books take a further refreshment break while this happens. Reviews are either written

messages or small pieces of art which are given to the Living Books by each group of readers as a symbol of what they have taken from the exchange. These reviews are not publicly shared but given to the Living Book in a sealed envelope during the plenary session (see item 6) to look at privately. Some Living Books may choose to look at them there and then, others may take them away to open afterwards (20 minutes).
6. A plenary session in which there is broad discussion of learning from experience, facilitated by librarians, about what readers have learned and how it may impact their future practice. Living Books listen, and add to this discussion if they wish. The plenary discussion refers to the Living Library reading exchanges in general terms, but student readers are specifically asked not to share any of the intimate detail from the readings in the plenary session, as these details are viewed as confidential between the reading group and Living Book (15 minutes).
7. Summary and closing of the Living Library, led by a librarian (five minutes).

The exchange of experiences between Living Book and reader is contained within the boundary of the particular book reading. This is an intimate learning experience between a Living Book and between four and six students. The exchange is private between a Living Book and their small group, and is therefore not mediated by an academic tutor. While tutors are present at the event, they do not listen to or oversee the detail of the group exchanges once the small groups have been organised. As a result, the ambiance of the learning experience changes, from the didactic learning associated with the formal classroom to a more personal and less regimented air of mutual exchange between Living Book and student readers. These small group exchanges are at the heart of the libraries. The setting provides the opportunity for safe disclosure of experience and their exploration. It may be one of the only times when equality of interaction occurs between students and people with experience of services in the social work curriculum. In this way, the experience is one of immense value.

The Human Library in Diaconia University of Applied Sciences

In spring 2017, students in the Bachelor of Social Services programme at Diak came up with the idea of organising a Human Library event as part of their learning on the course. The event was planned and implemented by students in collaboration with people with experiences of services, teachers, staff members, volunteers and professionals from various social organisations in Helsinki. One of the aims of the students was to develop tools to teach anti-oppressive methods in social work and to increase awareness of people with experience of services from diverse backgrounds.

The Human Library event brought together 19 Living Books and more than 120 readers. The Living Books included people from the LGBTQIA community, people with physical and mental health disabilities and people from different ethnic and religious backgrounds. Some of the Living Books had used social and health services, but not all. The readers were students, teachers, visiting teachers and other staff members in Diak University. The Living Books were recruited through organisers, social networks and Allianssi (the Finnish National Youth Council), who have a register of Living Book volunteers. Living Books received free refreshments during the event.

On that occasion, Living Books engaged in discussions with the readers using open dialogue. The Human Library at Diak managed to challenge many of the stereotypes about minority groups, served as a platform for introspection regarding marginalisation and helped students to practice many of the professional competencies needed in social services and social work (Pardasani and Rivera, 2017). It is also worth noting that students at Diak are themselves a diverse group of people in the first place. They come from different countries of origin and cultures, and have different beliefs, ages, political affiliations and sexual orientations. This variety already offers a unique opportunity to learn about different social interplays and processes (Pardasani and Rivera, 2017, p 11). The Human Library built on this opportunity.

Several of the international students enrolling in the Bachelor of Social Services degree programme come from societies in which the overt marginalisation of certain minority groups is still an ongoing human rights issue. This background offers a valuable motivation for personal and professional development and, in particular, for acquiring tools for implementing anti-oppressive practice as future professionals (Human Rights Centre, 2012, p 22). Sometimes the different values and traditions of students may be in tension with the values of social work and social services in Finland. This requires sensitive handling such that differential experiences and perspectives are acknowledged while the professional requirements of training to become a social worker in a Finnish context are also met. The Human Library provided an excellent illustration of a format in which such differences could be explored in a safe, respectfully challenging space.

The Human Library event was assessed via a summative evaluation wherein students collected both quantitative and qualitative feedback (Pardasani and Rivera, 2017, 29). The quantitative feedback consisted of the number of readers visiting the event, the number of readings and the number of Living Books. The qualitative feedback consisted of assessment questionnaires for readers and Living Books and a group discussion for readers. Feedback from readers of the books was positive and suggested that the exchanges had increased their awareness of the different life experiences of people receiving social work services. Feedback from Living Books revealed that the event was well organised and that they had welcomed the chance to meet readers from diverse backgrounds. Some of the Living Books reported that discussing important issues strengthened their own identity (Pardasani and Rivera, 2017, pp 28–33).

Readers (most of them bachelor-level students) gave positive feedback on the Human Library. For example, they felt that discussions with Living Books raised human rights issues. Some of the readers wanted to utilise this idea and arrange a Human Library event in their native countries in Africa and Asia. Many participants felt that 'diversity was celebrated' but also that misunderstandings, prejudice and conflicting ideas had been discussed (Pardasani and Rivera, 2017, pp 34–5). Most of the Living Books felt that they had received generic and expected questions. However, some of them felt surprised at the ignorant and judgemental views of some readers which arose from their belief systems (Pardasani and Rivera, 2017, p 34). This example shows that the learning experience is often mutual, and all parties learn something new, not only the readers.

Experiential knowledge can be a valuable resource and can help people respond to uncertain futures (Faulkner, 2017). It can help people to develop multifaceted responses to uncertain situations. Such knowledge is sometimes considered to be anecdotal, and is often viewed by policymakers with ambivalence. However, people with experience of receiving services have a greater understanding of many situations than do formal 'experts'. The Human Library format can provide an excellent opportunity for social work students to gain insight into many issues which affect broader society through the experiential knowledge of those who have received social work services.

Conclusion

The living libraries have attracted a wider number of people, with divergent experiences of social work, to become involved in social work education. The feedback from Living Books and readers on their experiences of the libraries is typically very positive (Sen et al, 2016; Pardasani and Rivera, 2017). Living Books' feedback has suggested that they have a sense of being heard and of making a difference to students' future practice. Students' narratives have suggested some long-lasting learning can arise from Living Library exchanges. Those participating in the living libraries have included people with physical and mental health disabilities, those with serious health issues, carers for people requiring social work services, people with prior experience of abuse and trauma, those who are seeking asylum or who are refugees, young carers, care-experienced young people and people who are LGBTAIQ. However, organisers of these events have also sought to challenge the stereotypes and assumptions that might pigeonhole the experiences of Living Books based on labels, appearance or presentation. Each Living Book brings rich individual human experience to the Library, beyond any category or label which formally defines them as a recipient of a particular service. Indeed, the Living Library model lends itself to the sharing of different life experiences, not just those of people with experience of social work services. Social work students should learn from these wider experiences as well. As a result, some living libraries have, for example, included lesbian mothers and transgender people who have had no direct experiences of social work per se. Suggestions for future living libraries have included the idea of building on this element by inviting professional carers, those in allied helping professions and those with experiences of particular health services to be Living Books.

There are challenges in recruiting Living Books from the full breadth of people who have received helping services. To illustrate: while at Sheffield there have been Living Books who have experienced involuntary statutory social work intervention due to mental health needs or child protection concerns, these have been a small minority. Volunteers with experience of services due to serious addiction or criminal activity have not been recruited. In order to address this issue, it will be necessary to look both at more successful outreach and also at other ways of developing the Living Library model. One possible extension could be the use of audio, video or written accounts from people who might find the idea of discussing their experiences in person too intimidating. The development of such learning artefacts would require the extension of the theoretical and pedagogical basis of the Living Library beyond that presented here. This modified conceptualisation would need to be flexible enough to capture how asynchronous, non-face-to-face encounters may also operate to break down preconceptions and barriers.

Whether living libraries may, unintentionally, exclude people who are traditionally left out of many of life's activities – for example, those with severe learning disabilities and autism – also requires consideration. In Sheffield, the ways in which Living Books could become involved was broadened in an attempt to address this. Tables of 'short stories' were offered instead of one Living Book. At these tables, members from particular groups in the city joined the Library, with a support worker who acted as their facilitator. Instead of one person telling one story, therefore, four or five people used the same amount of time to tell a couple of short stories each. For those who need less support, the possibility of co-authorship may be more appropriate: two people with the same experience working together and telling their contrasting stories of receiving services.

Finally, it is important to note that we recommend avoiding the claim that the Living Library is representative of any group. No Living Book has a mandate to represent anyone but themselves, and their stories and experiences are individual to them, and indeed individual, even, to a particular Living Library reading. The quality of the information given or received is subjective and of the moment. If a reader were to 'borrow' the same Living Book twice, their reading would be different: the story would differ, if only subtly; the reader would interact with it in a different way in this new exchange; and the interpretations of the exchange might be different in light of changed experiences. The subjective uniqueness of Living Library exchanges is one of their strengths, but through another lens this could also be viewed as a limitation. Importantly, while a Living Book's account should not be considered representative, the knowledge gained from the Living Library can be supplemented by students' engagement with web-based resources of user-led organisations, their wider personal and practical experiences and more traditional sources of academic learning. Such wider engagement allows students to contextualise learning gained from the Living Library among other sources of knowledge in the social work field. This task bears a similarity to that which faces social workers in practice, who must balance experiential knowledge with other sources of knowledge such as agency rules, policy and legal requirements, research findings, prior case knowledge and personal and professional values (Sen, 2018). This engagement also helps underpin the Living Library's status as a serious educational tool for student social workers. By taking part as readers, and subsequently contextualising the learning from the Living Library among other sources of social work knowledge, they are developing the skills, knowledge and mindset to become autonomous, critically reflective and empathic practitioners.

References

Allianssi (2020) 'Central information on youth work in Finland', The Finnish National Youth Council Allianssi. Available from: https://www.alli.fi/en/general-information-youth-work-finland

Allport, G.W. (1954) *The Nature of Prejudice*, Reading: Addison-Wesley.

Arnstein, S.R. (1969) 'A ladder of citizen participation', *Journal of the American Planning Association*, 35(4): 216–24. Available from: https://doi.org/10.1080/01944366908977225

Baines, D. (2011) 'An overview of anti-oppressive practice, roots, theory and tensions', in D. Baines, *Doing Anti-Oppressive Practice: Social Justice Social Work*, 2nd edn, Halifax and Winnipeg: Fernwood Publishing, pp 1–24.

Council of Europe (n.d.) 'Living Library', Council of Europe. Available from: https://www.coe.int/en/web/youth/living-library

Faulkner, A. (2017) 'Survivor research and Mad Studies: the role and value of experiential knowledge in mental health research', *Disability & Society*, 32(4): 500–20.

Human Library (n.d.) 'Welcome to the Human Library'. Available from: http://humanlibrary.org/about-the-human-library/

Human Rights Centre (2012) 'Human Rights Education in Finland'. Available from: https://www.humanrightscentre.fi/about-us/

Kendal-Raynor, P. (2009) 'Inquiry to investigate care of people with learning disabilities', *Nursing Standard*, 23(21): 10–1.

Levinas, E. (1969) *Totality and Infinity: An Essay on Exteriority*, Pittsburgh: Duquesne University Press.

Little, N., Nemutlu, G., Magic, J. and Molnar, B. (2011) *Don't Judge a Book by Its Cover! The Living Library Organizer's Guide 2011*, Budapest: Council of Europe – Youth Department. Available from: https://www.coe.int/en/web/youth/living-library

Marton, F. and Säljö, R. (1997) 'Approaches to learning', in F. Marton, D. Hounsell and N.D. Entwistle (eds), *The Experience of Learning*, Edinburgh: Scottish Academic Press, pp 39–58.

Merleau-Ponty, M. (2013) *The Phenemonology of Perception*, London: Routledge.

Orosz, G., Bánki, E., Bőthe, B., Tóth-Király, I. and Tropp, L.R. (2016) 'Don't judge a living book by its cover: effectiveness of the living library intervention in reducing prejudice toward Roma and LGBT people', *Journal of Applied Social Psychology*, 46(9): 510–17.

Pardasani, R. and Rivera, W. (2017) 'Human Library: an anti-oppressive tool; implementation guidelines of Human Library', thesis in Bachelor of Social Services, Helsinki: Diaconia University of Applied Sciences. Available from: http://urn.fi/URN:NBN:fi:amk-2017111717294

Schütz, A. (1967) *The Phenomenology of the Social World*, Evanston: Northwestern University Press.

Sen, R. (2018) *Effective Practice with Looked after Children*, London: Palgrave.

Sen, R., McClelland, N. and Jowett, B. (2016) 'Belonging to the library: humanising the space for social work education', *Social Work Education*, 35(8): 892–904, DOI: 10.1080/02615479.2016.1211098.

Valentine, G. (2007) 'Theorising and researching intersectionality: a challenge for feminist geography', *The Professional Geographer*, 59: 10–21, DOI: 10.1111/j.1467927.2007.00587.x.

8

Creating a platform together for the voice of the service user: inspiration for organising an event together with service users

Ruth Strudwick, Suzanna Pickering and Joep Holten

Summary

This chapter describes two annual conferences that are run in partnership with service users in both the United Kingdom and the Netherlands. The conferences have some differences in the way they are planned and delivered, but there are also many common themes. At both events, service users share their stories and interact with students. This chapter gives a description of both conferences and shares the experiences of the authors in organising an event with service users.

Introduction

There are many ways to involve service users in education. Approaches used by colleagues in different universities and countries can be a source of inspiration. It is possible to learn from their experiences and develop ideas and tips for your own situation. This happened when the authors of this chapter came together to write this chapter.

The conference at the University of Suffolk, UK, is an interprofessional event and is a mandatory part of the curriculum for all second-year students on the following undergraduate courses which lead to registration as health or social care professionals: adult nursing, mental health nursing, child health nursing, midwifery, operating department practice, paramedic science, social work, diagnostic radiography and therapeutic radiography. The post-graduate police students also attend. The conference has been running for four years and there are approximately five hundred delegates, including students and qualified professionals from the health service, the police and social services. The aim of the conference is to promote service-user involvement and to hear the voices of service users. The conference title reflects this: 'Can You Hear Me? The Voice of the Service User'. Due to the number of different professionals attending the conference, a wide range of service users from different backgrounds are involved. The conference structure consists of keynote speakers at the start of both the morning and the afternoon, each of which are followed by service users telling their stories to the delegates.

The conference at the Amsterdam University of Applied Sciences in the Netherlands is focused on the field of social work and is a mandatory part of a course for first-year students who study social work part time. In this course, the students develop a conference about homeless young people in Amsterdam. This conference is also organised and partly presented by the service users, who like to be referred to as 'youngsters'. The conference is organised annually and has been running for more than ten years. The involvement of service users is growing. Each year there is space for 150 delegates, including professionals, policymakers, researchers, the youngsters themselves and students. Although there is some space for keynote speakers and a plenary debate, the conference mainly consists of workshops that are organised by the youngsters and students.

At both universities, the idea of a conference came about during the planning of the courses when staff members were keen that students be enabled to interact with service users and hear their stories. It is an important part of the training to be a health or social care professional to be able to listen to service users and to understand their point of view (Costello and Horne, 2001; Frisby, 2001). A service user telling their own story is a lot more powerful than university staff talking about service-user experiences (Blackhall et al, 2012; Rooney et al, 2019).

Which service users are involved?

In both universities, the group of service users that participate in the conference is a mixture of people who are recovering and people still going through their experience. Striking a balance between engaging service users who are still experiencing issues and those who have recovered makes it a challenge to present authentic accounts to students while making sure that the service users who are involved are also supported when telling their stories (Unwin et al, 2018).

In the Netherlands, all the youngsters that are involved are experiencing challenges in finding a stable home, mostly in combination with different problems, and have a long history of broken homes. To the outsider, the conference appears to be organised in a semi-chaotic way, and there is not a structured method for finding youngsters willing to participate. Most youngsters are recruited by word of mouth and personal contact. Many of the youngsters have helped for a few years, although this is not a requirement. There is one organisation called Straatvisie which a lot of the youngsters attend each week. Straatvisie assists with the recruitment of the youngsters and provides a location to meet outside of the university building to plan the conference.

In Suffolk, service users participate in two different ways: some help with planning and hosting the event, others speak at the event. The service users who are involved in planning the delivery and hosting of the event come from a variety of backgrounds and have had different experiences with health and social care services. They form part of the university service-user forum. The service-user forum is a group of service users who are interested in public sector education and meet four times a year at the university. The forum has been in existence since 2000. As well as planning the conference, they are also involved in other activities within the university, including the recruitment and selection of students, course and curriculum design, attending meetings and speaking to students about their experiences. Service users who are involved in the forum do this because they feel that it is important for students to hear their stories and to understand how they feel. It also gives them a positive sense of self and of being listened to (McKeown et al, 2012).

There is a conscious effort made to invite service-user speakers who can be relevant to as many of the delegates as possible. The service users speaking have experienced a range of different services, and they are recruited via the service-user forum and through other contacts as well as from the police and health and social care. This is more of a snowball recruitment strategy. The reason for this is to involve service users with many different experiences of public sector services and emphasise the overlap and connectedness between different public sector professions. There is no formal recruitment process for speakers. The conference team, consisting of university staff and service users, decides which service users can speak, and this is largely based on the service users' experiences so that there is sufficient variety. There has not been any difficulty in recruiting service users to tell their stories at the conference to date.

Whereas in Suffolk there is a distinction between the two different ways in which service users participate – either helping with planning and hosting or speaking at the event – in Amsterdam the distinction between the different roles is less organised. Some of the youngsters are involved in planning the conference, but this is by no means a necessity. Sometimes the youngsters change their plans on the day of the conference and do not turn up, so the conference is organised in a way that this will not harm the programme. The reasons the cooperation is so loosely organised are that it is important that the youngsters are comfortable, are not put under pressure and that the conference provides an opportunity for important learning for them.

The conference in Amsterdam has been running for more than ten years. It has been noticed that the parts in which the youngsters have been involved (debates, for example) always provide inspiring insights for the participants. Over the years, the connection between the organisers of the yearly conferences and the youngsters has become stronger. For example, one of the themes used for the conference one year was housing. The conference featured five workshops in which delegates learned about the five steps that need to be taken by youngsters before they can live independently. The youngsters and students worked together in workshops to discuss this and came up with solutions. The workshops are much stronger if the youngsters are involved in the decision-making. This is also a good way of learning for the students involved. Although all the students are already active in the field of social work via their student placements, most of them are not used to working together with service users on a project. The conference provides a platform for listening to those service users' stories and an environment where students are able to engage in an important reflective process, where they can gain their own understanding of where power imbalances may lie between the professional and the personal, thus making essential links between their own experiences and those of service users. It is by focussing on personal and professional identities that student practitioners can begin to develop holistic models of self; integrated, informed and reflective, shaping the landscape for continuing professional development (Harrison and Ruch, cited in Lymbery and Postle, 2007).

The conference in Suffolk, over the past five years, has always involved service users in the planning and delivery of the event. This brings a different perspective to the conference and enables the university staff members to see things from a different point of view. The conference also enables discussion about learning objectives in order for students and service users to think and discuss together innovative ways of achieving them.

Service users have a lot to offer and contribute. They tell their stories and give an honest appraisal and overview of their own lived experiences (Unwin et al, 2018). Service users are experts about their own lives (Unwin et al, 2018). Their input is important to the development of students' learning and understanding. This extends their problem-solving skills and their ability to translate theory into practice. Service-user stories also enable students across professions to see where their role may begin and end, and to identify where other professional roles begin and end in the service-user experience. This understanding encourages different professions to communicate, to work together by closing the gaps between services and to move towards practice which is personalised and seamless to meet service users' needs. Students can also start to make more sense of the service users' 'journey' through different services, where different professionals are involved in the care of the service user and need to work together for the good of the service user.

Keynote speakers

In Suffolk, a decision was made to recruit high-profile keynote speakers and have a specific theme. The keynote speakers help to launch the event and provide a pull for external delegates to attend. They assisted in raising the profile of the event, and combined with press releases locally, national media interest was triggered.

The theme of the conference each year is key. It is imperative that the topic crosses professional boundaries. The first conference in 2016 needed to draw on the strengths of the county of Suffolk to launch a flagship for interprofessional practice. The theme of the Suffolk murders was chosen (BBC News, 2008). There had been a film and a play entitled *London Road*, and Ed Sheeran had written a song, 'The A Team', about prostitution. The Suffolk murders case was an excellent example of professionals working together across organisational boundaries and was worthy of being emphasised to highlight positive learning through reflection on good practice. This case was also something that everyone locally could recall and relate to. It emphasised the cohesion that had taken place between police and health and social care services.

In 2017, the University of Suffolk was reaching its tenth anniversary, and Lord Laming was invited to mark this occasion. Lord Laming, a former social worker, now a member of the House of Lords, chaired the public inquiry into eight-year-old Victoria Climbié's death in 2001, and in November 2008 he was appointed to investigate social services on a national basis in the UK following the death of Baby P. He did a real service to the university, placing this conference on the national stage. In 2017, the Prison Reform Trust's Laming report, *In Care, Out of Trouble* (Prison Reform Trust, 2016), was gifted by Lord Laming to all 500 delegates. The film director Mat Kirkby also introduced his Oscar-winning film *The Phone Call*.

Lord Laming wrote about the 2017 conference:

> The event yesterday that successfully brought together students from across all of the key services was both informative and inspiring. It encouraged me greatly. It was a real credit to the University of Suffolk. I do hope others will follow your lead. May I wish you continued success in your important work. (Lord Laming, 23 March 2017)

Ed Sheeran and Mat Kirkby both received honorary doctorates from the university. These conferences have offered an opportunity for them to showcase their contribution to students' learning and professional development.

In 2018, the theme was child sexual exploitation. Nazir Afzal, chief crown prosecutor in the Rochdale inquiry, was invited. The conference was based on a high-profile case that had been outlined in a BBC television drama,

Three Girls. Afzal stated: "Safeguarding is everybody's responsibility, not just the professionals, but we can learn from each other and this conference will drive up performance and awareness and protect even more."

Both Lord Laming and Nazir Afzal emphasised in their keynote speeches the importance of the voices of the marginalised, and they paved the way for service users to tell their stories. In 2019 the focus was on knife crime, gangs and county lines.

Each year, persuading a high-profile speaker to be the keynote has encouraged a wider audience, attracted media attention and most importantly attracted an audience that would listen to the stories and experiences of service users, placing human experience at the heart of inter-professional learning and practice across the East of England. However, the pull of the keynote speakers and the increasing popularity of the conference has become its downfall. It was no longer possible to accommodate all the delegates who wished to attend at the conference centre, and practical aspects such as catering became an issue. Changes had to be made to the conference.

Practicalities

Morgan and Jones (2009) suggest that service users need to be prepared for an experience with students. Therefore, service users who are speaking at the conference in Suffolk are briefed beforehand and intensively prepared by university staff. This preparation involves a briefing about the details and aim of the conference. These speakers are prepared and supported in speaking to a large audience of up to five hundred people. Speaking to large groups can be a challenge for some people, especially if they have never done it before, and preparation and support is needed (Scammell et al, 2015). The speaker can rehearse their speech and discuss any concerns that they might have. This reduces the possibility of anxiety (Le Var, 2002). Service users are also given the option to record their story if they are nervous or unable to attend the conference. This has been utilised by three service users so far. On the day of the conference, service users who are speaking are supported by one of the service users on the organising committee. They sit with the speaker during the conference, providing reassurance. Speakers are also given the opportunity to debrief with one of the conference organisers afterwards. This ensures that they have the chance to discuss the experience and any feelings this may have evoked (Frisby, 2001).

The service users who are involved in the planning of the conference and the service users who speak at the conference are paid expenses for travel, provided with lunch and paid for their time. Some service users do not want to be paid as this interferes with their benefit payments.

Students also need to be prepared for listening to service users' stories. Students may be affected emotionally by the stories they hear. Unwin et al

(2018) emphasise that students need to be fully briefed beforehand and debriefed afterwards. In Suffolk, the students are briefed before by university staff, and this is followed up at the start of the conference. They are encouraged to seek help and support should they become distressed during the day.

Student evaluations indicate that they would like to have the opportunity to ask questions of the service users. Over the past few years, this has not been part of the event, as service users have simply presented their stories to the audience and have only had 15 minutes to do this. However, in 2019 the format of the conference was changed, mainly because of practical considerations including funding the event and catering costs. For the 2019 conference, keynote sessions were in the morning, with all students together, and then in the afternoon students were divided into smaller groups and had two longer sessions with different service users. These sessions were video recorded so that students could watch them all, including sessions they did not attend. All sessions were facilitated by a member of university staff. This meant that there was more opportunity for discussion between service users and students, allowing students to ask questions and find out a bit more detail about service users' experiences. This change to the format was well received and students were happy that they could view the video recordings from all service-user sessions.

In terms of funding the event, this is a real challenge in Suffolk, as sponsorship needs to be obtained. Sponsorship comes from different health and social care organisations. Some are given a stand or exhibition at the conference in return for sponsorship money. Sponsorship and the exhibition of stands can be time consuming and challenging to organise. Until 2019, the conference was held at a conference centre away from the university, which needed to be paid for, but in 2019 it was decided to host the conference at the university to reduce costs and the need for sponsorship. The conference is free to attend for students, and external delegates pay a small fee.

When the conference moved to the university, there was no longer space to invite paying delegates. Therefore, the only delegates from 2019 onwards were the students, and the conference lost the input of external professionals in health and social care services. The loss of the professional delegates made a difference, as they showed by example, by learning alongside the students, that service users' voices needed to be at the centre of practice and to continue to be so beyond training. This was a shame as the conference had been an opportunity for alumni to return and to realign themselves to the importance of the service user voice.

The other tension was that other service users who were not involved in the planning of the conference or speaking at the conference wanted to attend as delegates. This was fine at the external conference centre as there was enough space. However, from 2019 there was not enough space to accommodate them.

In Amsterdam, the conference is connected to a course which is specially designed to teach students project management and at the same time to work with service users on an equal basis. This format provides a lot of benefits in terms of practicalities. The fact that students must meet weekly in class makes it easy to track progress. It is also easy for the service users to remember where to turn up and when as it has become a regular event. Each year some students and service users come up with good ideas to improve the conference, and each year organising the conference becomes less time consuming and stressful. One staff member (a lecturer) is in charge. He is the spokesperson for the conference and the person approaching the youngsters, inviting them to participate. The conference is held at the university campus which reduces the costs. All the things that can be done by the organising team are organised together with the service users and students to reduce additional costs; for example, registration on the day and sending out information beforehand. Thanks to connections in the city, most keynote speakers attend for free. There are still some costs however, and so a small contribution (€3000) is provided by a foundation (Bestuurlijk Overleg Zwerfjongeren) that represents some of Amsterdam's biggest social service organisations. This contribution allows delegates to attend the conference for free. The students and youngsters are responsible for the budget and are free to invest it in ways the lecturer and/or the foundation might disapprove of. Yet, the simple fact of being responsible makes the students and youngsters feel more involved. The conference contains elements of a didactical approach, such as learning communities. One of the characteristics of a successful learning community is that there are ways to evaluate the work done. Students are taught about group work both before and after the conference. In these evaluations, attention must be paid to the opinions of all stakeholders, including the youngsters, the students, the foundation, the lecturers and the conference attendees. Service users need to know in advance that their needs are being paid attention to, but that it is not possible to meet or fulfil them all.

For example, one of the service users stated in advance that she did not want to meet a certain social worker she knew from past experiences. Of course, this could not be promised or guaranteed, but in order to meet the service user's wish, the day before the conference she was shown the list of attendees so she could decide whether or not to participate.

One of the most important conference-related challenges concerns the availability of lecturers willing and able to organise an event with service users. Although most lecturers do agree with the concept, many of them feel more comfortable providing classical and didactic education. Co-creation with service users requires lecturers who are not afraid of uncertain working conditions.

A second challenge is the tension between providing enough learning opportunities to achieve specific learning objectives and providing important opportunities for dialogue between the service users and students. A final important challenge concerns the tension that might occur between the service users themselves. Where some service users are involved in an intensive way and work extremely hard, others turn up on the day of the conference or even disappear. Although this has no direct consequences for the organisation of the conference, this is noted in service users' evaluations.

Suffolk and Amsterdam: commonalities

When comparing the two conferences in Suffolk and Amsterdam, several common aspects can be identified:

1. the provision of a model of service-user involvement;
2. they are both annual events;
3. the conferences are co-created and planned by staff, students and service users; and
4. explicit attention is paid to avoiding tokenism.

It is important to provide an example to students about how to really involve service users, not in a tokenistic way but by engaging and listening to their voices. Relationships need to be built with service users to facilitate this (Cooper and Spencer-Dawe, 2006). It is hoped that this will be something that the students take into their own professional practice and that they continue to engage with and listen to their service users.

In recent years, austerity and managerialist perspectives have had an impact on health and social care practices. However, emerging from this has been renewed interest in relationship-based practice (Ruch et al, 2010; Dix et al, 2019). This offers practitioners an ethical and effective model that recognises the complexity of human behaviour while integrating with the professional landscape (Harrison and Ruch, cited in Lymberry and Postle, 2007).

For a relationship-based perspective to be realised, practitioners need to be able to acknowledge the uncertainty and unpredictability of service users' lives in order to engage effectively with the distress and disadvantage in which individuals and families may find themselves, and to be able to communicate well to establish meaningful professional relationships (Harrison and Ruch, cited in Lymberry and Postle, 2007).

Lessons learnt from planning and running the conferences

There is general agreement in the literature that service-user involvement of any form needs to be well organised and worthwhile (Repper and Breeze, 2007).

- Real collaboration and co-creation – no tokenism
  All of those involved in planning and delivering such a large-scale event (university staff, service users and students) need to have an input. Roles need to be clear and understood. Expectations need to be managed, and everyone needs to be briefed beforehand. For both conferences, the organisers agreed that it was important that the service users' voices were heard and that there were no assumptions made about service user's experiences or ideas. The conferences were co-produced with service users on an equal footing with university staff.
- Funding
  Ensuring that funding is secured is a key consideration. Conferences cost money to organise and deliver, and so funding needs to be in place.
- Preparing the service users
  This is important so that service users understand what is required of them and are prepared to speak to a large audience.
- Debriefing after the event
  Individual and group debriefs can take place. For service users, an individual debrief with someone who was present at the event is recommended. Service users may find that telling their story evokes an emotional response, and they will need time to discuss and deal with this. They need to be cared for. Students and staff members may also benefit from individual debriefing if they find that they have had an emotional response to the event. Group debriefing is useful in order for the organising committee to evaluate the event.
- Evaluation
  The organising committee should obtain feedback from all of those involved in the conference: service users, students and staff members. The feedback should be used to provide an evaluation of the conference and to make improvements for future delivery. It is important that any educational initiative that includes service users is evaluated so that its usefulness to students, staff members and service users can be assessed and captured (Jones et al, 2009).

Learning from experience and looking towards the future.

On reflection, both conferences provide an important learning experience for students, professional staff, university staff and service users. These conferences will continue to be successful, and continuous evaluation and reflection is key to their success.

Looking at the neighbours over your own institution's walls can offer insights and opportunities for improvement. For example, in Suffolk, a post-graduate programme is currently being developed. A joint community-development project between students and service users, for which a budget is managed, will be one of the planned learning activities; this is a lesson learnt from the Amsterdam conference. This will also enhance engagement with the local community and employers.

During the current COVID-19 pandemic, the use of technology and virtual environments has been developing at a fast pace. This should be a consideration for future conferences, as using an online platform would increase the reach of the conferences, reduce issues with space at the conference venues and allow more people to attend. It may also be an easier platform on which for service users to share their stories with no physical audience. A virtual platform is not a substitute for face-to-face interaction, but it would provide opportunities for international and shared events from different locations.

References
BBC News (2008) 'Suffolk murders trial', BBC News, [online] 3 April. Available from: http://news.bbc.co.uk/1/hi/in_depth/uk/2008/suffolk_murders_trial/default.stm
Blackhall, A., Schafer, R., Kent, L. and Nightingale, M. (2012) 'Service user involvement in nursing students' training', *Mental Health Practice*, 16(1): 23–6.
Cooper, H. and Spencer-Dawe, E. (2006) 'Involving service users in interprofessional education and narrowing the gap between theory and practice', *Journal of Interprofessional Care*, 20(6): 503–617.
Costello, J. and Horne, M. (2001) 'Patients as teachers? An evaluative study of patients' involvement in classroom teaching', *Nurse Education in Practice*, 1(2): 94–102.
Dix, H., Hollinrake, S. and Meade, J. (2019) *Relationship-Based Social Work with Adults*, Northwich: Critical Publishing.
Frisby, R. (2001) 'User involvement in mental health branch education: client review presentations', *Nurse Education Today*, 21(8): 663–69.
Harrison, K. and Ruch, G. (2007) 'Social work and the use of self: on becoming and being a social worker', in Lymbery, M. and Postle, K. (eds), *Social Work: A Companion to Learning*, London: Sage.
Jones, D., Stephens, J., Innes, W., Rochester, L., Ashburn, A. and Stack, E. (2009) 'Service user and carer involvement in physiotherapy practice, education and research: getting involved for a change', *New Zealand Journal of Physiotherapy*, 37(1): 29–35.
Le Var, R.M.H. (2002) 'Patient involvement in education for enhanced quality of care', *International Nursing Review*, 49: 219–25.
Lord Laming excerpts, young carers, debate in Lords Chamber, 23rd March' (2017) Available from: https://www.parallelparliament.co.uk/mp/lord-nash/debate/Lords/2017-03-23/debates/0C178D3A-0CF7-4146-B448-40D30FE0F6D2/YoungCarers

Lymbery, M. and Postle, K. (2007) *Social Work: A Companion to Learning*, California: Sage.

McKeown, M., Malihi-Shoja, L., Hogarth, R., Jones, F., Holt, K., Sulivan, P., Lint, J., Vella, J., Hough, G., Rawcliffe, L. and Mather, M. (2012) 'The value of involvement from the perspective of service users and carers engaged in practitioner education: not just a cash nexus', *Nurse Education Today*, 32(2): 178–84.

Morgan, A. and Jones, D. (2009) 'Perceptions of service user and carer involvement in healthcare education and impact on students' knowledge and practice: a literature review', *Medical Teacher*, 31: 82–95.

Prison Reform Trust (2016) *In Care, Out of Trouble*, London: Prison Reform Trust. Available from: http://www.prisonreformtrust.org.uk/Portals/0/Documents/In%20care%20out%20of%20trouble%20summary.pdf

Repper, J. and Breeze, J. (2007) 'A review of the literature on user and carer involvement in the training and education of health professionals', *International Journal of Nursing Studies*, 44(3): 511–19.

Rooney, J.M., Unwin, P.F. and Shah, P. (2019) 'Keeping us grounded: academic staff perceptions of service user and carer involvement in health and social work training', *Journal of Further and Higher Education*, 43(7): 929–41.

Ruch, G, Turney, D. and Ward, A. (2010) *Relationship-Based Social Work: Getting to the Heart of Practice*, London: Jessica Kingsley.

Scammell, J., Heaslip, V. and Crowley, E. (2015) 'Service user involvement in pre-registration general nurse education: a systematic review', *Journal of Clinical Nursing*, 25: 1–2.

Unwin, P., Rooney, J. and Cole, C. (2018) 'Service user and carer involvement in student's classroom learning in higher education', *Journal of Further and Higher Education*, 42(3): 377–88.

9

Reflections on inspiring conversations in social work education: the voices of Scottish experts by experience and Italian students

Susan Levy and Elena Cabiati with John Dow, Elinor Dowson, Keith Swankie and Gil Martin

Introduction

There is an increasing literature setting out models and good practice in service-user involvement in social work education (Skilton, 2011; Robinson and Webber, 2013; Tanner et al, 2015; Askheim et al, 2017; Duffy et al, 2017; Cabiati and Levy, 2020). Pedagogically this work is framed by approaches to integrating the voices, lived experiences and experiential knowledge of service users and carers into social work education. While these voices are becoming less marginal within social work education, the contribution of service users and carers as co-authors in this literature is less visible (McPhail, 2007; Fox, 2016; Bell et al, 2020; Levy et al, 2016, 2020). This chapter contributes to addressing this lacuna by being co-authored with three Scottish service users and/or carers, also called experts by experience. All three have written reflectively on their experiences of involvement in social work education and their perceptions of the impact of their involvement on students' learning, social work practice and on them personally. The chapter also includes reflective accounts written by Italian social work students as part of their course work. The EBE and students all used the concept of 'inspiring conversations' (Cabiati and Levy, 2020) as a starting point to explore and reflect on their experiences of user involvement in social work education.

'Experts by experience' (EBE), rather than 'service users', is used in this chapter as a term that more coherently conveys the essence of experiential and tacit knowledge; that is, knowledge acquired through living with a disability, being a family carer and/or receiving social services. The term EBE locates experiential, tacit knowledge in the experiences of service users, but is also inclusive of people who, for a variety of reasons, do not receive services (McLaughlin, 2009). More broadly, the term engages with the struggles, emotions and muted voices from the margins, and with people living precarious lives.

We start the chapter by discussing the concept of inspiring conversations; second, we contextualise the involvement of EBE in social work education at the University of Dundee, Scotland, and the Catholic University of Milan, Italy. We then present reflections from the three co-authors, Dow, Dowson and Swankie, and from student social workers. We close the chapter with some thoughts on the impact and outcomes of user involvement and propose inspiring conversations as a conduit for guiding the future inclusion of tacit knowledge in social work education across Europe.

Inspiring conversations on the involvement of experts by experience in social work education

The concept of inspiring conversations emerged from a comparative study (Cabiati and Levy, 2020) based on the involvement of EBE in social work education in Italy and Scotland. 'Inspiring' refers to how conversations between EBE and students, when framed within reciprocal, trusting and engaging relationships, can be stimulating and impactful for all involved: students, EBE and academics (Irvine et al, 2015; Driessens et al, 2016; Rooney et al, 2016; Duffy, 2020). For students, the participation of EBE in their social work studies can inspire reflection on their motivations for choosing a career in social work and on their relational and communication skills (Cabiati and Levy, 2020; Wilken et al, 2020). It can provoke a deeper and more intense level of learning which Duffy (2020) argues is most impactful when students are challenged to step out of their comfort zone through a 'pedagogy of discomfort' (Boler, 1999), an approach that can expose students to the 'strangeness' (Kreber, 2014) and uncertainty of social work practice, and unsettle and deconstruct stigmatising attitudes towards people in receipt of social services (Cabiati and Raineri, 2016). For EBE, involvement can be meaningful and inspiring. It can lead to increasing the self-confidence of EBE to manage independent lives, to the creation of a new support network (Rooney et al, 2016) and the development of new competencies (Wilken et al, 2020). These outcomes are achieved through involvement that highlights the strengths and capabilities of EBE, and through their contributions to students' learning being respected and valued. For academics, working with EBE can lead to reflections on their own personal biases (Duffy, 2020) and revisiting the pedagogy underpinning their teaching (Cabiati and Levy, 2020).

Experts by experience in social work education in Scotland and Italy

EBE have been participating in the learning journeys of social work students at the University of Dundee, Scotland, and the Catholic University of Milan, Italy, for over 17 years and 12 years respectively. In both institutions, EBE, academics and students work collaboratively across undergraduate and postgraduate qualifying social work programmes. While the context for involvement in the two institutions is quite different, pedagogically they are aligned (Cabiati and Levy, 2020). In Scotland, user involvement has been mandatory in qualifying social work programmes since 2003 (Scottish Executive, 2003). In Italy, as elsewhere in Europe, there is no such mandatory directive, and involvement has been at the discretion and commitment of academics.

In Scotland, at the University of Dundee, a carer and users (CU) group, made up of EBE, both service users and informal family carers, is actively involved in the social work programmes. Examples of CU group involvement include: sharing their experiential knowledge in lectures; role play; group work; joint presentations with students; assessment; recruitment; and fulfilling the role of the chair of the Programme Board. One module that is structured around the involvement of EBE is 'Caring within Integrated Services' (Gee et al, 2009; Levy et al, 2016; Cabiati and Levy, 2020; Levy et al, 2020). The module enables students and CU group members to meet on a weekly basis over a semester to co-produce an assessed group presentation. At the Catholic University of Milan, Italy, full-day meetings between students and EBE are one example of a successful model of involvement (Cabiati and Raineri, 2016; Cabiati and Levy, 2020). The full-day meetings are divided in two parts: in the morning, each student talks individually with an EBE for two hours. Following a shared lunch in the university canteen, all the participants (students, EBE and academics) meet to discuss and share their thoughts and feelings on the experience.

The two European universities base their involvement of EBE around coherence, prudence and sustainability (Cabiati and Levy, 2020) and the six key principles described in the following section. Coherence refers to the need to ensure that involvement is situated holistically within students' overall learning and that it has pedagogical rigor. Prudence is used to highlight the careful planning that is required to ensure involvement is meaningful and achieves learning outcomes. Sustainability is achieved through organisational support and commitment as well as resources.

Six key principles of user involvement

1. Human support to manage life challenges arise from a reciprocal relationship between social workers and people in need.

2. Conscientisation and education are conduits to enable people to become 'more fully human in the world in which they exist' (Nyirenda, 1995).
3. 'Experiential knowledge' and 'technical/methodological competences' are complementary and not antagonistic (Folgheraiter, 2004).
4. EBE are people from whom to learn for the promotion of anti-oppressive social work education, research and practice.
5. Social workers must be self-aware, sensitive and equipped with a strong sense of ethical and moral practice.
6. The role of education in achieving social change includes functions of advocacy (Cabiati and Levy, 2020).

In the following two sections, the concept of inspiring conversations is reflected on by those who have been actively involved in user involvement in social work education. First, Dowson, Swankie and Dow, members of the University of Dundee CU group, reflect on their experiences of sharing their tacit knowledge with students and contributing to social work education. Second, Italian social work students Luca, Michela and Giulia reflect on their experiences of full-day meetings with EBE.

Experts by experience: voices from Scotland

Two key questions shaped the following reflections by Elinor Dowson, Keith Swankie and John Dow: what inspired us to get involved? What inspires us to continue our involvement in social work education?

Elinor

As an unpaid carer/supporter of a relative with mental health needs I felt, even at the beginning of this journey, frustrated that human rights were being breached, that care in hospitals and in the community was frequently not recovery focused or person centred and that too often the balance of power lay with the establishment. When a carers' support worker suggested that I become involved with the CU group at the University of Dundee, I had no idea that such an opportunity existed. I soon realised that this was not tokenistic consultation as was happening elsewhere. This felt like a lifeline was being thrown to me. It was a chance to share my experiences of feeling helpless and alone when care in the hospital and community was inadequate, patchy or non-existent (and the behaviour of staff, often unknowingly, became part of the problem, rather than an aid to finding a solution).

Occasionally we encountered a social worker who inspired us with hope, who really lit up our lives, who listened and appeared to care, who wanted to help us progress and made us feel that our lives mattered. These experiences affected me deeply, and along with my own conversations with other EBE and practitioners, were to lead me to become passionate about how to effect change. When I joined the CU group, I realised this was a heartfelt opportunity. It offered time to share what had worked well for my relative and for me, what had hindered the steps on our journey and how these experiences had made us feel. My involvement was in the fervent hope that the students would be listening and would be the social workers to bring about the needed change of attitude and behaviour, to make the lives of those they encountered much more fulfilled.

The continuity over many years of the CU group means that members are now like a family, inspiring each other, engaging in friendly banter, helping with transport, being there for each other in times of joy and sorrow, delighted and encouraging when members gain in confidence and take on new roles. We are also proud and thankful when we meet a former student who tells us that our involvement made a difference to how they think and how they have used this to make a difference. Many of the CU group members have, through adversity, become experts in their own field. Our stories are constantly evolving, and I am now a carer/supporter for an elderly relative as well as being on the board of a mental health charity.

Keith

In 2014, my care manager asked if I wanted to join the CU group at the University of Dundee. She had studied social work at Dundee and had valued the input of EBE. Having had varying degrees of negative and positive experiences as a service user, I felt this was an opportunity to share those experiences with future social workers, to help them in their careers and explain the impact that they can have on service users, carers and their families. Having been a confident and successful manager for many years, I had not done anything like this since becoming ill in 2009. I felt apprehensive. Would I manage to help develop the students as I had previously with my staff? This was going to be another challenge for me personally after losing so much. Was I able to give back again?

My involvement in one module led to me receiving written communication from the students who had to write to a service user using one of four scenarios explaining what they, as a social worker, would do in that scenario. This activity was something new and uncharted, and I did not know how it would impact on the students or me. The students wrote their responses, and as far as they were concerned it was a paper exercise job done. Not so. Some months later, with a surprise visit from myself, I provided feedback to the class. I remember entering the room and it was silent; I had no idea how this was going to pan out. The students listened respectfully and acknowledged how what they had written could affect me. It was as if

I commanded the room; any doubts I had had about doing this were gone. I felt valued, and the positivity from the students was overwhelming. One student commented, 'I will always remember this and the impact from a real person giving real live feedback.' I knew then that I had nailed it. I was delighted that it had gone so well and the students had gained so much from my work. The time spent on this journey felt well used and it was inspiring to be able to deliver that developmental role again as I had in the past. I feel very privileged to have been on this journey, contributing to developing the practitioners of the future.

John

In 2002, I was approached by the University of Dundee and asked if I would consider being part of establishing a CU group to look at how 'user involvement could be central to social work education'. My name was mentioned as someone who was passionate about user involvement and working for change. My personal interest was driven by my complex needs as regards my physical and mental health, having previously been an inpatient at a large mental health hospital. I was already involved in various mental health groups ranging from a strategy group to an advocacy and support group. Yet, despite being involved in these groups and many positive meetings, there were, and are, times when I ask myself: 'When are we going to see real change from our involvement?'

I found that, working with the CU group, I had a real opportunity to not only be involved but to *influence* how change in social services could be achieved and moved forward. Another bonus for me was that, unlike other groups I was involved with, working with the CU group would not be 'the never-ending story' where we simply sit in meetings and decide when the next meeting will be. This feeling of *influence* and not just involvement was then and still is my main reason for wanting to be an active member of the CU group. We influence how social work students learn, and they hear about what it is really like to receive services. This leads to considerably enhancing students' learning experience. However, to see real, demonstrable change in practice, we need to continue to reaffirm what has been learned and show the real value and influence of EBE.

Social work students: voices from Italy

After the full-day meetings with EBE at the Catholic University of Milan, students write personal reflections on the learning experience. The following are extracts from the reflective accounts of three students. The students gave their permission to use their work, and the names of students and EBE have been anonymised using pseudonyms.

Luca

The involvement of EBE in the university programme represented a great opportunity for my learning journey. Last Saturday I met Agostino, and the activity was inspiring, even if challenging in some aspects. Initially, I felt curious about the EBE and their life stories, but also afraid of what I should do in the interactions with unknown people that I was only meeting for the first time. I was worried that I would not be up to the situation, would not be able to control my emotions and the moments of silence and that I was not ready to interact in the right way. These worries were based on my never having talked before with a person who has lived with drug addiction or mental health problems. The encounter with Agostino has been an unforgettable experience. I can only thank him, because on a day like any other, he gave me a profound life lesson. The idea of involving all the family members in the helping process was a discovery for me: I believed that if a person has a problem (alcohol addiction), he/she must receive help. Agostino made me consider the sides of the social work profession that I had not yet considered. Speaking with my peers after the experience, I discovered that the contribution of each EBE was a gift for each student. The full-day meeting with EBE left its mark on each of us. For me, the day with Agostino made the difference for my future as a social worker.

Michela

As a first point, the conversations with the EBE inspired me to reflect on my own story. During the conversation with Angela, I spontaneously shared my personal experiences with her, both positive and negative. She inspired me to revisit my behaviour and personal life. I opened up to the EBE and I shared my family story because I felt that she understood me and was not judging. When I was recounting painful events from my life, I felt I could relate to Angela as a person just like me. I was surprised about what was happening during the conversation, because I understood Angela's feelings, and Angela understood my feelings in a way that very few people had. The conversation with Angela increased my confidence in working with people in need, and I fully admired her strength. Listening to her story I felt small in front of the courage, strength and willpower of this woman. As I listened to Angela, I wondered what I would do in her place. I learned a lot about drug addiction, self-help and mutual aid groups, but the true value of the activity was at a human level. At the end of the day, I only whispered thanks to Angela. I wanted to say more, but the strong emotions I was feeling prevented me from articulating anything else. I hope to meet her again. This experience confirmed and increased my personal motivation to become a social worker. After the encounter with Angela, I am more passionate about social work and I am more convinced of the path I have chosen for my future. I want to support people in a respectful way, as Angela yesterday respected my feelings and thoughts.

Giulia

The encounters with my EBE inspired me to be aware that during the educational path, before becoming a social worker, we must take care of ourselves and reflect on our personal experiences. For some of us (as for me), our conversation with the EBE generated feelings of discomfort because it touched traumatic memories. Participating in this activity was not easy for me, because during the conversation my EBE spoke about problems that I could relate to in my family. When I was speaking with Mario, I had the feeling that I had to walk away into a room and be alone because the emotions were so strong. Reflecting on Mario's experience and on my personal experience, I understood that people who ask for support are asking for their words to be heard. The conversation with Mario made me understand how to handle my emotions in the face of huge suffering. The encounter with an EBE was a unique experience and it should be mandatory for all students who want to become a social worker. This opportunity has led to my deepest learning during my first year at university. I returned home with an inexhaustible inner richness. I fully understood that in our future as social workers it is essential to put aside the presumption that we will know what people want and need in their life. I'm grateful to the EBE who I was fortunate to talk with, and I hope there will be similar opportunities in the coming years.

Outcomes and impacts from student and expert-by-experience encounters

The narratives of Dowson, Swankie and Dow convey effect and impact across three interconnected areas: students' learning, future practice and personal fulfilment. All three authors were motivated by a commitment to social justice, and refer to their experiences of involvement as being meaningful and inspiring, the antithesis of tokenism (Arnstein, 1969). In the words of Dow, 'this was a feeling of influence and not just involvement', and Dowson, 'I soon realised that this was not tokenistic consultation as was happening elsewhere'. Dowson refers to her experiences of social workers 'who inspired us with hope, who really lit up our lives', and how these positive experiences, coupled with negative experiences, inspired her to share her experiential knowledge with student social workers. There is optimism in the three reflections that the students' learning, from spending time with the EBE and other members of the CU group, will lead to social workers who are able to 'bring about the needed change of attitude and behaviour, and make the lives of those they encounter much more fulfilled'. At a personal level, the narratives highlight the significance of effective communication and relationships in achieving positive outcomes in the lives of the people that social workers engage with, and the importance of creating space where good practice can be modelled in the classroom.

For the students, the conversations with the EBE were inspiring in three interconnected areas: developing professional competencies, challenging established perceptions of service users and at a personal level. The time spent with the EBE resonated with and impacted meaningfully on the Italian students. The students saw the EBE as people who were bravely sharing their life experiences and their tacit knowledge to support their learning and future practice. The meetings provided a safe space to listen to the stories of the EBE, and within this space, they saw reflected in each other another human being. This process was acknowledged as being unsettling, but as such, it was also a source of deep learning.

To prepare students for practice it is important that they acquire a realistic picture of themselves, of their values and biases, and are open to these being challenged. As Gambrill (2013) argues, critical self-knowledge and self-awareness are 'vital'. Jeffery (2005, p 416) refers to 'heightened awareness' achieved through learning 'to be' with another person in a caring, attentive way no matter the differences that lie between them. The encounters with EBE appeared to stimulate students to feel better prepared for meeting and managing strong emotional content in practice (Smith, 2013). Removing barriers between EBE and students, and the honesty that this requires, led students to mirror the EBE, to share their own stories. The students reflected deeply on the similarities and differences in how they would behave if they were in the shoes of the EBE; how they would cope or have coped. This led to the students seeing the person first, and not their disability or label; to their respecting, valuing and being inspired by the EBE's uniqueness, courage and determination (Corrigan and Penn, 2015; Cabiati and Raineri, 2016). Giulia succinctly articulates the kernel of listening to and involving EBE in social work education and practice: 'It is essential to put aside the presumption that we will know what people want and need in their life'.

Conclusion

This chapter has presented insights into the meaning, impact and outcomes of EBE being integral to the learning journeys of social work students in two European countries. The voices of the Scottish EBE and Italian social work students provide a unique and powerful insight into the potential for user involvement in social work education to achieve impact and outcomes on multiple levels (Irvine et al, 2015; Driessens et al, 2016; Rooney et al,

2016; Duffy, 2020). The reflections respond to questions about whether user involvement in social work education is 'meaningful' and 'effective', and 'meaningful' to who: students, service users and carers or practitioners? And 'effective' where: student learning, social work practice, the everyday lives of service users and carers?' (Levy et al, 2016, p 868). The word 'inspiring' captures how involvement can be meaningful and effective. Furthermore, 'inspiring', we argue, is a modest yet powerful conduit for guiding future collaborative involvement of EBE in social work education across Europe.

References

Arnstein, S.R. (1969) 'A ladder of citizen participation', *Journal of the American Planning Association*, 35(4): 216–24. Available from: https://doi.org/10.1080/01944366908977225

Askheim, O.P., Beresford, P. and Heule, C. (2017) 'Mend the gap: strategies for user involvement in social work education', *Social Work Education: The International Journal*, 36(2): 128–40.

Bell, J., Fraser, M., Hitchin, S., McCulloch, L. and Morrison, L. (2020) 'Planning and delivering a skills practice workshop', in H. McLaughlin, J. Duffy, P. Beresford, H. Casey and C. Cameron (eds), *The Routledge Handbook of Service User Involvement in Human Services Research and Education*, Abingdon: Routledge, pp 239–349.

Boler, M. (1999) *Feeling Power: Emotions and Education*, London: Routledge.

Cabiati, E. and Levy, S. (2020) '"Inspiring conversations": a comparative analysis of the involvement of experts by experience in Italian and Scottish social work education', *British Journal of Social Work*, 51(2), 487–504.

Cabiati, E. and Raineri, M.L. (2016) 'Learning from service users involvement: a research about changing stigmatizing attitudes in social work students' attitudes in social work students', *Social Work Education: The International Journal*, 35(8): 982–96.

Corrigan, P.W. and Penn, D.L. (2015) 'Lessons from social psychology on discrediting psychiatric stigma', *Stigma and Health*, 1: 2–17.

Driessens, K., McLaughlin, H. and Van Doorn, L. (2016) 'The meaningful involvement of service users in social work education: examples from Belgium and the Netherlands', *Social Work Education: The International Journal*, 35(7): 739–51.

Duffy, J. (2020) 'Service user involvement in countries of conflict', in H. McLaughlin, J. Duffy, P. Beresford, H. Casey and C. Cameron (eds), *The Routledge Handbook of Service User Involvement in Human Services Research and Education*, Abingdon: Routledge, pp 339–46.

Duffy, J., McKeever, B., McLaughlin, H. and Sadd, J. (2017) 'Service user and carer involvement in social work education: where are we now? – Part 2', *Social Work Education: The International Journal*, 36(2): 125–27.

Folgheraiter, F. (2004) *Relational Social Work: Towards Networking and Societal Practices*, London: Jessica Kingsley.

Fox, J. (2016) 'Being a service user and a social work academic: balancing expert identities', *Social Work Education: The International Journal*, 35(8): 960–69.

Gambrill, E. (2013) *Social Work Practice: A Critical Thinker's Guide*, New York: Oxford University Press.

Gee, M., Ager, W. and Haddow, A. (2009) 'The caring experience: learning about community care through spending 24 hours with people who use services and family carers', *Social Work Education*, 28(7): 691–706.

Irvine, J., Molyneux, J. and Gillman, M. (2015) 'Providing a link with the real world: learning from the student experience of service user and carer involvement in social work education', *Social Work Education: The International Journal*, 34: 138–50.

Jeffery, D. (2005) '"What good is anti-racist social work if you can't master it"?: exploring a paradox in anti-racist social work education', *Race Ethnicity and Education*, 8(4): 409–25.

Kreber, C. (2014) 'Rationalising the nature of "graduateness" through philosophical accounts of authenticity', *Teaching in Higher Education*, 19(1): 90–100.

Levy, S., Aiton, R., Doig, J., Dow, J., McNeil, R., Brown, S. and Hunter, L. (2016) 'Outcomes focused user involvement in social work education: applying knowledge to practice', *Social Work Education: The International Journal*, 35(8): 866–77.

Levy, S., Ferrier, C., Dowson, E. and Risbridger, J. (2020) 'Social pedagogy, collaborative learning and outcomes in service user and carer involvement in social work education', in H. McLaughlin, J. Duffy, P. Beresford, H. Casey and C. Cameron (eds), *The Routledge Handbook of Service User Involvement in Human Services Research and Education*, Abingdon: Routledge, pp 371–83.

McLaughlin, H. (2009) 'What's in a name: "client", "patient", "customer", "consumer", "expert by experience", "service user" – what's next?', *British Journal of Social Work*, 39(6): 1101–17.

McPhail, M. (2007) *Service User and Carer Involvement: Beyond Good Intentions*, Edinburgh: Dunedin Academic Press.

Nyirenda, J.E. (1995) 'Evaluation of the utilisation of mass media for civic education in Zambia', *International Journal of University Adult Education*, 36(1): 10–26.

Robinson, K. and Webber, M. (2013) 'Models and effectiveness of service user and carer involvement in social work education: a literature review', *The British Journal of Social Work*, 43: 925–44.

Rooney, J.M., Unwin, P. and Osborne, N. (2016) 'Gaining by giving? Peer research into service user and carer perceptions of inclusivity in Higher Education', *Social Work Education: The International Journal*, 35(8): 945–59.

Scottish Executive (2003) *The Framework for Social Work Education in Scotland, Edinburgh*, Richmond: The Stationery Office.

Skilton, C.J. (2011) 'Involving experts by experience in assessing students' readiness to practice: the value of experiential learning in student reflection and preparation for practice', *Social Work Education: The International Journal*, 30(3): 299–311.

Smith, M. (2013) 'Involving child protection service users in social work education', *The Journal of Practice Teaching and Learning*, 11(2): 77–91.

Tanner, D., Littlechild, R., Duffy, J. and Hayes, D. (2015) 'Making it real: evaluating the impact of service user and carer involvement in social work education', *British Journal of Social Work*, 47(2): 467–68.

Wilken, J.P., Knevel, J. and van Gijzel, S. (2020) 'Lessons of inclusive learning: the value of experiential knowledge of persons with a learning disability in social work education', in H. McLaughlin, J. Duffy, P. Beresford, H. Casey and C. Cameron (eds), *The Routledge Handbook of Service User Involvement in Human Services Research and Education*, Abingdon: Routledge, pp 385–402.

10

Joint workshops with students and service users in social work education: experiences from Esslingen, Germany

Thomas Heidenreich and Marion Laging

Introduction

Service-user involvement in social work education has gained widespread attention in various countries in Europe and worldwide (Chiapparini, 2016). Although the term 'service-user involvement' suggests a common approach, it encompasses a number of different approaches with varying aims and scope. One important distinction is the view of service-user involvement as taking place either from an empowerment perspective or from an educational perspective (Laging and Heidenreich, 2019): from an empowerment perspective, the main aim of service-user involvement is to mobilise and empower service users by including them in as many domains as possible (for example, curriculum development, seminars or administration). From an educational perspective, the emphasis of service-user involvement in social work education is on the students' perspective, especially on skills development. In this chapter, we will focus on the latter perspective.

Service-user involvement from an educational perspective

In the German context, social work as an academic discipline has developed relatively late (Kruse, 2004; Hamburger et al, 2015). Thus, academic knowledge plays a major role in the study courses. However, conducting social work is a complex task that requires skills from a variety of domains. The German 'Qualification Framework for Social Work' (QFSW, Qualifikationsrahmen Soziale Arbeit), edited by the Social Work Faculty Council, defines a number of these skills: besides more academic content, 'professional general abilities', 'attitudes in social work' and 'personal characteristics and attitudes' (see Bartosch et al, 2008) play a major role. The development of these skills could be impacted by service-user involvement: due to its experiential nature, it lends itself to the development of important interpersonal skills that are highly relevant for social work. On a more practical note, the most important experience for students might be to collaborate with service users on eye level (Askheim, 2012), that is, by working together with service users on a specific topic rather than lecturing them on knowledge they have gained in their studies. The specific knowledge that service users bring into the interchange (Utschakowski et al, 2016) can be distinguished from academic knowledge: experiential knowledge is more subjective, grounded in personal experience and 'hands-on', while academic knowledge is often of a more generalised (and less emotional) kind.

Including service users in social work education needs careful consideration in terms of ethical issues. Besides the danger of instrumentalisation and exploitation of service users, power and power imbalance within a given faculty have to be addressed. Also, the potential vulnerability of service users, especially in the context of higher education, which in many cases is not familiar to them, must be considered.

Joint seminars of service users and students

Planning service-user involvement requires decisions about suitable areas in the curriculum. Also, it must be decided how participatory the respective courses are going to be. In Esslingen, we asked students to identify areas in the bachelor's degree programme in social work that they considered appropriate for service-user involvement. Thus, our project was organised as a series of student projects, that is, during the fifth and the sixth semesters of the bachelor's course at our university, students develop individual projects in small groups of three to six students supervised by professors. The general aim of the project seminar, as set out in our curriculum, is to draw on the experiences gained during the internships in the fourth semester and the theoretical content of the earlier semesters by initiating a project that brings together theory and practice. More specifically, students are expected to plan, conduct and evaluate a joint enterprise based in an area of social work, combining elements of theory and practice. This module offers ample opportunities for both teachers and students (and, in this case, service users) to design a project that is in line with basic ideas of service-user involvement and which can be understood as an attempt to 'mend the gap'. Areas where gap-mending seemed especially relevant were the gaps between the professional role and the person of the helper, between professionals and clients and also between teachers and students.

As shown in Table 10.1, service users have regularly come from the mental health field as well as from an addictions background. However, other service-user groups, such as adolescents in foster care and single parents, were involved recently.

Table 10.1: List of service-user involvement seminars at Esslingen University

Years	Service users involved	Format	Products
2014–15	People with alcohol dependencies, people with psychiatric problems (EX-IN)	Joint workshop over several days on the topic 'What is good social work?'; post-workshop evaluation meeting	Teaching film with interview comments made by service users on the topic
2015–16	People with psychiatric problems	Joint workshop over several days on the topic 'Achieving a fit between service users and the university'	Creation of profiles/record cards on service users who are qualified and motivated to take part in teaching at the university; creation of a Facebook group for ongoing communication
	People with a criminal record using probation services	Joint workshop over several days on the topic 'Discrimination and stigmatisation'	Joint talk with the press
	Families, especially lone parents in residential facilities for young people	Joint workshop over several days, and interviews on the topic 'Social work between help and coercion: role conflicts'	Talk at a scientific conference; specialist article
2016–17	People with alcohol dependencies, people with psychiatric problems (EX-IN)	Joint workshop to prepare and implement a seminar in the modules 'Interviewing clients' and 'Client counselling'	Teaching concepts; evaluation concepts for seminars
	People with alcohol dependencies, people with psychiatric problems (EX-IN)	Joint workshop to prepare a national conference	Conference with other universities, service users and students; creation of a national network with representatives from universities, service users and students
2017–18	Women living in poverty	Joint workshop with interviews	Documentation of experiences
	Young people in residential care	Joint workshop to explore earlier experiences of service users	Animated film based on experiences from service users in residential care

Overall, during the past four years, roughly 60 to 70 students were included in the projects. During the first student projects, exactly the same number of students and service users participated (eight), whereas the student numbers were usually slightly higher than the service users in later projects. Nevertheless, we estimate that about 40 to 50 service users were included with a varying degree of intensity (that is, with regular contact with service users from an EX-IN background versus one-session contact with other service users). EX-IN trains people who have experienced (treatment in) mental health services to take the role of a peer who helps others in the process of recovery, thus gaining insights into their own problems.

Users' experiences with services were quite varied, but the majority described mostly positive interactions and the impression of having found help (for some, however, after an arduous number of contacts). Attempts to contact service users with more negative experiences proved challenging as they, understandably, do not tend to organise strongly. Overall, as can be expected, the most stable connections were those between individual service users and associations such as EX-IN (Jahnke, 2012; Utschakowski et al, 2016) that already have a high level organisation.

Recruitment of service users took place via professional and personal contacts: during past years, building on professional relations that had been developed over much longer timeframes, contacts with organisations such as EX-IN and self-help groups were initiated by teaching staff. Other service-user groups were recruited via personal contacts of students, mostly from their internships. Also, service users were encouraged to report their areas of expertise and settings they are comfortable with (such as the number of students and/or professionals in a group). Currently, Esslingen University of Applied Sciences does not offer training opportunities for service users; however, there is a strong collaboration with EX-IN which provides a sophisticated curriculum for people with psychiatric experiences to develop professional skills both to help other people with similar problems and to publicly talk about their experiences (such as in schools). It is a comprehensive training programme that aims at opening up new vocational and personal perspectives for people with experiences of psychiatric treatment. Experiences with mental crises and psychiatric services are discussed and reflected upon in these courses, and they form the foundation for students to work as recovery companions and/or lecturers. EX-IN graduates are aware that their personal and reflected history may be important for others in teaching situations and for educational aims. Thus, graduates of EX-IN courses are very well prepared to participate in service-user involvement seminars. These courses exist in a high number of federal states in Germany. In Baden-Wuerttemberg (the federal state where Esslingen is located), there is the special situation that the EX-IN course is run by a self-help group of persons experienced with the psychiatric system.

The degree of responsibility of service users in the seminars depended on the context of involvement in different seminar formats. Service users from an EX-IN background were regularly active as co-teachers in seminars, while at the same time there were other joint activities involving service users, such as organising lectures and workshops. One important area of involvement was in collaboratively developing teaching materials with students (such as the DVD, *What Is Good Social Work?*), whereas in other seminars, service users' main task was to provide feedback to students regarding their professional interpersonal skills, such as their initiating and maintaining professional contacts.

As we conducted a number of different seminars, the themes and topics were quite varied: besides the question 'What is good social work?' (or more precisely: Which aspects of users' experiences with social work and social workers are/were helpful and which were not?), other topics included stigmatisation, the question of help versus control in professional relationships as well as the question of 'what factors are helpful to you for/hindering you from relating to participation in service user involvement activities in social work courses'.

Wherever possible, service users, students and professors entered the discussions on an equal footing, for instance when discussing experiences with social work; all groups were encouraged to report on their personal experiences. Power imbalances were addressed early on and rules for the interactions were defined (such as the urging of students and professors to use appropriate language instead of professional jargon, or the right of all participants to stop the discussion and ask for clarification and so on).

Evaluation of service-user involvement seminars

All the activities reported so far were carefully evaluated using different methodological approaches. As an example, we will report on service-user and student feedback from the first project seminars. We will then evaluate and critically reflect on our approach to service-user involvement, and will discuss implications for the future. Both the methods and results of this study are described in detail in earlier papers (Heidenreich and Laging, 2016; Laging and Heidenreich, 2017) and will only be briefly summarised here.

To evaluate the project seminars, both service users and students were asked for feedback immediately after the workshop. The service users' comments in semi-structured interviews were analysed using qualitative methods. The service users' responses were coded using MAXQDA. A number of major categories were identified:

- the importance of exchange with students and gaining new perspectives;
- knowledge about social work theories;

- practical experience, such as getting to know other service users;
- personal benefits from the seminar;
- experiencing a university setting; and
- future expectations, especially the hope that this newly formed collaboration would continue.

The results confirmed that all the service users that were interviewed responded positively. The students' feedback on both the seminar and the whole project was positive (see also Heidenreich and Laging, 2016; Laging and Heidenreich, 2017): most of all, the students valued having the opportunity to get into direct contact with service users. One special effect of this contact was diminished anxiety when anticipating working with service users in the future. Several students pointed out that they were impressed with what service users had told them about the course of their lives and the obstacles they had had to overcome. It became clear that students reported feeling more connected to service users after the seminar.

The aim of another project was to find out in which ways service users could be involved in social work education. For this project, service users, students and teachers were brought together. One very important result of this project was the realisation that personally 'matching' service users and teachers is important in order for service-user involvement to succeed. To find possible matches, a large amount of information, discussion and preliminary work is necessary. On the other hand, experience showed that participation – in this case the participation of students in shaping their lessons – mobilised extraordinary resources of energy. For further developments in service-user involvement, including students more systematically should also be considered.

The added value derived from service-user involvement in social work education is that students develop much deeper levels of understanding with regard to users' lives and experiences. While in their internships (usually during the fourth semester) students came to learn quite a lot about service users' problems and how to professionally deal with them, they reported that in spite of these experiences they were rarely able to fully appreciate the life conditions of individual service users. The intense work in service-user-involvement seminars enabled them to assume this perspective more readily and, in many instances, led to profound changes in their perception of roles and what it means to be professional.

Service users who participated in our courses were usually paid as guest lecturers, and thus had the same status as professional lecturers who appear in courses once or for a limited time during the semester. In other instances, such as when working with adolescents on the question of how they experienced the helping system, service users received payment in vouchers that they could use for buying things they value.

Challenges to implementing joint seminars of service users and students

Currently, involving service users in social work education is very much determined by the interest and engagement of individual teaching staff. On an organisational level, EX-IN (see Jahnke, 2012; Utschakowski et al, 2016) is a close cooperation partner. On the level of our university, and in cooperation on a national level, EX-IN is systematically included and addressed, such as in roundtable discussions, workshops and in newsletters. To mend one of the existing gaps between training in Social Work and Service Users, we are currently working on a Facebook page which is designed to simplify communication between the university and service users (for instance by posting interesting events). These are the first steps towards anchoring service-user involvement in social work education in Esslingen in a broader and more systematic way.

We experienced obstacles in the work with service users on a number of levels: First, it should be kept in mind that even though service users are highly motivated to take part in social work education (and in this case even had special training), the stresses and strains they may experience in their daily lives necessitate careful planning so that the experience is not overwhelming. Furthermore, on a conceptual level, as briefly discussed in earlier papers (Heidenreich and Laging, 2016; Laging and Heidenreich, 2017), a broader adoption of service-user-involvement principles by the faculty (that is, in other areas of the BA curriculum) raises a number of questions that need answering before these principles can be realised in more depth. One of these questions concerns the possible role of service users in academic areas such as exams (as in the UK). Also, empowering service users to participate in social work education as equals will be an important issue because, after their experiences with hierarchical structures, discussions with professionals on an equal footing can be highly challenging.

Conclusion

Conducting joint workshops and seminars with service users is a promising perspective. Our experiences show that both service users and social work students experience joint workshops as very helpful. When planning joint workshops, it must be ensured that these are conducted on 'eye level', with both the service users and students contributing. Currently, we are continuing our work on joint workshops with service users and students, and we will expand the range of service users that we will include: in the last seminar as of this writing (late 2019 and 2020), we will conduct joint workshops with refugees, queer young adults and students in secondary education.

References

Askheim, O.P. (2012) '"Meeting face to face creates new insights": recruiting persons with user experiences as students in an educational programme in social work', *Social Work Education*, 31(5): 557–69. Available from: https://doi.org/10.1080/02615479.2011.590972

Bartosch, U., Maile, A., Speth, C., Buttner, P., Knauer, R., Knösel, P. and Welz, S. (2008) *Qualifikationsrahmen Soziale Arbeit (QR SArb) Version: 5.1*. Available from: https://scholar.archive.org/work/j7k2ihhjfjfyzgtwtqdhqt3yb4/access/wayback/http://www.fbts.de/uploads/media/QRSArb_Version_5.1.pdf

Chiapparini, E. (ed) (2016) *The Service User as a Partner in Social Work Projects and Education. Concepts and Evaluations of Courses with a Gap-Mending Approach in Europe*, Leverkusen: Budrich-Verlag.

Hamburger, F., Hirschler, S., Sander, G. and Wöbcke, M. (2015) 'Ausbildung für soziale arbeit in Europa' (Education for social work in Europe)', in H.-U. Otto and H. Thiersch (eds), *Handbuch Soziale Arbeit*, München: Ernst Reinhardt, GmbH & Co KG, pp 123–30.

Heidenreich, T. and Laging, M. (2016) 'Germany: service user involvement at Esslingen University of Applied Sciences: background, concept and experiences', in E. Chiapparini (ed), *The Service User as a Partner in Social Work Projects and Education: Concepts and Evaluations of Courses with a Gap-Mending Approach in Europe*, Leverkusen: Budrich-Verlag, pp 106–23.

Jahnke, B. (2012) *Vom Ich-Wissen zum Wir-Wissen: Mit EX-IN zum Genesungsbegleiter*, Neumünster: Paranus-Verlag der Brücke.

Kruse, E. (2004) *Stufen zur akademisierung: wege der ausbildung für soziale arbeit vonder wohlfahrtsschule zum Bachelor-/Mastermodell* (Steps toward academisation: ways of social work education from the welfare school to the Bachelor/Master model), Wiesbaden: VS Verlag für Sozialwissenschaften.

Laging, M. and Heidenreich, T. (2017) 'Service user involvement in social work education: experiences from Germany and implications for a European perspective', *European Journal of Social Work*, 20(3): 387–95. Available from: https://doi.org/10.1080/13691457.2017.1283586

Laging, M. and Heidenreich, T. (2019) 'Towards a conceptual framework for service user involvement in social work education', *Journal of Social Work Education*, 55(1): 11–22. Available from: https://doi.org/10.1080/10437797.2018.1498417

Utschakowski, J., Sielaff, G., Bock, T. and Winter, A. (eds) (2016) *Experten aus Erfahrung: Peerarbeit in der Psychiatrie*, Köln: Psychiatrie Verlag.

11

Service users, students and staff: co-producing creative educational activities on a social work programme in the UK

Kieron Hatton, Kevin Holmes and Pete Shepherd

Introduction

From limited beginnings service-user/carer involvement has become central to the accreditation and validation of social work programmes in the UK (Hatton, 2015). The extent and depth of service-user/carer involvement varies widely across the country and in many, but not all, cases focuses on the involvement of service users/carers in the traditional elements of the programme – admissions interviews, guest teaching and as expert speakers. This chapter suggest that if we are to make service-user/carer involvement meaningful, we need to develop a more holistic and complex way of understanding how service users/carers can contribute to social work education. This will involve seeing service users/carers as co-producers and partners in the educational experience rather than seeing their involvement as a way of legitimising our commitment to inclusion. To achieve this, this chapter argues that we need a more developed analysis of power, agency, imagination and creativity. The chapter uses the phrase 'service users/carers' for clarity, although it fully recognises that: a) service users/carers are not a homogenous grouping, and b) the very words are themselves contentious (McLaughlin, 2009). In current discourses, service users/carers are more often referred to as experts by experience or people with lived experience (PWLE). The authors also recognises that service users/carers have multiple identities beyond their status as service users/carers, and that many of these roles intersect (Hill Collins and Bilge, 2016) and cause contradictions/conflicts. This is the content of a recently published companion piece (Hatton, 2020).

The development of service-user involvement in the UK

Over the last 20 years, service users/carers have at last been recognised as having a significant role in the delivery, management and development of welfare services. This is reflected in the attention given to service-user involvement in both the legislative and policy contexts. These debates cut across all service boundaries and raise questions about service-user representation (Hatton, 2015), the efficacy of current initiatives and the usefulness of the service-user perspective across a range of service-user areas.

The drivers behind these initiatives have often been service users themselves. The role of disability activists in creating the political climate to support anti-discriminatory legislation around disability is well known, as was their role in ensuring that the Disability Discrimination Act 1995 (subsequently the Equality Act 2010) was amended to give disabled people the right to enforcement action if their entitlements were not met.

The development of services incorporating personalisation and co-production has provided an important motor for this enhanced move towards empowering people in the adult social care sector. This approach was further developed in the proposals around co-production which placed the emphasis on users and user-led organisations. The Social Care Institute for Excellence (SCIE) (2013) produced a guide to co-production which suggests that it is possible to identify some key features. Co-production, they suggest, defines people who use services as assets with skills, and breaks down the barriers between them and professionals.

Three features of personalisation as an important way of empowering people – design, commission and delivery – are critical to our ability to distinguish whether involvement has any meaning. The key elements of co-production involve promoting people's strengths, reciprocity and mutuality, and the idea of people as change agents. Ideas of co-production link closely to the concerns within this chapter about how we develop meaningful ways of securing the involvement of service user/carers in the delivery of social work education.

Service-user/carer involvement in social work education

Within social work there has been a clear articulation of the importance of securing service-user/carer involvement (Anghel and Ramon, 2009). This is reflected in teaching (Waterson and Morris, 2005), assessment and peer review (Humphreys, 2005; Skoura-Kirk et al, 2013), face to face interactions between service users/carers and students and the use of video and other tools (Waterson and Morris, 2005). As Irvine et al (2015) argue, the students they looked at had a 'strong perception that their practice was improved by the input they had been given from service users and carers' (Irvine et al, 2015, p 148 – see reflections below).

The Portsmouth experience

The Social Work Inclusion Group (SWIG) at the University of Portsmouth has been established in slightly different forms since June 2004, with the support of money provided by government agencies to secure the involvement of service users in programme design and delivery (previously known as the Service User Inclusion Group; SUIG, 2005). At the University of Portsmouth this has taken a variety of forms as illustrated in Table 11.1 below.

Service-user/carer involvement in the social work programmes in Portsmouth has as its central aim the development of creative teaching artefacts with which to engage with students in a critical and empowering way. The example of the CREATE day (in the BSc programme) demonstrates how the aim of producing a creative artefact was achieved through the co-production of activities by students, service users and staff. Inspiration for the potential outcomes was often initiated by service users, with the students then coming on board to work out how to best achieve the suggested outcomes – whether using film, theatre, dance, poetry or other forms of performance. The staff then offered facilitative support to achieve the desired outcomes delivered by students and service users in small group presentations to the whole cohort.

Table 11.1: Service-user/carer involvement in creative activities at the University of Portsmouth

• Interviewing and admissions procedures	• Teaching – the group trained service users to teach in the social work degree programmes
• Redesigning the curricula	• Assessing students 'readiness for practice' at the end of the first year (undergrad) or first semester (postgrad)
• Producing a video, 'What I want from a social worker', and a series of DVDs for Palgrave's Social Work Toolkit	• Assessing student presentations
• Developing a range of drama and cultural activities for use in social work training: a) a CREATE day; b) *Perspectives* project (Hatton, 2013); c) 'debate days' for first-year students	• Assessing presentations by applicants seeking academic positions
• Small-scale research around homelessness	• Auditing work placements – designing an audit tool to assess whether placement agencies meet students' learning needs
• Attending and contributing to team meetings	• Attending and contributing to course validation and other events

Source: see www.swig.uk.net

The BSc students were also asked to engage in a debate day in which two groups would present different aspects of a key issue facing service users. The groups were co-facilitated by a member of SWIG and a member of the academic staff. The students were allocated groups, so would sometimes be asked to present arguments which they may not have been supportive of. Such an approach encouraged students to step out of their comfort zone and research and engage with ideas they may not have been familiar with. The combination of these activities developed the students' critical abilities and their confidence in engaging and communicating with service users in a way the presence of service users as teachers (an approach also used) could not replicate.

The Perspectives project, (attached to an empowerment unit) sought to adopt a similar approach. Students, service users and carers, in small groups, co-produced a piece of theatre, film or similar artefact which was presented to the whole year group. The outcomes were often powerful and gave a voice to service users/carers who are often under-represented in academic discourses (for examples see swig.uk.net).

Conceptualising the involvement of people using services in social work education

The theoretical underpinning for such an approach has frequently been under-conceptualised. Generally involvement has been seen as good and part of a broader inclusion agenda which seeks to engage with the empowerment of people using social work services. The inclusion agenda has focused on the importance of power relationships (Tew, 2006), and the need for service-user 'voice' (Beresford, 2013), and has been critical of managerialist and procedural approaches to engagement with people using social work services, particularly in the age of austerity (Jordan and Drakeford, 2012). However, these areas could be further developed. Power discourses have drawn on a range of writers from across the social and political sciences.

Foucault (1991) reminds us that power operates in a complex way, that we need to interrogate our understanding of power at macro and micro levels and that people need to have

> the right to speech and political imagination [which] must be returned to them ... the complexity of the problem will be able to appear in its connection with people's lives ... the object is to proceed a little at a time, to introduce modifications that are capable of, if not finding a solution, then at least changing the givens of a problem. (Foucault, 1991, pp 158–9)

Foucault's comments can be seen as a prime legitimation of our concern with involving people who use social work services in making decisions about their lives. Work with service users and carers is specifically about releasing people's political imagination so that they can envision an alternative experience, a different way of experiencing and delivering welfare and social work services. It is concerned with changing the way issues are framed so that service users are not seen as 'problems' or 'clients' but rather as active partners in changing the services they directly experience.

Engaging and creating partnerships with people who use social work services has a change dimension; it is essentially political, which means that when examining service-user/carer involvement we need to ask whether the involvement we are discussing is real or tokenistic (Webber and Robinson, 2012). To achieve real inclusion/engagement we need to have a multi-dimensional concept of power which incorporates a range of variables (see Figure 11.1).

This concept of power includes inclusion/participation, the link between theory and practice, the actualisation of personal and political power through creativity and artistic action and an underpinning commitment to the recognition of agency as the determining factor in people realising their potential.

Figure 11.1: A dynamic view of power

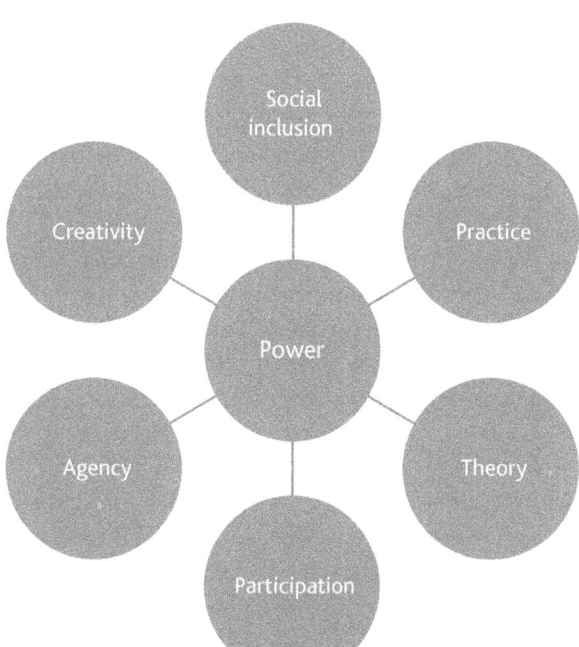

SWIG members attribute great importance to their having a significant role in training and educating social workers. Their concern is not just to highlight issues but to contribute to the development and improvement of services. Such an involvement is essential if services are to be able to meet the demands placed on them in the new welfare mix.

Creating new forms of power

We need an analysis of the way in which ideas emerge which challenges the idea that service users are passive in the face of the institutional power of large social work or professional agencies. Service users/carers struggling to have their voices heard need to be recognised themselves as change agents.

We can do this by seeing service users as people with the capacity to bring about change not only in their own individual circumstances but in the broader institutions and structures against which they struggle. Empowerment becomes central to the service-user/carer experience (Hatton, 2015).

Promoting meaningful change

To make involvement and participation real, we need to look not just at how power can be exercised but also at how it can be resisted. How can we develop strategies to promote meaningful change? Giddens's analysis of agency and structure can provide some pointers as to how this may occur. He refers to power as 'the transformative capacity of human action' (Cassell, 1993, p 109). This, Giddens (1979) suggests, is the key element in the notion of praxis – the creation of a radical practice based on notions of overcoming discrimination/oppression and the creation of new cooperative social relationships, which is at the heart of any theory of social action. Similar ideas can also be seen in Freire's idea of 'conscientisation', the notion that when a person becomes aware of the way their oppression is determined they develop the capacity to take action to change their situation (Freire, 1972).

Power should be viewed as a dynamic concept in which individuals 'are always in the position of simultaneously undergoing and exercising power … [they] … are the vehicles of power, not its application' (Foucault, 1980, p 98). This is the agency that we, as social workers, academics and users/carers, are looking for, the sense that service users can resist and reframe their experience in a way that can change the way services are delivered.

There is a need to identify why people act or fail to act to redress any disadvantage they experience. Underpinning the need for a focus on participation/inclusion is a commitment to recognising the agency of service users. Giddens's concept of agency is of 'human action', or what Fook (2002) has characterised as a 'sense of responsibility, of agency, an appreciation of how each player can act upon it to influence a situation' (Fook, 2002, p 200). Central to this is the development of a consciousness which can imagine another, different way of doing things, a point similar to that attributed to Foucault (Foucault, 1980). Hatton (2015) has suggested that this would enable 'the creation of a radical practice based on notions of overcoming oppression ... and the creation of new cooperative social relationships, [which are] at the heart of any theory of social action' (Hatton, 2015, p 113).

Service-user involvement and social pedagogy

One way in which this development of a new consciousness can be seen is through the prism of the European concept of social pedagogy (Hatton, 2013), which is defined by Hamalainen (2003) as the intention 'to promote people's social functioning, inclusion, participation, social identity and social competence as members of society' (Hamalainen, 2003, p 76). This commitment to social action is recognised as a central tenet of social pedagogy by a number of writers (Hatton, 2013). This is also reflected in Vygotsky's idea of the 'creative imagination', which occurs 'whenever a person imagines, combines, alters and creates something new' (Vygotsky, 2004, p 11). This will involve setting agendas for change, not just responding to the agenda of those with power, (Jordan and Drakeford, 2012) and developing new participatory organisations and practices which signify real and lasting change. This illustrates Foucault's point about individuals simultaneously undergoing and exercising power, and would help us understand the way power operates (Foucault, 1980).

Central to a pedagogues' activity is the use of head, heart and hands. The former enables the pedagogue to develop an understanding of the reasons for their intervention, the heart indicates the regard for and empathy with the person or group with whom the pedagogue is intervening and the hands indicate the range of practical activity and creativity which the pedagogue uses in any intervention (Boddy and Statham, 2009).

These features need to be incorporated into a change agenda and be central to fostering engagement between service users/carers, students and academic staff.

From understanding to action

An important influence on Danish pedagogy has been the work of Freire (Eriksson and Markstrom, 2003; Hatton, 2017). Freire (1972) argues that a key way in which people without power are marginalised is through a process in which their behaviour becomes pathologised and their human nature is constructed in a distorted way through a process of indoctrination, manipulation and 'dominated consciousness'. He argues that as a result, people lack the consciousness or understanding to decode their situations. He argues, therefore, that we should encourage people to see the commonality of their situation, and that this focus on the common interest can only be achieved through a process which he describes as *conscientanzo*. This is a process through which people not only become aware but act on that awareness.

The role of creativity

An important element of this approach is a focus on creativity. Vygotsky's focus on creativity and imagination suggests a way forward. Our creative actions are, he argues, based on our use of imagination which is 'the basis of all creative activity ... an important component of all aspects of cultural life, enabling artistic, scientific, and technical creation alike ... whenever a person imagines, combines, alters and creates something new' (Vygotsky, 2004, p 11).

To free the creative imagination is to challenge the organisation of the society in which we live and to improve the life chances of the people we work with. Vygotsky concludes by advocating the particular importance of cultivating creativity (Vygotsky, 2004, p 87).

A creative approach can have relevance across the helping professions. As the work of SWIG demonstrates, play, music, drama and awareness of the body can be employed in work with siblings, mental health users, people with physical and intellectual disabilities and in the care of older people. An understanding of the theory behind creative activity can promote reflection and learning in a variety of contexts (Hatton, 2020).

The Creativity, Inclusion, Social Pedagogy model

A model which suggests a way of linking these divergent thoughts together is the one which lies behind the service-user/carer involvement work in Portsmouth. The Creativity, Inclusion, Social Pedagogy (CRISP) model is an attempt to build a model of social theory and practice which makes explicit the need for creativity and inclusion to be part of the pedagogic/social work task (Hatton, 2013, p 17). The approach advocated suggests that the missing link between creativity, which is essential to empowering practice, and social pedagogy is the notion of inclusion. Creativity suggests a way of realising the potential of people working in and making use of welfare services. Social pedagogy is predicated on equal partnerships between people working in and using welfare services. Both are central to the idea of inclusion. Inclusion provides the philosophical, practical and professional rationale for joining together creativity and social pedagogy and achieving a 'politics of liberation'.

A focus on inclusion is central to good social-professional practice (Beresford and Hoban, 2005; Hatton, 2015). Those involved with radical social and community work will appreciate the difficulty of achieving real inclusion rather than the often tokenistic attempts at inclusion which agencies seek to perpetuate (Ferguson and Woodward, 2009; Hatton, 2015).

It is now recognised by the institutions of the state (government departments and Social Work England), higher education institutions, academics, students and users of social work services that the involvement of service users/carers in social work education is a good thing. Clearly there is evidence of a recognition of power relationships, of the need for inclusion and for an understanding of the importance of service-users'/carers' voice. This chapter seeks to build on these insights to suggest a conception of involvement which develops these concerns and provides a deeper conception of power, the importance of involvement, inclusion and participation and the need for us to embrace creativity as a way of enhancing such involvement.

Some reflections from the Portsmouth experience

During our work with service users/carers and students at the University of Portsmouth, we asked participants in the creative work we undertook to comment on their experiences.

Social Work Inclusion Group members

SWIG members have reflected positively on the importance of working in this inclusive and creative way. One of the co-leaders of the SWIG group noted:

> 'The reason we do creative work is that it has proved to be the best way to educate future social workers as the feedback proves – it isn't until they sit down and see life through our eyes that they get a real understanding of the issues around social work. If you want to change the way social work operates, care workers turning up at a time to suit the agency rather than the client, it's time to start listening to the client. It's not until they can put themselves in our place that they realise the impact of bad practice and accept that they wouldn't put up with it.'

Another member, recalling her experience of co-producing a short drama, commented on the way her and her husband's story impacted on the students:

> 'The most enjoyable for me I think was last year I worked with a group ... I did a sketch on my life, because I receive care through agency care system and that has its drawbacks, because I'll have them in the morning and evening and they will come in the early evening, sometimes when

I had to go out. I mean, I remember once or even twice going to choir practice in my pyjamas … it was really embarrassing … (they, the students, got that). Most of it is … I feel very useful. It helps them develop as social workers. I really think it works.'

Another commented on the importance of creativity in their work with students:

'I like the emphasis on creativity because it does force people to think outside the box … how to communicate with people with a disability. I like the fact that [through their engagement with Create] … I think the students have an edge when they go out into the workforce … if you come across somebody … who has got a social work degree … from another institution where they don't demand that they interact with people with a disability, they … are going to be at a disadvantage because they're going to come with absolutely no idea about what to do.'

Students

One student talked of how co-producing creative artefacts led them to

'see [service users] differently. And seeing people with a disability not as people with disabilities but just as people … it's more than just tokenistic. It's actually, from the get go, working together, coming up with ideas together. Producing what you produce together. And really using the service user's knowledge, their skills, to come up with something at the end.'

The students saw this as more than just being partners; it was also about critical engagement:

'The challenging part was the questions from the service users, because they could really analyse what we were saying. It's OK to talk about it and advocate for people, but unless we had that experience we would never know completely how it feels … the questions from them were much more real and challenging.'

Another student said:

'Although we talk about person-centred practice, in reality it does not always happen as you say. Service users are heard but for some reason their voice gets lost further down the process … this creative work has [taught me] ... as social workers, we need to be challenging managers and higher authorities and say, well Ok but the service users say this.'

Discussing their collaborative work on the debate days, one of the students commented:

'I needed to have that experience before going into practice. Because now, it wouldn't phase me, but if someone had said to me, right, I am putting you straight into practice with people with disabilities, I would have become quite anxious, but now I know I have nothing to be anxious about.'

These brief insights from students who have studied in the Portsmouth social work programmes provide concrete illustrations of the debates framed in this chapter and suggest a way we can achieve change in student outlook and practice if we meaningfully engage service users/carers in our programmes.

Academic staff

Academic staff can find this work equally challenging. One of the staff involved with SWIG's creative work suggested a need to recognise

'the staff time and commitment needed to facilitate this complex process. Also, an acknowledgement of the pivotal role someone like Kevin has played in managing and supporting a service user group hub, etc. From my previous experience of trying to initiate, support and facilitate the involvement of new and established service users to contribute to teaching on a social work programme, I am aware of the considerable time, resource and capacity issues this can bring.'

They added,

'In terms of content, this was often highly critical in highlighting the failures of agencies and in some cases particular unnamed practitioners. These narratives were often raw, challenging and in need of an understanding of context, history and circumstance for some less experienced students to take on board in a positive way. Whilst they were extremely positive in terms of promoting service-user involvement, giving voice and challenging students' attitudes and knowledge, the issues associated with this process needed ongoing monitoring and an established infrastructure of support.'

Another member of staff explained the challenges engagement with service users can pose:

> 'I think student groups need to be prepared sometimes for that variability of experience and the different ways SWIG members come across. I think sometimes they can expect SWIG members to be more like lecturers and don't really understand co-production from the start ... I've seen students just taking notes and waiting for the SWIG member to say something so they take some notes rather than doing a dialogue. So ... it's been difficult, and different student groups have been really different [in their responses].'

Reflecting further she said:

> 'It's not just an add-on that enhances it and makes it pretty ... it has to be grounded in the voices of service users, and we have to work at it together. There would be no point in having a social work course without that ... I can't imagine a social work course without service-user involvement.'

Another staff member spoke about the commitment entailed in real engagement/involvement: "It is actually easier just to tick the box to say that you've spoken to a service user than actually to work out how you've engaged with them and how you have transformed things."

Conclusion

This chapter draws on debates around creativity, models of social pedagogy and the experience of delivering a creative agenda at the University of Portsmouth. It is suggested that we need to fuse together a multi-dimensional analysis of power (with a particular focus on the idea that we co-produce learning activities and experiences), a recognition of the degree of agency exercised by people using social work services and a commitment to using our own and our collective creative (and political) imaginations to work in new ways. This means moving beyond traditional measures of involvement such as teaching assessment and interviewing to a wider concept that positions us all as drivers of the learning experience and as creators of the curricula. Most importantly, it gives meaningful voice to the people involved in the creative and inclusive work undertaken by service users/carers, students and academic staff engaged in this process.

To this extent, this chapter should be seen as an exploratory discussion which raises important issues about the centrality of service-user/carer involvement in social work education. The reflections from a small number of service users, staff and students experiencing the Portsmouth social work programmes highlight the impact that such involvement can have on the profession and on the lived experience of people using social work services.

References

Anghel, R. and Ramon, S. (2009) 'Service users and carers' involvement in social work education: lessons from an English case study', *European Journal of Social Work*, 12: 185–99.

Beresford, P. (2013) 'Service user issues: rights, needs and responsibilities', in B. Littlechild and R. Smith (eds), *A Handbook for Inter-Professional Practice in the Human Services: Learning to Work Together*, Harlow: Pearson, pp 187–99.

Beresford, P. and Hoban, M. (2005) *Participation in Anti-Poverty and Regeneration Work and Research: Overcoming Barriers and Creating Opportunities*, York: Joseph Rowntree Foundation.

Boddy, J. and Statham, J. (2009) *European Perspectives on Social Work: Models of Education and Professional Roles*, London: Thomas Coram Research Unit, Institute of Education.

Cassell, P. (ed) (1993) *The Giddens Reader*, Basingstoke: Macmillan.

Eriksson, L. and Markstrom, A.M. (2003) 'Interpreting the concept of social pedagogy', in A. Gustavsson, H.E. Hermansson and J. Hamalained (eds), *Perspectives and Theory in Social Pedagogy*, Gotenburg: Bokforlaget, DaidLOS, pp 9–22.

Ferguson, I. and Woodward, R. (2009) *Radical Social Work in Practice: Making a Difference*, Bristol: Policy Press.

Fook, J. (2002) *Social Work: Critical Theory and Practice*, London: Sage.

Foucault, M. (1980) *Power/Knowledge: Selected Interviews and Other Writings*, Brighton: Harvester Wheatsheaf.

Foucault, M. (1991) *Remarks on Marx*, New York: Semiotext Books.

Freire, P. (1972) *Pedagogy of the Oppressed*, London: Penguin.

Giddens, A. (1979) *Central Problems in Social Theory*, Basingstoke: Macmillan Education.

Hamalainen, J. (2003) 'The concept of social pedagogy in the field of social work', *Journal of Social Work,* 3(1), 70-80.

Hatton, K. (2013) *Social Pedagogy in the UK: Theory and Practice*, Lyme Regis: Russell House Publishing.

Hatton, K. (2015) *New Directions in Social Work Practice*, 2nd edn, London: Learning Matters/Sage.

Hatton, K. (2017) 'A critical examination of the knowledge contribution service user and carer involvement brings to social work education', *Social Work Education,* 36(2): 154–71. Available from: https://doi.org/10.1080/02615479.2016.1254769

Hatton, K. (2020) 'A new framework for creativity in social pedagogy', *International Journal of Social Pedagogy*, 9(1): 16. Available from: https://doi.org/10.14324/111.444.ijsp.2020.v9.x.016

Hill Collins, P. and Bilge, S. (2016) *Intersectionality*, Cambridge: Polity.

Humphreys, C. (2005) 'Service user involvement in social work education: a case example', *Social Work Education*, 24: 797–803.

Irvine, J., Molyneux, J. and Gillman, M. (2015) '"Providing a link with the real world": learning from the student experience of service user and carer involvement in social work education', *Social Work Education*, 34: 138–50.

Jordan, B. and Drakeford, M. (2012) *Social Work and Social Policy under Austerity*, Basingstoke: Palgrave Macmillan.

McLaughlin, H. (2009) 'What's in a name: "client", "patient", "customer", "consumer", "expert by experience", "service user" – what's next?', *The British Journal of Social Work*, 39(6): 1101–17. Available from: https://doi.org/10.1093/bjsw/bcm155

Pauvels, L. (2010) 'Visual sociology reframed: an analytical synthesis and discussion of visual methods in social and cultural research', *Sociological Methods and Research*, 38: 545–81.

Service User Inclusion Group (2005) *Training Service Users to Become Actively Involved in the New Social Work Degree*, London: TOPSS England.

Skoura-Kirk, E., Backhouse, B., Bennison, G., Cecil, B., Keeler, J., Talbot, D. and Watch, L. (2013) 'Mark my words! Service user and carer involvement in social work academic assessment', *Social Work Education*, 32: 560–75.

Social Care Institute for Excellence (2013) *Co-Production in Social Care: What It Is and How to Do It, SCIE Guide 15*, London: Social Care Institute for Excellence.

Tew, J. (2006) 'Understanding power and powerlessness: towards a framework for emancipatory practice in social work', *Journal of Social Work*, 6: 33–51.

Vygotsky, L. (2004) 'Imagination and creativity in childhood', *Journal of Russian and East European Psychology*, 42: 7–97.

Waterson, J. and Morris, K. (2005) 'Training in "social" work: exploring issues of involving users in teaching on social work degree programmes', *Social Work Education*, 24: 653–75.

Webber, M. and Robinson, K. (2012) 'The meaningful involvement of service users and carers in advanced-level post-qualifying social work education: a qualitative study', *British Journal of Social Work*, 42: 1256–74.

PART II

Collaborative models in research and policy

12

The co-researcher role in the tension between recognition, co-option and tokenism

Ole Petter Askheim

Introduction

The importance of involving users of welfare services in research is receiving increasing attention in public policy documents and in academic literature (Macaulay et al, 2011; Hancock et al, 2012; Heaton et al, 2016). Nowotny et al (2001) describe this tendency as a shift of mode in knowledge production. In the traditional scientific paradigm (mode 1), science is produced within an academic sphere separated from the influence of external society. The new paradigm (mode 2) is defined by research practices performed in dialogue with their implementation. Such research practices require researchers to step down from their ivory towers and recognise that knowledge is produced in arenas other than academia.

The significance of user participation is embedded in strong egalitarian rhetoric and positive concepts such as democratisation and research quality improvement. As Goldstein (2000, p 517) comments: 'Collaborative research has become as universally loved as Mom and apple pie.' Nevertheless, in practice, participation by co-researchers is essentially limited (Abma and Broerse, 2010; Hancock et al, 2012; Fleming et al, 2014). In general, researchers set the premises and decide the role expected of co-researchers.

Thus, while participation and co-production often appear to be fine words encompassing very different kinds of participation by actors outside the researcher community, in this way they may conceal the exercise of power and make hierarchical structures invisible (McLaughlin, 2009; Frankham and Tracy, 2012; Phillips et al, 2013). Nevertheless, the limited participation of co-researchers with service-user backgrounds has only been put on the agenda to a small degree (Abma, 2009; Brett et al, 2012). Frankham (2009) claims that there is resistance to such criticism, and Hodgson and Canvin (2005, p 48) comment that 'the value of user participation currently occupies a "morally imperious" position and is "increasingly resistant to criticism".'

Critics advocate that research proclaiming user involvement be deromanticised and subject to greater criticism. Important questions include: Behind the apparent recognition of service users' experiences and competence, is their participation in reality symbolic, serving mainly to legitimise projects that in practice are controlled by the researchers? If so, why? Is it mainly because researchers are sceptical of non-researchers as equal actors in the research process? Alternatively, is it primarily because of possible challenges when actors with different backgrounds and expectations meet to co-produce knowledge?

The chapter will closely examine the tensions and dilemmas that may arise when people with service-user experiences are involved in the research process. Based on the main challenges that appear, it will discuss actions to resolve tensions and dilemmas in a constructive way, so that cooperation can lead to a democratisation of knowledge production.

Co-production: a challenge for established research

The involvement of non-academics in research challenges established research in a couple of ways: it breaks with academic traditions and the kind of research that has status. Hodgson and Canvin (2005) claim that participation by 'outsiders' will remain symbolic as long as a traditional view of science dominates and theoretical knowledge and the established language of scientific method have hegemony. Co-researchers will then be seen as lacking sufficient skills and qualifications for research, and as underestimating the complexity of the implications of research activity (Boote et al, 2002; Hancock et al, 2012; Case et al, 2014). Furthermore, they will be seen as partisan representatives threatening the objectivity of research. Stoecker (2008, p 108) claims that in some research institutions, participation by users is still looked upon as 'community housework' and not valued, and consequently receives little attention. He claims that the reward system of universities weakens the possibilities of cooperation with users.

However, researcher scepticism about user involvement could also be about attitudes, prejudices and stereotypes concerning co-researchers (Abma, 2009). For instance, researchers may consider that the co-researchers are too subjective and too emotionally involved in their projects, therefore it would be difficult to include them in the research process. Not least, researchers could see this as a problem when persons who have experiences as service users are recruited as co-researchers.

It could also be that researchers find themselves losing control over their research projects (Faulkner, 2009). Benoit et al (2005) claim that the researchers may feel alienated from their data if they do not conduct interviews personally.

In what ways do co-researchers participate?

The main questions when co-researchers are involved in research projects concern their degree of involvement and what they do. This determines whether their participation is real or symbolic.

A review of articles on how user participation is implemented and its potential benefit indicates two main strategies of collaboration: consultative and integrating strategies (Østensjø and Askheim, 2019). Examples of consultative strategies include inviting users to take part in advisory boards, such as a user panel, and seeking their input at different stages of the research process. Integrative projects, on the other hand, are initiated or developed in collaboration between the researchers and other actors, with the aim of integrating different types of knowledge.

In general, the consultative model predominates. The researchers set the premises and decide on the role of the co-researchers. Cornwall (2008) claims that the most common form of participation of non-researchers in projects is 'functional participation': people are invited to participate so goals may be achieved more effectively after significant decisions are made by the research leaders. Sometimes, toward the end of the application process, the researchers seem to be reminded that they must have some kind of user participation to receive funding for a project. The following quote from an experienced co-researcher seems to be a typical description of the situation:

> 'Since user participation or user involvement has been established as a requirement in research, I have been contacted several times by researchers needing people with experience as service users so that they can document in their project plans that they have met the demand for user participation. The project description and design have almost always been decided, so I have little influence on either the issues that need to be researched or on the role meant for me.' (Raak Høiseth, in Askheim et al, 2019, p 217)

Time and economy as the main challenges

The literature on user involvement in research stresses that co-producing research is resource intensive and emphasises the importance of being aware of this when planning and implementing projects (Nolan et al, 2007b; Minkler and Corage Baden, 2008; Case et al, 2014). McLaughlin (2006) claims that the need for additional resources in order for co-researchers to participate is often insufficiently recognised. Such recognition is important for a number of reasons. First, it is important to have and make time available to clarify the expectations for the project, its goals and the role of the different actors. Furthermore, sufficient time provides the opportunity to build good, trustful and confident relationships between the participants and to provide the necessary training and help or support to the co-researchers. It is also important that sufficient resources are set aside for co-researchers in order for them to obtain fair and acceptable remuneration for their work. Fair remuneration signals that the co-researchers and their contributions to the projects are taken seriously. As McLaughlin (2006, p 1395) concludes: 'If the costs in terms of resources, training, support, timescale and remuneration are not addressed, the research will be undermined and in danger of becoming tokenistic.'

The importance of making good collaborative relationships

Creating good relationships between the participants from the start of the research process is seen as a key investment for the success of the project (Nolan et al, 2007b; Cossar and Neil, 2015). Sufficient time for contact and discussion with the co-researchers is important for building trust and good relations so that the co-researchers feel taken seriously, recognised and valued. Furthermore, it is important to give priority to building good relations in order for co-researchers to understand the role of researcher and to be able to perform it optimally.

Giving priority to establishing contacts and building good collaborative relations is also seen as important because co-researchers may be sceptical about academics. The academic culture and jargon can be unfamiliar and frightening (Benoit et al, 2005; Banks et al, 2014). Hodgson and Canvin (2005) claim that scientific terminology can generate exclusion and alienation rather than affiliation. Scepticism could also be the result of negative research experiences and the feeling of not being taken seriously or of having been abused in research (Wallerstein and Duran, 2008; Frankham, 2009).

Different expectations for the research process

Establishing relationships of trust between participants is also an important precondition for clarifying actors' expectations of the research process. There may be fundamental tension related to the participants' expectations for both the research process and its results. When service users engage in research projects, their interests will often be linked to action and the possible effects of the research in their lives (Strier, 2007; Abma, 2009). Consequently, they will often be disappointed with the actual contribution of the research. They will often experience frustration about time-consuming processes and the time it takes to make the results of the projects public. Furthermore, the results often do not provide clear answers. Reservations are expressed in different ways. Minkler and Corage Baden (2008, p 256) describe the tension as between 'the necessary scepticism of science and the action imperative of communities.'

For co-researchers, the long period from the end of a project to the publication of the results, which is often written in unfamiliar academic jargon, will be experienced as frustrating (Minkler and Corage Baden, 2008; McLaughlin, 2009). As Benoit et al (2005) see it, the main challenge is to present the results in a language that is understandable to lay people but at the same time appreciated by the academic community.

The importance of training and support

Co-researchers without any research experience need training because research is new to them. As McLaughlin (2009, p 36) comments: 'Poor quality training is likely to lead to poor quality research.' Co-researchers need training in what research is about, methodological approaches and ethical issues (Hancock et al, 2012). Furthermore, Hancock et al (2012) state that training should be practical, varied, and presented in an understandable way that recognises the prior knowledge of the co-researchers. This is important in order for users to experience equality in the research process.

Part of the training should be a discussion about the implications of the researcher role in relation to a user role, an activist role or an advisory role. From time to time, researchers notice that their co-researchers have difficulty leaving such roles. Forbat and Hubbard (2015) show that when co-researchers interviewed other service users, they occasionally returned to their user role and spoke to informants from their user identity rather than as co-researchers. As a result, the co-researchers did not follow up on the utterances of the informants. Instead, they gave the informants advice or related the answers to their own experiences, which did not match with those of the informants. In a number of cases, the interviews developed into parallel conversations instead of dialogue, and the co-researchers lost opportunities to have the informants elaborate on their experiences and opinions.

Although the importance of training is emphasised, there are also warnings that excessive professionalism of users in research projects may separate them from the people they should represent (Abma, 2009; Natland et al, 2017). In other words, it undermines the co-researchers' ability to represent the groups from which they are recruited.

Especially for co-researchers recruited from user groups that could be characterised as marginalised, there may be a need for positive support in the research process. Researchers should be aware that the research process may involve emotional reactions that need to be managed (Benoit et al, 2005; Mjøsund et al, 2016). Abma (2009) shows that for co-researchers, interviewing people with service-user experiences similar to their own may trigger emotional tensions as they are reminded of painful experiences from their own lives, and may lead to feelings of despair and powerlessness.

Recognition instead of tokenism and co-option: what should be done?

Prioritising resources in the form of time and economy so that co-researchers can do meaningful work can create dilemmas for researchers. They may experience tension between different interests and loyalties. Resources from scarce funds must be used for training, follow-up and remuneration of the co-researchers. This will limit the degree to which the researchers feel they can involve the co-researchers (Abma, 2009). Researchers feel the need to prioritise between spending scarce resources in order to achieve constructive cooperation with co-researchers on the one hand, and accommodating academic expectations and demands while protecting their own research ambitions on the other.

If the involvement of persons with service-user experience as co-researchers is to imply recognition beyond tokenism and co-option, the dominant paradigms of research should be challenged. What are the practical consequences of the shift from mode 1, with a traditional scientific paradigm, to mode 2, with a recognition of the importance of knowledge produced in non-academic arenas? What consequences would there be for the initiation, organisation and implementation of research projects?

The importance of early involvement

A fundamental prerequisite for the equitable participation of co-researchers is that they be involved from an early stage of the research process. This should imply involvement of the co-researchers in the design of applications, sketches and plans when the premises of the projects are largely determined. However, in the application process, this may create dilemmas for the researchers because much time and resources are required for good applications and in a hectic work situation too little time is often allocated. For instance, in the Norwegian Research Council's welfare research programme plans (Norges forskningsråd 2017a, 2017b) it is stated that 'the users should be involved in all parts of the research process', and that 'a lack of involvement especially must be justified.' However, there are no specific measures to facilitate user involvement in the planning and application phase. Consequently, adaptions in the initial phases should be made to facilitate co-researcher involvement. A solution could be to announce funds for preliminary projects developing ideas and plans that could later develop into more extensive projects. This development of ideas and preliminary projects then could be more easily developed in cooperation between research communities and relevant actors.

In some of the other Norwegian Research Council programs, this idea has been tried out with some success.

Clarifying expectations

For successful cooperation, it is considered crucial for researchers and co-researchers to spend time together to clarify their expectations and the co-researchers' role (Sullivan et al, 2001; Fleming et al, 2014; Greenhalgh et al, 2016). This means open discussions about the goals of the project, the expectations of and commitments between the actors and how to manage conflicts (Phillips et al, 2013). Making formal agreements and contracts may be important both to formalise the collaboration and because the preparations for such agreements provide a good opportunity to discuss the form of cooperation in the project (Frankham, 2009; Fleming et al, 2014).

Prioritising relation building

As mentioned above, building good and trusting relations between researchers and co-researchers is seen as key for the recognition of co-researchers and for their sense of being taken seriously. Banks et al (2013, p 4) describe this process as the development of 'everyday ethics': 'The daily practice of negotiating ethical issues and challenges that arise through the research project.'

Chávez et al (2008, p 91) compare the cooperative relations between academic researchers and user representatives to a dance. Dancers from different cultures learn from each other's movements, rhythms and meanings.

> Like dancing, CBPR [community-based participatory research] has the potential for making research partners feel exhilarated, awkward, controlled and free. The dance involves being aware of differences and respecting that although some people appear to be 'natural' dancers, others need more time and instructions as they experiment with movement. Dancers complement each other's steps, sometimes leading, sometimes following; they are aware of each other, navigating the dance floor while trying not to step on each other's toes.

In the same paper, Chávez et al (2008) state that conscious efforts to create trusting relations improve research because the co-researchers will then behave more honestly in the research process. Not least, participants from so-called marginalised groups may otherwise tend to do and say what they believe the researchers expect from them.

With a background in action research, Herr and Anderson (2005) outline different forms of validity that should inform co-produced research and its evaluation. Besides the importance of valid results, they highlight a 'process validity', which concerns the way in which relations between participants are established and sustained so they contribute to an ongoing learning process. Furthermore, they describe a 'democratic validity', concerning the degree to which different voices are heard and considered in the research.

Equality does not mean equal contributions

Co-produced research does not imply that everyone contributes in the same way or to the same degree (Frankham, 2009; Fleming et al, 2014). McLaughlin (2009) claims that it would not be right to ask co-researchers to perform tasks that do not interest them or for which they are unqualified. He reminds us that not all co-researchers are interested in participating in all phases or parts of the research process. What it is about is developing a 'complementary collaboration, based on complementary expertise.' Such complementary expertise should preferably also be related to the mediation of the research.

Conclusion

Co-produced research intended to create equality between actors creates challenges for both researchers and co-researchers. However, as the researchers invite the co-researchers to enter their territory, they assume primary responsibility. Based on a review of 66 scientific articles of PPI (patient and public-involvement_ projects from the healthcare area, Brett et al (2012) summarise particular considerations for successful cooperation:

> The evidence demonstrates that the better the training, planning and procedures that are put in place, the clearer the definition of roles, the more positive the attitudes towards PPI and the greater trust and respect that parties (users, researchers, clinicians, funders, policy makers) have with each other, which may lead to more potential for beneficial impact. (Brett et al, 2012, pp 645–6)

This conclusion is consistent with the main points of this chapter. However, if tokenism and co-optation should be avoided and the abovementioned principles realised, it is still necessary to debate the more fundamental issue of what constitutes valuable knowledge and how it is created (Hodgson and Canvin, 2005; Owen, 2005; Nolan et al, 2007a, 2007b). Research is still dominated by discourses, methods and language that do not sufficiently value the competence of people outside academia. Paradoxically, while the research community lauds user participation and different forms of knowledge, these factors are not reflected in rewards or status. In this way, researchers are exposed to tensions between opposing expectations. If the contributions of co-researchers are to be recognised, it is important to discuss what valuable knowledge is and how knowledge is produced. Recognition and reevaluation of different knowledge forms are crucial in order to avoid user involvement being seen as 'secondhand research' or what Stoecker (2008) refers to as 'community housework'.

At the same time, it is important to point out that recognition and reevaluation of co-researchers' knowledge do not mean that co-produced research should evade the same level of critical investigation as research based on other paradigms.

> To merely argue that the involvement of service user co-researchers will naturally improve a research project is as misguided as believing only academic researchers can undertake 'real' research … We should pay such research the same respect we pay other research and examine its methods and claims critically and avoid giving it a 'soft touch' because it is undertaken in collaboration with or by service user researchers. (McLaughlin, 2010, pp 1600–3)

Evading critical examination of the research will also mean that co-researchers' competence is not taken seriously or recognised as an important contribution to research and knowledge production.

Acknowledgements

An extended version of the chapter has been published in Norwegian in the book *Samproduksjon i forskning: forskning med nye aktører* (Co-production in Research. Research with new actors) (Askheim and Raak Høiseth, 2019).

References

Abma, T.A. (2009) 'Patients as partners in responsive research: methodological notions for collaboration in mixed research teams', *Qualitative Health Research*, 19(3): 401–15.

Abma, T.A. and Broerse, J.E.W. (2010) 'Patient participation as dialogue: setting research agendas', *Health Expectations*, 13: 160–73."

Askheim, O.P. and Raak Høiseth, J. (2019) 'Medforskerrollen – i spenningsfeltet mellom anerkjennelse, kooptering og "tokenisme"', in O.P. Askheim, I.M. Lid and S. Østensjø (eds), *Samproduksjon i forskning: Forskning med nye aktører*, Oslo: Universitetsforlaget, pp 214–30.

Banks, S., Armstrong, A., Carter, K., Graham, H., Hayward, P., Henry, A. and Strachan, A. (2013) 'Everyday ethics in community-based participatory research', *Contemporary Social Science*, 8(3): 263–77.

Banks, S., Armstrong, A., Booth, M., Brown, G., Carter, K., Clarkson, M. and Russel, A. (2014) 'Using co-inquiry: community-university perspectives on research', *Journal of Community Engagement and Scholarship*, 7(1): 37–47.

Benoit, C., Jansson, M., Millar, A. and Phillips, R. (2005) 'Community-academic research on hard-to-reach populations: benefits and challenges', *Qualitative Health Research*, 15(2): 263–82.

Boote, J., Telford, R. and Cooper, C. (2002) 'Consumer involvement in health research: a review and research agenda', *Health Policy*, 61: 213–36.

Brett, J., Staniszewska, S., Mockford, C., Herron-Marx, S., Hughes, J., Tysall, C. and Suleman, R. (2012) 'Mapping the impact of patient and public involvement on health and social care research: a systematic review', *Health Expectations*, 17: 637–50.

Case, A.D., Byrd, R., Claggett, E., Deveaux, S., Perkins, R., Huang, C. and Kaufman, J.S. (2014) 'Stakeholders' perspectives on community-based participatory research to enhance mental health', *American Journal of Community Psychology*, 54: 397–408.

Chávez, V., Duran, B., Baker, Q.E., Avila, M.M. and Wallerstein, N. (2008) 'The dance of race and privileges in CBPR', in M. Minkler and N. Wallerstein (eds), *Community-Based Research for Health*, San Francisco: Jossey-Bass, pp 91–106

Cornwall, A. (2008) 'Unpacking "participation": models, meanings and practices', *Community Development Journal*, 43(3): 269–83.

Cossar, J. and Neil, E. (2015) 'Service user involvement in social work research: learning from an adoption research project', *British Journal of Social Work*, 45: 225–40.

Faulkner, A. (2009) 'Principles and motives for service user involvement in mental health research', in J. Wallcraft, B. Shrank and M. Amering (eds) *The Handbook of Service User Involvement in Mental Health Research*, Chichester: Wiley-Blackwell, pp 13–24.

Fleming, J., Beresford, P., Bewley, C., Croft, S., Branfield, F., Postle, K. and Turner, M. (2014) 'Working together: innovative collaboration in social care research', *Qualitative Social Work*, 13(5): 706–22.

Forbat, L. and Hubbard, G. (2015) 'Service user involvement in research may lead to contrary rather than collaborative accounts: findings from a qualitative palliative care study', *Journal of Advanced Nursing*, 72(4): 759–69.

Frankham, J. (2009) *Partnership Research: A Review of Approaches and Challenges in Conducting Research in Partnership with Service Users*, Southhampton: ESRC National Centre for Research Methods.

Frankham, J. and Tracy, F. (2012) 'Troubling the field of service user involvement in research', *Contemporary Social Science*, 7(1): 73–89.

Goldstein, L.S. (2000) 'Ethical dilemmas in designing collaborative research: lessons learned the hard way', *International Journal of Qualitative Studies in Education*, 13(5): 517–30.

Greenhalgh, T., Jackson, C., Shaw, S. and Janamian, T. (2016) 'Achieving research impact through co-creation in community-based health services: literature review and case study', *The Milbank Quarterly*, 94(2): 392–429.

Hancock, N., Bundy, A., Tamsett, S. and McMahon, M. (2012) 'Participation of mental health consumers in research: training addressed and reliability assessed', *Australian Occupational Therapy Journal*, 59: 218–24.

Heaton, J., Day, J. and Britten, N. (2016) 'Collaborative research and the co-production of knowledge from practice: an illustrative case study'. *Implementation Science*, 11: 20.

Herr, K. and Anderson, G. (2005) *The Action Research Dissertation: A Guide for Students and Faculty*, London: Sage.

Hodgson, P. and Canvin, K. (2005) 'Translating health policy into research practice', in L. Lowes and I. Hulatt (eds) *Involving Service Users in Health and Social Care Research*, Routledge: London, pp 48–65.

Macaulay, A.C., Jagosh, J., Seller, R., Henderson, J., Cargo, M., Greenhalgh, T. and Pluye, P. (2011) 'Assessing the benefits of participatory research: a rationale for a realist review', *Global Health Promotion*, 18(2): 45–8.

McLaughlin, H. (2006) 'Involving young service users as co-researchers: possibilities, benefits and costs', *British Journal of Social Work*, 36: 1395–410.

McLaughlin, H. (2009) *Service User Research in Health and Social Care*, London: Sage.

McLaughlin, H. (2010) 'Keeping service user involvement in research honest', *British Journal of Social Work*, 40: 1591–608.

Minkler, M. and Corage Baden, A. (2008) 'Impact on academic researchers, research quality and methodology, and power relations', in M. Minkler and N. Wallerstein (eds), *Community-Based Participatory Research for Health: From Process to Outcome*, San Francisco: Jossey-Bass, pp 243–84.

Mjøsund, N., Eriksson, M., Espnes, G.A., Haaland-Øverby, M., Liang Jensen, S., Norheim, N. and Forbech Vinje, H. (2016) 'Service user involvement enhanced the research quality in a study of interpretative phenomenological analysis: the power of multiple perspectives', *Journal of Advanced Nursing*, 73(1): 265–78.

Natland, S., Tveiten, S. and Ruud Knutsen, I. (2017) 'Why should patients participate in research?' *Tidsskriftet for Den norske legeforening*, 137(3): 210–12.

Nolan, M., Hanson, E., Grant, G., Keady, J. and Magnusson, L. (2007a) 'Introduction: what counts as knowledge; whose knowledge counts? Towards authentic participatory enquiry', in M. Nolan, E. Hanson, G. Grant and J. Keady (eds), *User Participation in Health and Social Care Research*, Berkshire: Open University Press, pp 1–14.

Nolan, M., Hanson, E., Grant, G. and Keady, J. (2007b) 'Conclusions: realizing authentic participatory enquiry', in M. Nolan, E. Hanson, G. Grant and J. Keady (eds), *User Participation in Health and Social Care Research*, Berkshire: Open University Press, pp 183–203.

Norges forskningsråd (2017a) *Programplan 2017 – Gode og effektive helse-, omsorgs- og velferdstjenester – HELSEVEL*, Oslo: Norges Forskningsråd.

Norges forskningsråd (2017b) *Programplan 2017 – Program for Bedre helse og livskvalitet – BEDREHELSE*, Oslo: Norges Forskningsråd.

Nowotny, O., Gibbons, M. and Scott, P. (2001) *Re-Thinking Science: Knowledge and the Public in an Age of Uncertainty*, Cambridge: Polity Press.

Østensjø, S. and Askheim, O.P. (2019) 'Forskning med nye aktører – forskningskvalitet og forskningsnytte', in O.P. Askheim, I.M. Lid and S. Østensjø (eds), *Samproduksjon i forskning. Forskning med nye aktører*, Oslo: Universitetsforlaget, pp 231–45.

Owen, J. (2005) 'Users, research and "evidence" in social care', in J. Burr and P. Nicolson (eds), *Researching Health Care Consumers, Critical Approaches*, Basingstoke: Palgrave Macmillan, pp 155–79.

Phillips, L., Kristiansen, M., Vehviläinen, M. and Gunnarsson, E. (2013) 'Tackling the tension of dialogue and participation', in L. Phillips, M. Kristiansen, M. Vehviläinen and E. Gunnarsson (eds), *Knowledge and Power in Collaborative Research*, London: Routledge, pp 1–18

Stoecker, R. (2008) 'Are academics irrelevant?', in M. Minkler and N. Wallerstein (eds), *Community-Based Research for Health*, San Francisco: Jossey-Bass, pp 107–20.

Strier, R. (2007) 'Anti-oppressive research in social work: a preliminary definition'. *British Journal of Social Work*, 37: 857–71.

Sullivan, M., Kone, A., Senturia, K.D., Chrisman, N.J., Ciske, S.J. and Krieger, J.W. (2001) 'Researcher and researched-community perspectives: toward bridging the gap', *Health Education & Behavior*, 28(2): 130–49.

Wallerstein, N. and Duran, B. (2008) 'The theoretical, historical and practice roots of CBPR', in M. Minkler and N. Wallerstein (eds), *Community-Based Research for Health*, San Francisco: Jossey-Bass, pp 25–46.

13

Community of development: a model for inclusive learning, research and innovation

Jean Pierre Wilken, Ellen Witteveen, Carla van Slagmaat, Sascha Van Gijzel, Jeroen Knevel, Toinette Loeffen and Els Overkamp

Introduction

In our Research Centre for Social Innovation, which is part of Utrecht University of Applied Sciences (the Netherlands), we are developing ways to involve service users in education and research in the field of social work. There are several reasons for this development. Firstly, we believe in the value of social inclusion. Since social workers promote 'social cohesion based on principles of social justice, human rights, and respect for diversity', according to the international definition (IFSW and IASSW, 2014), social workers by default contribute to social inclusion. We believe that students should not only be taught theories about social inclusion but should also experience what inclusion and exclusion mean in the daily lives of service users. This means that stories of people experiencing exclusion should be part of education. The second reason is that the best way to hear stories and to acquire understanding about discrimination and stigmatisation is to listen directly to people with these experiences and engage in dialogue. Therefore, we invite people into the classroom, or vice versa, the students into the places where people live. We often use the tandem model developed in Flanders by Driessens and others (Driessens and Van Regenmortel, 2006; Vansevenant et al, 2008) for working together with people with mild intellectual disabilities. We also use gap-mending principles as developed in Sweden and throughout the PowerUs network (Heule et al, 2017; Askheim et al, 2018;).[1] More and more we use the experiences of students themselves; for instance, their experiences with illness, impairment or family care. We do this, for example, in a peer-supported recovery course for students with mental health experiences (Karbouniaris and Wilken, 2019), and in our learning teams, small groups of students form a learning and support group throughout the programme (Van Slagmaat and Karbouniaris, 2020). Social work students (and professionals in the field) need to learn how to engage in an equal partnership to be able to work together on well-being, recovery and participation (Wilken and Den Hollander, 2019). The best way to learn about partnership is to create 'inclusive learning environments'. By doing this, we can not only improve the quality of our education but also the quality of our research. Experts by experience are valuable as co-researchers because it is often easier from them to connect with respondents and, for example, to help create questionnaires that are easy to understand for people from different backgrounds.

Community of development

One of the ways to involve service users is to invite them to participate in a 'Community of development' (CoD). The CoD is a learning community in which service users participate as co-researchers and co-designers. As students often take part in this group, it is also a way of learning from the experiences of service users.

A CoD is a variant of a 'community of practice' (CoP) as described by Etienne Wenger and colleagues (Lave and Wenger, 1991; Wenger, 1998, 2002). CoPs are 'groups of people who share a concern or a passion for something they do and learn how to do it better as they interact regularly' (Wenger, 1998). There are three characteristics that define a community as a CoP. Firstly, there must be an identity that is defined by a shared domain of interest. Membership therefore implies an involvement in the *domain* and thus the sharing of knowledge that distinguishes the members from other people. Secondly, in pursuing their interest in their domain, members engage in a *community* of joint activities and discussions, helping each other and sharing information. They build relationships that enable them to learn from each other. Thirdly, members share a *practice*, a repertoire of resources, such as experiences, stories, tools and ways to address recurring problems. This takes time and long-term interaction. Wenger states: 'It is the combination of these three elements that constitutes a community of practice. And it is by developing these three elements in parallel that one cultivates such a community' (Wenger, 1998, p 2). As far as the service users are concerned, it is obvious that since the quality of social, mental health or disability services is the main theme of the CoD, this is their domain of interest. If people have been using services for a long time, they have gained a lot of knowledge about the services and can tell many stories that express their experiences.

There are some additional features that distinguish a generic CoP from a CoD. Firstly, in a CoD more attention is paid to learning. This, by so-called facilitator-supported learning (see more on this in the next section), is not only about content and the need to develop innovations but is also about learning to work with a diversity of people with multiple perspectives.

A second characteristic is that research and development are an inherent part of a CoD. We usually combine 'participative action research' and 'design research'. Action research is defined as an interactive inquiry process that seeks a balance between problem-solving actions implemented in a collaborative context and data-driven collaborative analysis that enables personal, professional and organisational change (Reason and Bradbury, 2007). Action research is a combination of research, reflection, learning and change to improve a (professional) practice. Design research is aimed at designing improvements for current practice. According to Van Aken and Andriessen (2011), design research is driven by the desire to solve field problems, working from the perspective of the practitioners dealing with these field problems. This research method is therefore solution-oriented and initially strives for pragmatic validity, which means that the CoD's products must deliver the intended improvement in practice. Academic researchers actively participate in the community to help shape innovation. They also contribute with knowledge from research, for example about what is known about effective interventions or effective ways of organising services.

A third characteristic of a CoD is the combination of different kinds of knowledge: experiential knowledge, professional knowledge and scientific knowledge. Each voice and all sources of knowledge are of equal value. Although this sometimes requires a great deal of effort in terms of language, communication and understanding, this principle is essential to entering a co-creation process. Peter Beresford states about the experiential knowledge of service users: 'One key quality distinguishes such knowledge from all others involved in social care and social policy provision. They alone are based on direct experience of such policy and provision from the receiving end. Service users' knowledges grow out of their personal and collective experience of policy, practice and services' (Beresford, 2000, p 493).

An important principle of CoDs is to articulate not only the overt knowledge but also the knowledge that is 'embodied' in the participants. Often the participants have to (re)learn how to express the tacit knowledge they possess. Our evaluations show that participants engaged in this process not only experience appreciation and recognition of their knowledge and experience but also learn to discover existing strengths and to acquire new knowledge.

Facilitator

A CoD is supported by a so-called 'facilitator', who is an expert in coaching learning and innovation processes. In this process, the facilitator challenges individuals and the group to actively reflect on practice and to think outside the box about new solutions. A facilitator offers guidance, inspiration and encouragement. He/she is a competent coach or supervisor and is familiar with the group dynamics and design thinking. He/she also acts as a role model, and is committed, curious and creative. Especially in the beginning, the facilitator needs to develop a good learning mode. As with any form of group work, participants should get to know and feel safe with each other. The facilitator contributes to a friendly and safe atmosphere. It is an advantage if he/she is also familiar with the theme of the community. For example, if the theme of the CoD is improving care for people with brain damage, it is an advantage if the facilitator is familiar with problems related to brain damage and how care for people with brain damage is organised. He/she has the task of ensuring that the CoD develops and pursues the desired outcomes. A facilitator can also be regarded as a pro-active entrepreneur who is creative in suggesting ideas for the development and testing of the prototype. Facilitators make use of many different interventions, which differ according to the phase of the CoD, the development of the group as a learning community and the competencies of the CoD members (Witteveen and Wilken, 2015). Examples of interventions include providing a structure for discussing cases, mediating tensions within the group, guiding discussions on ethical dilemmas and summarising conclusions.

A facilitator must therefore be a highly skilled person and be able to connect in a neutral but committed way with all the actors involved, taking into account the great diversity in the group. He/she must be able to work with passion regarding the content and the different processes that are going on and can be initiated. A culture is needed in which everyone knows that they are heard, seen and that they matter, with all their talents and limitations. When people feel encouraged to take steps towards the goals that are intended, this enhances engagement and empowerment. In the trainings and peer-supervision we provide for new facilitators, we pay a lot of attention to highlighting the strengths, talents and passions of the participants in order to stimulate a creative process. We do this, for example, by making so-called 'rich pictures'. A rich picture is a drawing of a situation that illustrates the main elements and relationships that need to be considered in trying to intervene in order to create some improvement. It consists of pictures, text, symbols and icons. It is called a rich picture because it illustrates the richness and complexity of a situation (Brouwer and Woodhill, 2016). In this way you can get inspired to create beautiful processes and products.

Working on better practices

The model of the CoP provides one of the ways we can work with service users on social innovation. Murray et al (2010) describe social innovation as: a) new ideas (products, services, and models) that b) simultaneously meet social needs (and are more effective than alternatives), and c) as a process of creating new or better social relationships or collaborations. This definition was also adopted by the European Commission (2011). The authors state that social innovations should not only be good for society but should also enhance society's capacity to act. These three characteristics are an integral part of the CoD model. We use the experiences of service users to generate new ideas and to develop better social work practices. At the same time, we learn how to work better together. We believe that social work practitioners, academics and students need to be in a continuous dialogue with service users and carers, learning with and from each other (McLaughlin et al, 2018, p 2).

Composition

A CoD consists of a group of five to 15 people. In this group, all perspectives relevant to the practice are represented. The core consists of social workers, service users and our researchers, but formal and informal network members, managers of services and municipality workers can also be part, as well as students. As far as the background of the service users is concerned, people can have experiences with mental health problems, intellectual disabilities, physical disabilities, dementia, homelessness and poverty.

Prior to the actual start of the group, good preparation is crucial. It is important to clarify in advance what is required of the participating organisations and the participants. At this stage, the necessary conditions are laid down, such as the commitment of the parties participating in the project, ensuring joint responsibility and being clear about objectives, roles and tasks. Candidates for participation must be well informed and prepared. They must know what a CoD is about and what 'mindset' and efforts it requires. Expectations must correspond to the objectives of the project. In the event that a candidate's expectations and motivations do not match, it is recommended they not particpate in the CoD. Although education level is not an exclusion criterion, participants should be able to communicate about their own practice and reflect on their own experiences. Curiosity, commitment to the goals of the CoD and eagerness to learn seem to be the most important prerequisites.

Involvement

The inclusion of service users is in line with the adage of the global user movement 'Nothing about us without us' (McLaughlin et al, 2020). Together with other participants, they are engaged in a collective learning process. This requires a safe and open atmosphere, the willingness to work together on equal terms and the eagerness to develop innovation. In the first phases of the group process, participants need to get to know each other to build up a sense of trust. Participants must have an open and inclusive mind' and be willing to collaborate with people from different backgrounds and with different experiences and ideas. One of the things to deal with is the differences in status and power, which obviously are always present, but which can be more pronounced in a group with great diversity. It is the task of the facilitator to deal with this and coach the group in adopting an inclusive way of working. This is part of the learning process.

> Ten years ago, we had a project with three CoDs in different parts of the country on the social inclusion of people with disabilities in art centres. Many experiences (and expressions of art telling personal stories) were collected and exchanged. One of the participants expressed how she felt: 'If you ask me what good I could do for society; I think it is so hard just to maintain myself. To have a guiding influence in the world. If you want to have an influence in the human world, you have to be there. That means that you have to have people who support you, as a back-up, because you have to deal with people who have different opinions and different interests. They want other things and that means that you have to be very strong to deal with all those tensions. You have to be able to discuss with people and to be strong as an actor.' (Van Biene et al, 2010, p 26)

Involvement is also related to engagement with each other and with the topic and ambition of the CoD. The enthusiasm and drive to work together to improve a social work practice is also a bonding energy. Equal involvement and enthusiastic engagement can be enhanced by choosing ways of working and communicating that suit the learning styles and preferences of the participants. In several groups, we use methods such as art-based research, storytelling, photovoice and cartoons.

Use

We started using the CoD model in 2005. Over the past 15 years it has been applied in many different settings, such as vocational rehabilitation for mental healthcare users, care for people with brain injuries and the social inclusion of people with intellectual disabilities (Wilken et al, 2008; Dankers et al, 2010; Wilken and Dankers, 2010; Witteveen et al, 2010; Knevel and Wilken, 2015; Knevel et al, 2020). We have applied the model in both semi-residential and community settings. Approximately 30 CoDs have been run, involving about three hundred participants. We have learned that although it takes considerable efforts to run a successful CoD, the model offers great potential for service-user participation. Together with other ways of involving service users as experts by experience, we have gradually increased the interest in our university, in service user engagement. It is, however, a slow, step-by-step process to structurally embed service-user participation in our educational programmes.

The value of the model

Over the years, we have refined the methodology underlying the model and investigated factors that we assume make the model effective. In 2011, we conducted a meta-analysis to explore the effective factors of the model, including ten CoDs in four different projects (Van Gijzel et al, 2011; Wilken et al, 2013). In 2014 and 2015, we published analyses from three CoDs on the interplay between formal and informal care (Witteveen, 2014; Witteveen and Wilken, 2015). We recently published a report on a new meta-analysis looking at effective elements of the model (Kloppenburg et al, 2020).

The studies show that CoDs generate a number of positive outcomes. A CoD provides a rich learning environment to share and develop professional knowledge and to improve professional practice. The CoDs have delivered a variety of products that can be used for reflection, assessment and service provision. Examples include a protocol for describing and reflecting on cases, assessment tools, working methods, guidelines, e-learning modules and manuals. Often, these products are also used in bachelor's and master's programmes. Professionals indicated that the CoD has improved their awareness and increased their knowledge and skills. A CoD offers the opportunity to discuss at a different level than the usual daily outine. A professional:

> The effect of learning and working in a community of development is that you can wrestle with different people about certain issues you are struggling with in your practice. Collaboration is established. We are no longer islands. We no longer think we know everything better. We learn how to work better with clients. And the informal caregivers and experts by experience point out our language use, they keep us sharp in our actions. They don't settle for "I always do it that way". Actually, you always need such a place of learning. I wish everyone this experience. (Witteveen and Wilken, 2015, p 42)

Other participants, such as service users and family carers, appreciate the opportunity to contribute to improving practices from their perspective and that their experiences are valued. For professionals, the experiences of users and family members often provide new insights (Witteveen, 2014). At the level of the methods of the professionals, most CoDs have led to new or improved ways of working. CoDs have also played an important role in improving collaboration between professionals from different disciplines and organisations, for example in new forms of outreaching care. This knowledge can be used in the curricula of social work programmes: 'The project has greatly contributed to a better understanding and trust among professionals from different organisations. One of the effects is that there have been more, and more effective referrals from clients and caregivers' (Witteveen et al, 2010).

At the level of the individuals receiving the services of professionals, several CoDs show positive results, for example in terms of increased participation and better working methods: 'Clients were given specific support to realize their wishes regarding community participation, started to undertake activities such as leisure and voluntary work, and got new social contacts' (Dankers et al, 2010).

A point of discussion is whether CoDs only generate valuable contextual knowledge or to what extent this knowledge is generally applicable. We could say that the innovation of a local practice is valuable in itself. The applicability of the results strongly depends on the type of product being developed and whether there is sufficient evidence to support generalisability on a larger scale. The latter may be the case if, for example, a multisite study with different CoDs is conducted.

Challenges

One of the major challenges for organising and running a CoD is involving service users and ensuring full participation. Service users can be recruited in different ways. Both our research centre and the School for Social Work maintain collaborations with a number of service-user and advocacy organisations. With some of them we have formal agreements to hire experts by experience in our curriculum and research projects. This is the case, for example, with the LFB, a national advocacy organisation run by people with intellectual disabilities. Part of the agreement is that people receive compensation. Another condition is that people receive the support they need to perform in our academic environment. This means that we have to invest in 'tandem constructions'.

Especially for people with an intellectual disability, it is important that they work closely with a lecturer, for example when preparing a classroom activity or a research activity. Other examples include our collaboration with MIND, a national association of mental health service users, and our cooperation with the local Poverty Coalition. The Poverty Coalition is a network of service providers and experts by experience in the city of Utrecht. We have set up a CoD with the ambition of improving the understanding of poverty in people's everyday lives. The Poverty Coalition has invited experts by experience from their midst to participate in this CoD. Participants receive a small financial compensation for their participation. Another way to invite service users to participate is by having professionals from social service agencies approach their clients.

It is not easy to involve service users or neighbourhood representatives (Geelhoed et al, 2018; Knevel et al, 2020). We have experienced that professionals can be reluctant to ask clients to participate in projects. The reasons for this range from their feeling safer in the group without the presence of clients to the assumption that participation is too difficult or too stressful for clients. When family carers are involved, professionals may be afraid that they will be too critical of their work. It often takes time to convince professionals or managers that the presence of service user and family carer representation is an immanent feature of the CoD model.

Like social workers, service users can be hesitant, for obvious reasons: they are not used to being asked to participate in research projects; they fear tensions in their relationship with the service they are currently using; or the group size may deter them. This therefore requires a careful approach. Sometimes, it helps if service users are accompanied by a family member who can help the person express themself or speak on his/her behalf: 'It is important that participants are approached carefully and thoughtfully. They also need to be well informed. A good introduction and trust building are important' (Loeffen, 2010).

In order to prepare the users of services and other participants, it may be useful to organise an introductory programme. Several topics can be covered in this programme, such as the way of working in the CoD, the support of the facilitator and the renumeration. Training can also be part of the programme.

During the work of the CoD, it can be quite a challenge to keep everyone on board on an equal basis. A facilitator states:

> The use of language can be a problem, for example in a group with residents with addiction problems and a mild intellectual disability, policy makers, and social workers. During a coffee break, one of the social workers told me that two residents had left because the session was too long for them. Even though we used very interactive ways of working and short activities, the participants with learning difficulties said it was a lot of talking and listening. So, involving the residents was difficult but also fascinating because they had a very different input than the others. They find other things important in these homes than social workers and policy makers. (Kloppenburg et al, 2020, p 46)

We sometimes opt for flexible forms of organisation for the CoD, so that everyone can feel comfortable and at the same time we can ensure that all voices are heard. For example, in a project on the social inclusion of people with learning disabilities, a separate group of users was formed. This allowed not only more people to participate – more voices! – but also enhanced the quality of the contributions. Two representatives of the group, supported by the facilitator and the researcher, forwarded the contributions to the rest of the community (in this case professionals and volunteers). In projects involving people with mental health experiences, we used art-based methods (Biene et al, 2010; Weerman et al, 2019).

Opportunities

At our university, the awareness of the value of service-user involvement is slowly but surely growing. We have a core group of people who are constantly creating awareness and developing, evaluating, improving and introducing methods for experiential learning and experiential knowledge (for instance, Boer et al, 2018). There are also promising developments on a national level. Already ten years ago, we set up a national network of universities that are on the same path, with, for example, associate degree programmes for students who want to develop and use experiential knowledge professionally. Currently, ten universities are members.

Two national associations of service providers and the National Association of Mental Health and Addiction Care have recognised the value of experiential expertise and created a professional profile (Van Bakel et al, 2013). At the moment, around two thousand people with service-user experience are already employed by services.

Conclusion

A CoD is a model that combines learning, research and development. It is a useful model for working on social innovation. It is a multi-actor model in which different sources of knowledge come together: professional knowledge, experiential knowledge and scientific knowledge. Experiential knowledge is brought in by service users, carers and professionals. Service-user experience is indispensable for assessing and improving the quality of services. This model can be used to develop a better or new social practice. The CoD serves as a space or living lab in which it is possible to share each other's knowledge, reflect on dilemmas, pitfalls and challenges, find creative solutions and freely experiment with these solutions. It is a non-competitive arena in which participants work as a team towards good results and are coached by a facilitator and supported by researchers. A well-trained and enthusiastic facilitator, preferably someone who is familiar with the theme of the CoD, is important in order to bring all voices together and support the development process, which can lead to results that have a positive impact on the service. The inclusion of the experiences of service users is not always easy. It requires sound ethical standards, careful preparation and personal support.

Note
1 www.powerus.org

References

Askheim, O.P., Beresford, P., and Heule, C. (2018) 'Mend the gap: strategies for user involvement in social work education', in H. McLaughlin, J. Duffy, B. McKeever and J. Sadd (eds), *Service User Involvement in Social Work Education*, pp 151–63.

Beresford, P. (2000) 'Service users' knowledges and social work: theory, conflict or collaboration?', *British Journal of Social Work*, 30: 489–503.

Boer, M., Karbouniaris, S. and de Wit, M. (2018) *Didactiekboek van Levenservaring naar ervaringsdeskundigheid,* Oud Turnhout/'s Hertogenbosch: Gompel & Svacina.

Brouwer, H. and Woodhill, J. (2016) *The MSP Guide: How to Design and Facilitate Multi-stakeholder Partnerships*, Wageningen: Wageningen UR.

Dankers, T., van Slagmaat, C., Brettschneider, E., Karbouniaris, S., Oosterink, M. and Wilken, J.P. (2010) *Ondersteuning en Participatie. Eindrapportage*, Utrecht: Kenniscentrum Sociale Innovatie.

Driessens, K. and Van Regenmortel, T. (2006) *Bind-Kracht in Armoede: Leefwereld en hulpverlening*, Leuven: LannooCampus.

European Commission (2013) *Guide to Social Innovation*, Brussels: EU Commission.

Geelhoed, S., Gademan, M. and Sprinkhuizen, A. (2018) *De Boomberg: Ontmoeten in de tussenruimte van zorg en de wijk*, Utrecht: Kenniscentrum Sociale Innovatie.

Heule, C., Knutagård, M. and Kristiansen, A. (2017) 'Mending the gaps in social work education and research: two examples from a Swedish context', *European Journal of Social Work*, 20: 396–408.

IFSW and IASSW (2014) *International Definition of Social Work*. Available from:

Karbouniaris, K. and Wilken, J.P. (2020) *Evaluatie Peer Supportgroep Social Work*, Utrecht: Kenniscentrum Sociale Innovatie.

Kloppenburg, R., De Jonge, E. and Greven, K. (2020) *Wat werkt in ontwikkelwerkplaatsen? Een verkennend onderzoek naar werkzame factoren*, Utrecht: Kenniscentrum Sociale Innovatie.

Knevel, J. and Wilken, J.P. (2015) *Inclusie, (on)gewoon doen!*, Utrecht/Amersfoort: Kenniscentrum Sociale Innovatie.

Knevel, J., Gademan, M. and Roelfsema, H. (2020) *Meedoen en erbij horen: Maatschappelijke participatie van jongeren met een licht verstandelijke beperking in de gemeente Utrecht*, Utrecht: Kenniscentrum Sociale Innovatie.

Lave, J. and Wenger, E. (1991) *Situated Learning: Legitimate Peripheral Participation*, Cambridge: Cambridge University Press.

McLaughlin, H., Duffy, J., McKeever, B. and Sadd J. (eds) (2018) *Service User Involvement in Social Work Education*, Oxfordshire: Routledge.

McLaughlin, H., Beresford, P., Cameron, C., Casey, H., Duffy, J. (2020) *The Routledge Handbook of Service User Involvement in Human Services Research and Education*, Abingdon: Routledge.

Murray, R., Caulier-Grice, J. and Mulgan, G. (2010) *The Open Book of Social Innovation*, London: National Endowment for Science, Technology and the Arts.

Reason, P. and Bradbury, H. (2007) 'Introduction to groundings', in P. Reason and H. Bradbury (eds), *The Sage Handbook of Action Research: Participative Inquiry and Practice*, London: Sage.

Vansevenant, K., Driessens, K. and Van Regenmortel, T. (2008) *Bind-Kracht in Armoede: Krachtgerichte hulpverlening in dialoog*, Leuven: LannooCampus.

Van Aken, J. and Andriessen, D. (2011) *Handboek ontwerpgericht wetenschappelijk onderzoek: wetenschap met effect*, Amsterdam: Boom uitgevers.

Van Bakel, M., Van Rooijen S., Boertien, D., Kamoschinski, J., Liefhebber, M. and Kluft, M. (2013) *Beroepscompetentieprofiel Ervaringsdeskundigheid*, GGZ Nederland, Trimbos-instituut, HEE!, Kenniscentrum Phrenos. Available from: https://www.trimbos.nl/aanbod/webwinkel/product/dl019-ervaringsdeskundigheid-beroepscompetentieprofiel

Van Biene, M., de Bruijn, P., Haker, J., Loeffen, T., Oosterink, M., van Slagmaat, C., Sparreboom, H., de Vos, K. and Wilken, J.P. (2010) *Kansen in kunst. Kunst door mensen met speciale wensen*, Utrecht: Kenniscentrum Sociale Innovatie.

Van Gijzel, S., Koraichi, N. and Vriend, L. (2011) *Samen stilstaan bij voortuitgang, een meta-evaluatie van de Community of Development*, Utrecht: Kenniscentrum Sociale Innovatie.

Van Slagmaat, C. and Karbouniaris, K. (2020) 'Van ervaring naar ervaringskennis en ervaringsdeskundigheid: over het begeleiden van een bijzonder leerteam', *Tijdschrift voor Begeleidingskunde*, 9(2): 38–46.

Wenger, E. (1998) *Communities of Practice: Learning, Meaning, and Identity*, Cambridge: Cambridge University Press.

Wenger, E., McDermott, R. and Snyder W. (2002) *Cultivating Communities of Practice: A Guide to Managing Knowledge*, Harvard: Harvard Business School Press.

Wilken, J.P. and Dankers, T. (eds) (2010) *Schakels in de buurt: op weg naar nieuwe vormen van zorg en welzijn in de wijk*, Amsterdam: SWP.

Wilken, J.P., Van Slagmaat, C. and Van Gijzel, S. (2013) 'The best practice unit: a model for learning, research and development', *Journal of Social Intervention: Theory and Practice*, 22(2): 131–48.

Wilken, J.P. and Den Hollander, D. (2019) *Handboek Steunend Relationeel Handelen*, Amsterdam: SWP.

Wilken, J.P., Knevel, J. and Van Gijzel, S. (2020) 'Lessons of inclusive learning: the value of experiential knowledge of persons with a learning disability in social work education', in H. McLaughlin, P. Beresford, C. Cameron, H. Casey and J. Duffy (eds), *The Routledge Handbook of Service User Involvement in Human Services Research and Education*, Abingdon: Routledge, pp 385–402.

Wilken, J.P., Dankers, T., Karbouniaris S. and Scholtens, G. (2008) *De Omgekeerde Weg. Eindrapportage onderzoek*, Utrecht: Kenniscentrum Sociale Innovatie.

Witteveen, E. (2014) 'Leren in netwerken: de praktijk van leerwerkplaatsen', *Sociale Vraagstukken*, 7. Available from: https://www.socialevraagstukken.nl/sociale-praktijk/leren-in-netwerken-de-praktijk-van-leerwerkplaatsen/

Witteveen, E. and Wilken, J.P. (2015) 'Werken en leren in ontwikkelwerkplaatsen: innovaties in het samenwerken van formele en informele zorg rondom mensen met cognitieve beperkingen. Hoofdstuk 3', in A. Kooiman, J.P. Wilken, M. Stam, E. Jansen and M. Van Biene (eds), *Leren transformeren: hoe faciliteer je praktijkinnovatie in tijden van transitie?*, Utrecht: Wmo-Werkplaatsen/Movisie, pp 30–49.

Witteveen, E., Visser, H. and Wilken, J.P. (2010) *Goeie Snap van Elkaar: verbetering van de communicatie in en rond de zorg voor mensen met niet aangeboren hersenletsel*, Utrecht: Kenniscentrum Sociale Innovatie.

14

Dialogue, skills and trust: some lessons learned from co-writing with service users

Sidsel Natland

Introduction

Collaborative research is aimed at co-producing knowledge, which refers to the ways in which service users (or other participants) can be involved in collaborative partnerships with conventional researchers to develop research, new types of knowledge and practice (Needham, 2009). This represents a transcendence of the traditional distinction between researchers and service users. Collaborative research is recognised as part of a 'dialogic turn' in which communication is approached as a dialogue between the participants in the research group. The knowledge production should be approached as an intertwined process (Phillips, 2011). Co-produced knowledge potentially increases the relevance for both users and the field of practice, and aims to have an empowering effect on users, allowing their experiential knowledge to be acknowledged.

Users can be involved at different levels and stages of the research process, ranging from the planning of projects, design and research questions to data production, analysis and interpretation (McLaughlin, 2010). There is a large body of literature available on the benefits, barriers and potential outcomes of collaborative research and user involvement. However, the final phase of a research process, that is, the writing and dissemination of results, is less explored. Writing academic articles and reports is a task that conventional researchers are trained in and are expected to carry out in order to meet academic, societal and funders' needs and requirements. How can co-writing be carried out without positioning the researcher as the expert and overruling the user? I will describe some of the lessons learned from co-writing, with the aim of turning them into learning experiences that may be useful for future collaborative research.

Theoretical underpinning of service users' involvement in knowledge production

Co-production of knowledge, dialogue and participation as signifiers of collaborative research can be linked to the influential ideas put forward by Nowotny et al (2001), which claim that we no longer live in a society where academia maintains control over how, where and by whom knowledge is produced. We live in a knowledge society, characterised by the transition from mode-1 to mode-2 knowledge production. Whereas mode 1 is characterised by theory formation and testing within a discipline towards the goal of universal knowledge, mode 2 is characterised by knowledge produced for application. In mode 2, knowledge is produced by different stakeholders, in new domains, and is increasingly validated on the basis of its transferability to practice. User involvement in social work research is part of this approach to knowledge production.

Another theoretical framing is Flyvberg's concept of 'science of the concrete', whereby one agrees to see matters from the point of view of others (1998). This requires equal opportunities to participate and be included. Further, Habermas's theory of 'communicative action' underlines how agreement between subjects facilitates action in the world. Service user and researcher may both think from their individual, idiosyncratic point of view, but together they form a community in which they can help each other to think, negotiate, elaborate and reposition their viewpoints. The participants must argue their points of view and agree on a common conclusion. Subsequently, it is important to be sensitive to how differences in roles and power relations can influence the research process. Knowledge is not objective, because power can influence the (co)production of knowledge (Heizmann and Olsson, 2015). In all participatory research, power relationships are important to recognise, as the most powerful participants are perhaps the most powerful in defining reality. This calls for 'reflexivity' as a means of dealing with participatory research practices (Phillips, 2011).

Collaborative writing

Writing is a complex process containing moments of both joy and frustration. When more than one individual participates in writing, the process increases in complexity and can be overwhelming in terms of interactions, coordination, perspectives and inputs. Lowry et al (2004) describe different forms of co-writing, among them 'sequential' (each person adds their work, passes it on to the next person who can edit it freely) and 'stratified division' (with each partner writing on those parts or sections in which they feel most competent or talented). Ritchie and Rigano (2007) define two approaches: 'cooperative writing', in which the participants negotiate which sections to write and one of the authors merges the sections and voices produced, and 'lead writing', wherein one person takes responsibility for writing the first draft, which is then rotated.

Ens et al (2011) highlight general aspects of co-writing in terms of expertise, negotiation, emotional investment and quality. Group dynamics, writing styles, benefits of writing and responsibility are important topics to discuss. All these aspects require social skills and the ability to create trust among the co-writers. Johnson and Walmsley (2003) find that power differences between participants can both be confirmed and created when aspects of the work are assigned to people for whom the task is routine. For example by leaving the analysis, interpretation and writing to the researcher. Important insights can then be missed. Different ways or genres of writing and representation of knowledge allow different discourses to emerge (Archer, 2006).

Research context: the University Research Program to Support Selected Municipal Social Service Offices

In Norway, as in other Western countries, the social welfare system has become increasingly entangled in political pressure to reform the system and increase the quality of public social services. The government has initiated several programmes to achieve these goals. The programme in the focus of this chapter was named the University Research Program to Support Selected Municipal Social Service Office(HUSK). HUSK was launched by the Directorate of Health and Social Care, and was linked to the National Strategy for Quality Improvement of Health and Social Services. The HUSK programme called for research and development projects aimed at achieving three strategic goals:

1. Promoting structures and arenas for equal cooperation between municipal social service providers/social workers, social service users, social work researchers and educators;
2. Strengthening practice-based social research; and
3. Strenghtening knowledge designed to inform practice.

The programme provided funding (€8.97 million) for six years (2006–11). Four universities in different regions of Norway were selected to lead the HUSK projects regionally. Unique to HUSK was the requirement for the active involvement of service users in the design and delivery of research and development projects. The ideal of 'equal collaboration' was particularly emphasised by the directorate. Up to then, service users had been involved in education by being invited to lectures, contributing with insight into how they have experienced encounters with welfare systems, drivers and barriers to receiving the help they needed and so on. This time they were involved as co-researchers. Their contribution was offset by allowances and gift vouchers. The outcomes of the programme were evaluated externally. The conclusion was that HUSK strengthened the value of service users' experiences, but concrete results, such as new models that can be applied in practice, were not implemented (Gjernes and Bliksvaer, 2011).

Case 1: Service users' book project – the researcher as an outsider

The HUSK programme provided a research context in which new forms of research could be explored and in which traditional roles and power relations between the participants were challenged, not least because of the involvement of service users as equal partners. HUSK worked closely with the user organisation Creativity and Diversity in Work Life (translated from Norwegian), which was given the opportunity to arrange its own 'Empowerment training seminars' targeted at long-term users of social services. Participants were trained in the narrative methods, focusing functions and narrative structures of the fairy tale. They were then instructed to use the method to 'retell' their lives like a fairy tale, placing themselves as the hero. The method was claimed to help the service users gain a deeper understanding of their life stories, and was part of an empowering process. The underlying idea was that narratives facilitate a fruitful way of expressing one's own experiences as a service user, improving the understanding social workers' understanding of them and their needs.

In order to document this as part of the HUSK research, the users asked for support in publishing a book on the narrative method, including a collection of the users' fairy tales. They were very clear: this book should represent users and *their voices*. The service users wanted to challenge the traditional image of social service users. Their wish was approved and I was asked by the regional project leader to participate in this project. It was not specified what my role and tasks would be, but it was indicated that I would be responsible for securing the process in terms of time, deadlines, reading drafts and so on.

The user representatives in the project group approved of my participation. They had already started working on the book, and invited me to a project meeting. The various meetings in HUSK most often took place at the researchers' workplace, at the Oslo campus. However, this meeting took place in a city outside Oslo, where most of the participating users were located. Upon arrival, there were many user representatives present; some just seemed to hang around, while others were busy working, talking, sitting behind their computers. I was not introduced and did not know who was participating in the book project. I felt lost, but after a while the group got together at a table. Nobody took the lead or started the meeting, and I thought it was wrong for me to do so – would that not help confirm the traditional roles between researchers and service users? I saw this as a user-led project.

Some of the participants started a discussion about the layout. They wanted something different from the "boring" academic journals with only text. They wanted pictures, drawings, a mix of letters in style and format and empty pages in between where readers could write their own thoughts. Another participant suggested the need to work with a timetable, and presented a self-designed schedule with an overview of content, responsible persons and deadlines, all marked in different colours. I felt confused and I started to worry about what I could contribute and what they wanted this book to be. I struggled to understand where they were in the process and what they had decided about the content of the book. Did they expect to publish the whole collection of fairy tales from the empowering training seminars or did they want some sort of review process? If so, on what terms and by whom? My head filled with questions.

I decided I had to take the lead, raised my voice and suggested we start the meeting. I complimented the participants on all their energy, ideas and the hard work done. I shared with them my need to understand more. I introduced my academic background and my interest in narratives. I honestly positioned myself as the unknown outsider who needed their help to contribute. I suggested spending some time clarifying expectations about both the book and my role in it. To make the discussion more concrete, I asked how many fairy tales the sample contained and if they could give me access so I could familiarise myself with them. I asked to take a closer look at the timetable, as it included their ideas about the content. This gave me more clarity about their expectations for the book.

After this meeting we continued with only two to three of the most dedicated users. First we read the fairy tales critically to decide which ones should be published. We decided that the leader of the user organisation and I should co-write a small and easy-to-read introduction about fairy tales. The users with competence and interest in creative contributions (photos and drawings) decided what they would produce and use as illustrations. They also suggested making a CD on which the fairy tales would be told in order to secure access for people struggling with reading. The book was published (Dalen and Natland, 2011), and the users were satisfied with the result.

My description of the first meeting clearly shows how it forced me to leave my comfort zone. What I want to emphasise is how it was an important reminder of the significance of roles and relationships in collaborative knowledge production, and of where a project meeting takes place. The sudden shift in roles, the users in the majority and in the leadership of the project, the unfamiliar place and me as the last person on board the project were all an important eye-opener. It got me reflecting on how the representatives of the users always had to deal with this – going to the capital, to the university, sometimes struggling to find the right entrance or floor, entering meeting rooms where academics were in the majority. This experience has affected me and humbled me with regard to how it feels to enter a project meeting, perhaps also to experience how it feels when many plans and decisions have already been made by other, more powerful stakeholders.

Case 2: Article for a scientific journal – the researcher back on stage?

The following case represents an 'academic follow-up' to the fairy tale book project – an article for the *Journal of Evidence-Informed Social Work*'s special issue on the HUSK project (Austin and Johannessen, 2015). The editors invited different stakeholders of the HUSK project (researchers, educators, members of the advisory board and two user representatives). They strongly requested an article written by the service users to pinpoint how user involvement and the recognition of experiential knowledge had been a crucial marker for the HUSK project. The editors decided which topics they wanted the various authors to cover. The users were asked to contribute with an article on their fairy tale method and the empowering training seminars. This was an opportunity to disseminate their project to an international audience and in an academic context.

All authors were invited to a writing seminar organised by the journal editors. All had shared their article drafts before the seminar. Unfortunately, the two service users had to cancel due to practical problems, and later one of them left the writing process. In their absence, their submitted draft was discussed, and the seminar participants agreed that it was not yet acceptable for a scientific journal. The editors suggested that it was necessary to involve a researcher in the process, and asked me because I was interested in co-writing and had already worked with them on the fairy tales book. Although the editors greatly appreciated the perspective of the users, it was clear that they would have to adhere to the academic context and requirements if they wanted to have the article published.

The co-writing process became a collaboration between me and the same user representative as in the fairy tale book project, as the other representative had left the process. I was aware that this co-writing process would be different. Time limits were shorter, resources were scarcer and the genre was different. I also had to find a balance between the demands of the editors and the importance of building a reliable collaboration with the co-writer. I was responsible for keeping to deadlines, monitoring quality, ensuring that both academic and user voices were reflected and adhering to the requirements of analysis and reliable interpretations. My co-writer agreed with the editorial requirements because it was important that their contribution to the research was recognised and published in a scientific and international journal.

As far as the writing process was concerned, we divided the tasks according to our stated competencies in different aspects of the process. We agreed which parts we would start with in order to keep up the pace and the writing motivation. We agreed which fairy tales we would select for the article. We asked for feedback from the users who had written the selected fairy tales to make sure they felt comfortable with our presentation and interpretation.

Nevertheless, writing for a scientific journal can be both stressful and tiring. Managing the editors' expectations of academic rigour and my co-writer's wishes and later the energy to stay in the process proved to be critical aspects of the co-writing process. I felt uncertain about how to react to the content and style of my co-writer's drafts. Moreover, during the writing process, I noticed that my co-writer seemed to be losing energy because we were working on "the same" over and over again. In order to improve the quality of the text, I often suggested other words, more academic formulations, while at the same time taking care not to compromise and leave out the voice and "footprint" of the users in the text. This is both time-consuming and patient work. We also discussed the need to adopt a distant approach and to allow a critical reading of the findings and conclusions.

Another challenge was that deadlines were not always achievable. My co-writer was actively involved in many projects and did not always have the time to write. I started to worry, but did not want to take an easy solution by leading the process. That would have been a failure both of the co-production of the text and of my ability to ensure good user involvement. Nevertheless, I reached a point where I decided that I had to take responsibility for getting the process back on track. Then I got the idea to apply the same techniques as I had observed my co-researcher using in the empowerment training seminars (see case 1), focusing individual resources and competencies. I asked: "How can we cooperate in a way that gives you energy to persevere? Which parts of the text give you the most energy to work on? What should *I* do now?" We had an honest and constructive discussion where I suggested this:

FIELD DIARY
29 October 2013

Write on the sections and parts of the text that give you energy to continue. Do not think about academic style or theoretical concepts. Approach it as a story you want to tell. What do you want the reader to learn? What is your message? Then I can read and work to find the "academic style" without compromising the content you find important to underline. We do this in close cooperation to ensure that both voices are heard.

I managed to put strength into the parts that gave her energy and the will to proceed. This also gave me new encouragement, because now I received texts written with commitment and energy. The article appeared as planned (Natland and Dalen, 2015). The users who knew the writing process called it "our PhD dissertation" with humour, because they thought it was long, detailed and academic – but it also had a positive connotation because they considered the publication to be a recognition of their knowledge within the academic community.

Discussion

Power, roles and relationships can influence knowledge production as well as new contexts for research production. Both cases can teach us something about the conditions required for co-writing processes to work, but also about the underlying values on which such collaboration should be based. The fairy tale book project was highly user led and usually followed a stratified co-writing process, in which each participant contributed to the parts that he/she felt most competent in (Lowry et al, 2004).

However, it is important to note that the process included more than just writing; the users employed creative and artistic ways to communicate the findings (layout, drawings, photo, colours). As for the short introduction on the function of fairy tales, it was drawn up by one user representative in a 'lead process' (Ritchie and Rigano, 2007) and then handed over to me. As it turned out that we approach fairy tales from different angles (I was trained in folklore studies and the user geared towards therapeutic and self-help literature), we had to communicate clearly in order to merge them into one final text.

The co-writing of the article, on the other hand, started in a more hierarchical way, even though it was the two users who had led and written the first draft. The sudden appointment of me as 'the expert', as well as the demands of the editors, could easily have led to a confirmation of the power differences between us as authors and between academic and experiential knowledge and writing styles (Johnson and Walmsley, 2003). The requirement to adhere to the academic style of writing and the editorial demands left the users little room to manoeuvre. If they did not comply, they would no longer be able to publish in an international scientific journal.

To ensure an equal co-writing process, I had to use communication skills to build trust and facilitate dialogue. Faced with challenges due to a lack of available time and enduring strength, I had to take the lead, but I tried to do it in a sensitive way by focusing on dialogue and with a particular focus on individual resources and talents (Johnson and Walmsley, 2003; Ens et al, 2011). This laid the foundation for the continuation of a stratified co-writing process in which we wrote the parts in which we felt most competent, and in which I, in sequences, merged sections and voices to ensure that we could both find our imprint in the written text.

Co-writing with users should embrace a polyphony of voices. This does not exclude critical reflections or the validation of results. A complex task for the researcher co-writing with users is to find a balance between exercising too much and too little control over the co-writing process. This was especially clear in the academic article, for which I had to be distant enough to guarantee academic standards but also be empathic and close to assure that the user's objectives were included and recognised. The role aligns with the concept of the 'critical friend' (Foulger, 2010). This denotes a middle position that allows the researcher to ask critical questions and read data from a different perspective while at the same time being the person who fully understands the context of the work and what the other persons/groups are pursuing with the project. Criticism in this context should be approached as a creative and positive activity – something the researcher does to clarify and improve, not to undermine (Foulger, 2010). Power relations in collaborative research often arise in the operational phase. Emerging situations need to be resolved before they become conflicts and obstacles to collaboration (Natland, 2020). Soft skills, trust and open discussions are important to ensure a co-writing process in which all voices are heard. It is my understanding that we avoided such tensions in both cases because we used the time to reach a common understanding and agreement on the exact purpose of our writing. Then we divided the tasks and activities, planned the process, set a deadline and decided whether anyone should have lead authority to ensure that the process takes place (and if so, who).

Finally, my experiences with the co-writing projects shed an interesting light on topics related to communication and dissemination of research results.

User involvement can be a challenge for the traditional ways of publishing within the academic context. Involving users in HUSK brought with it a demand for alternative and creative ways of communicating results, as well as the need to communicate them to readers other than researchers and practitioners. The fairy tale book is a good illustration of this.

The users' wish to disseminate results and represent knowledge creatively constituted an epistemic clash between the academic and user views of 'proper research dissemination'. Nevertheless, the project leader gave his consent and supported the idea. In my opinion, this is a sign of real commitment to the ideals of equal cooperation and recognition of the service users' knowledge and competencies which goes beyond rhetorical expressions and buzzwords. This allowed different discourses to emerge and be explored (Archer, 2006). The journal article, on the other hand, was produced within an academic discourse and it is less likely that all service users read or have access to such journals.

For the researcher, co-writing processes force a thorough reflection on extra time consumed and resources needed. The researcher is imbedded in an academic context where publication in highly rated journals is important for his or her own academic development and for the institution. This may conflict with the expectations and aspirations of the users regarding the genre and the target group. If funders and the academic world expect projects to be completed within traditional academic constraints, this can be an obstacle to securing users' involvement. It should also be noted that not all researchers will co-write texts that are not ranked in the academic counting system.

As funders of research are placing increasing demands for user involvement, it must be recognised that more time and resources are needed to explore co-production, co-writing and alternative ways of publishing the results. In this regard, the experiences described in this chapter illustrate a clash between different knowledge production discourses regarding expectations for what the research should result in, what funders of research expect and how they regard scientific knowledge. When policymakers and other funders of research demand user involvement, they should also acknowledge that collaborative research, grounded in qualitative methods and epistemologies, is also imbedded in ideals of dialogue and participation. This research also places a strong emphasis on softer outcomes such as processes and empowering the participating users. If calls for research projects aimed at enhancing services increasingly ask for research grounded in neo-positivistic ideals with the aim of measuring effects (as for example RCTs), or projects grounded in epistemologies where users' experiental knowledge is not validated, there is an epistemic clash between what the funders expect and what they inevitably also must acknowledge if they, at the same time, demand user involvement. Respect for knowledge diversity should be a core value, both ethically and epistemologically. To gain and maintain *epistemic justice* (Fricker, 2009), user involvement in research must therefore also include the writing, reporting and publishing part of the research project.

Conclusion

The experiences discussed in this chapter illustrate how co-writing and the co-construction of knowledge are still new, and that action and learning take place during the process. I have approached the co-writing process as knowledge production within communicative spaces and in dialogical interaction. This context creates conditions for the transcendence of traditional academic writing, as 'expert knowledge' is challenged and broadened by the impact of other voices as a result of service users and other lay people participating in research. This illustrates how co-writing should be explored and approached as part of the development of *participatory epistemology*. Such epistemology should be grounded in a democratic ethos, challenging the knowledge monopoly of universities and bringing forward discussions and distinctions between academic knowledge and everyday/experiential knowledge (Heron and Reason, 1997; Biesta, 2007,). Mode-2 knowledge (Nowotny et al, 2001) and reflexive analyses of positions, roles and power (Phillips, 2011, Natland, 2020) are useful as epistemological and methodological frameworks for understanding this knowledge production.

We all need recognition and to build trustful relations in our encounters with co-writers, but also with editors and other critical voices. Academics and research funders need to realise that service-user involvement is a transcendence of the traditional distinction between participants in research, but also understand *how* this is played out in concrete projects.

Co-writing is an underresearched topic in the literature on collaborative research and user involvement. This chapter aims to contribute to fill this gap. The experiences shared in this chapter illustrate the importance of trust and dialogue to ensure a collaborative process in which writing is worthwhile for all and that the research is carried out within a democratic ethic of knowledge production. This knowledge production must be approached critically as a process in which power and position play an important role. For future research, more ethnographic and thick descriptions and context-sensitive analyses of the co-production of knowledge are needed to inform collaborative research.

References

Archer, A. (2006) 'A multimodal approach to academic "literacies": problematising the visual/verbal divide', *Language and Education*, 20(6): 449–62.

Austin, M. and Johannessen, A. (eds) (2015) 'Enhancing the quality of public social services through the involvement of users: the Norwegian HUSK projects', *Journal of Evidence-Informed Social Work*, 12(S1): 1–6.

Biesta, G. (2007) 'Towards the knowledge democracy? Knowledge production and the civic role of the university', *Studies in Philosophy and Education*, 26: 467–79. Available from: https://doi.org/10.1007/s11217-007-9056-0

Dalen, H. and Natland, S. (2011) *Eventyr fra virkeligheten* [Fairy tales from the real world], Bergen: Fagbokforlaget.

Ens, A.H., Boyd, K., Matczuk, L.A. and Nickerson, W.T. (2011) 'Graduate students' evolving perceptions of writing collaboratively', *Canadian Journal of Higher Education*, 41(2): 62–81.

Foulger, T.S. (2010) 'External conversations: an unexpected discovery about the critical friend in action research inquiries', *Action Research*, 8(2): 135–52.

Fricker, M. (2009) *Epistemic Injustice: Power and the Ethics of Knowing*, Oxford: Oxford University Press.

Geertz, C. (1973) 'Thick description: toward an interpretive theory of culture', in C. Geertz (ed), *The Interpretation of Culture*, New York: Basic Books, pp 3–30.

Gjernes, T. and Bliksvaer, T. (2011) *Nye samarbeidsformer – nye læringsformer: Sluttrapport fra evalueringen av forsøket Høgskole- og universitetssosialkontor (HUSK)*, (New collaborations – new learning: evaluation of the HUSK program), NF-report, Bodø: Nordland Research Institute.

Heizmann, H. and Olsson, M.R. (2015) 'Power matters: the importance of Foucault's power/knowledge as a conceptual lens in KM research and practice', *Journal of Knowledge Management*, 19(4): 756–69.

Heron, J. and Reason, P. (1997) 'A participatory inquiry paradigm', *Qualitative Inquiry*, 3(3): 274–94.

Johnson, K. and Walmsley, J. (2003) *Inclusive Research with People with Learning Disabilities: Past, Present and Futures*, London: Jessica Kingsley Publishers.

Lowry, P.B, Curtis, A. and Lowry, M.R. (2004) 'Building a taxonomy and nomenclature of collaborative writing to improve interdisciplinary research and practice', *The Journal of Business Communication*, 41(1): 66–99. Available from: https://doi.org/10.1177/0021943603259363

McLaughlin, H. (2010) 'Keeping service user involvement in research honest', *The British Journal of Social Work*, 40(5): 1591–608. Available from: https://doi.org/10.1093/bjsw/bcp064

Natland, S. (2020) ' "Recently, I have felt like a service user again": conflicts in collaborative research, a case from Norway', in H. McLaughlin, P. Beresford, C. Cameron, H. Casey and J. Duffy (eds), *The Routledge Handbook of Service User Involvement in Human Services Research and Education*, Abingdon: Routledge, pp 467–76.

Natland, S. and Dalen, H. (2015) 'Service users' self-narratives on their journey from shame to pride: tales of transition', *Journal of Evidence-Informed Social Work*, 12(1): 50–63.

Needham, C. (2009) *Co-production: An Emerging Evidence Base for Adult Social Care Transformation*, London: SCIE.

Nowotny, H., Scott, P. and Gibbons, M. (2001) *Re-Thinking Science: Knowledge and the Public in an Age of Uncertainty*, Cambridge: Polity Press.

Phillips, L. (2011) *The Promise of Dialogue: The Dialogic Turn in the Production and Communication of Knowledge*, Amsterdam: John Benjamins Publishing Company.

Ritchie, S.M. and Rigano, D.L. (2007) 'Writing together metaphorically and bodily side-by side: an inquiry into collaborative academic writing', *Reflective Practice*, 8(1): 123–35, DOI: 10.1080/14623940601139087.

15

Participatory pathways in social policymaking: between rhetoric and reality

Peter Beresford and Heidi Degerickx

Introduction

Since the 1990s more attention has been focused on the 'participation paradigm' in the making of social policy (Carr, 2007). In existing research, the participation of people in poverty has been framed as a promising anti-poverty strategy, entailing explicit recognition of the voices and life knowledge of poor people in the realm of social policymaking (Beresford, 2001; Krumer-Nevo, 2005, 2008).[1] It has been argued that 'they have the capacity to place, and indeed sometimes to force, life knowledge on the political, professional, academic and policy-making agenda' (Beresford, 2000, p 493). As a radical shift from the prevailing paradigm, in which poor people are predominantly treated as objects, this emphasis on their participation in social policymaking recognises them as subjects shaping their own lives (Lister, 2002). The question remains, however, whether this popular principle of participation has actually produced a democratic shift in power and contributed to a social justice agenda. Here, we accordingly engage in a critical investigation of the complexities at stake in 'the politics of participation', as many authors highlight the danger of participation being 'tokenistic' (Beresford, 2010), 'more rhetoric than reality' (Adams, 2008) or a mere 'buzzword' (Cornwall and Brock, 2005).

Our research study concerns two exemplary historical cases: the disabled people's movement in the UK in the 1970s, and the fourth world movement in the 1990s in Belgium. Both zoom in on *how* the concerned people themselves, in a political dialogue with many other societal stakeholders, challenged the pejorative rhetoric on *their* impairment or *their* poverty towards a rhetoric of participation, equality and respect from a human rights perspective.

Case 1: *The Fundamental Principles of Disability* (1976)
Impacting on social policy by redefining ourselves

This UK case study is about a group – disabled people – predominantly living in poverty, who challenged their cultural and policy conceptualisation and representation and thus had profound effects on public policy, their life chances and ultimately international understandings of them and how they were best able to live their lives to the fullest extent.

Historically, social policy has often been shaped by one group of powerful people – policymakers – determining interventions affecting many others, often including disempowered and devalued groups, like homeless and unemployed people, older, sick and disabled people, at-risk children and young people. What has tended to unify these different groups is the high levels of poverty and deprivation with which they are associated. While the intentions of such policymakers are often benign, as with the creation of the European post-war welfare states, their approach has often been paternalistic and reflective of the discriminations and exclusions characterising their societies (Beresford, 2016).

The emergence of the UK disabled people's movement in the 1970s highlighted this status quo. It argued that the prevailing perspective on disability was to understand it in terms of personal tragedy. Disabled people were framed as dependent and the issue interpreted though a medicalised individual model of disability which tended to lump together and segregate disabled people into separate schools or training centres, residential institutions and impoverished lives on welfare benefits. Levels of employment were low and levels of low income were high (Oliver, 1983). The nascent disabled people's movement, particularly through a new self-organised grouping, the Union of Physically Impaired Against Segregation (UPIAS), challenged this.

There are two particular points of interest in their challenge. First, it was documented in a unique way, and second, it was based on a paradigm change as to how disability should be understood and policy developed, as well as in the nature of such policy (UPIAS/Disability Alliance, 1976). It offers a unique window on how service users have become involved in policymaking and the radical implications such involvement can have.

The occasion was a meeting between UPIAS and the Disability Alliance to explore how disabled people could 'become more active in the disability field' and explore 'a long term programme of action' to make that possible (UPIAS/Disability Alliance, 1976, p 3). While UPIAS was an organisation controlled by disabled people, the Disability Alliance was founded and led by Peter Townsend, the famous non-disabled social policy academic. A report of their meeting was agreed on by the two organisations and published as *The Fundamental Principles Of Disability* (1976).

What this actually showed was the massive gulf between traditional policy assumptions and the ambitions of disabled activists. UPIAS criticised Townsend and the alliance for focusing narrowly on poverty and taking control from disabled people, seeing them as:

- pursuing the income issue in isolation – 'It is only one aspect of [disabled people's] oppression';
- maintaining an approach with 'a small number of [non-disabled] experts having the central role and most disabled people left "largely passive"';
- seeking to educate the public through 'expert' information, with a 'narrow concentration on parliamentary pressure' (UPIAS/Disability Alliance, 1976, p 4) rather than working for the 'mass participation of disabled people';
- not making serious efforts to involve disabled people (UPIAS/Disability Alliance, 1976, p 4).

UPIAS saw Townsend's and the Disability Alliance's focus on a comprehensive state income for disabled people as perpetuating their dependence. It regarded the alliance's reliance on a medically based model for assessing disability – what people 'could not do' – as keeping control with policymakers and away from disabled people. UPIAS were critical of what they saw as 'the willingness of the incomes "experts" to use disabled people to give authority' to their own agendas and control (UPIAS/Disability Alliance, 1976, p 16).

Not surprisingly, the two organisations and their leaders could not come to any agreement. There was a massive gap between them. This reflected the gulf between traditional disability policy and its assumptions and those of the new disabled people's movement. UPIAS rejected this past policy approach as that of 'a small group of non-disabled "experts" [who] write, discuss and print pamphlets advocating State Charity. These are then circulated to the public in the name of disabled people before we have had a chance to evaluate their contents critically' (UPIAS/Disability Alliance, 1976, p 17).

Adam Lent's study of modern 'new social movements' (NSMs) concluded their meeting 'was supposedly designed to see whether UPIAS could join the Alliance and whether Alliance members would be allowed to affiliate to UPIAS. In effect, however, it simply emphasised the irreconcilability of the old moderate approach and the new, self-organised radicalism' (Lent, 2002, pp 107–8).

Reflecting this, Vic Finkelstein, a leader of the international disabled people's movement and spokesperson for UPIAS called for a radical revisiting of disability: 'Unless you raise and investigate these questions, "what is disability, and how come we are impoverished in the first place", you are not going to deal with the causes of disability, and it may well be that your approach will help to perpetuate them' (Lent, 2002, p 7).

UPIAS set a precedent, built on by the international disabled people's movement, of disabled people developing their own understanding of disability, based on lived experience and experiential knowledge rather than any claim to professional 'expertise'. This social understanding of disability was first set down in the UPIAS/Disability Alliance document: 'In our view, it is society which disables physically impaired people. Disability is something imposed on top of our impairments, by the way we are unnecessarily isolated and excluded from full participation in society' (Lent, 2002, p 3).

This contrasts sharply with the traditional, individual model of disability which saw the problem as lying in the disabled person. The new social model, elaborated by Mike Oliver and others, first drew a distinction between:

- impairment or perceived impairment: the absence or lack of functioning of a person's limb or sense; and
- disability: the negative societal response to people seen as having such impairments, reflected in the negative and discriminatory attitudes, barriers and exclusions they face (Oliver, 1990).

Over the years, the social model has been critiqued, developed and extended and has increasingly addressed diversity. Interest in such a social model has extended to other service-user groups, from mental health service users and people with learning difficulties to people with alcohol and drug problems and those living with dementia (MHF, 2015). Its initiators have always argued that it was not intended as a comprehensive theory and its critics have attacked it for failing to be one (Shakespeare, 2002; Thomas, 2007; Oliver, 2013). More significantly, it has played a key role in international activism and been central to both major policy reform and disabled people's own self-reconception.

Instead of internalising the individualising message that they were necessarily damaged, inferior and incompetent, disabled people have instead increasingly recognised the effects on them of societal and attitudinal discrimination, and their movement fought to challenge this. They argue that it is not their need to use a wheelchair that limits their mobility but the failure to provide access; it is not because they are blind, sign or cannot communicate verbally that there are barriers but because equal communication access is not ensured by policymakers.

The vehicle that they have used in struggling for equality and against discrimination is the associated philosophy of 'independent living'. In this, disabled people internationally have turned traditional understandings of independence on their head. Instead of taking independence to mean people managing on their own and 'standing on their own two feet', the disabled people's movement has reinterpreted it to mean people having the support to live their lives on equal terms with non-disabled people. Such support can extend from personal support to help them with the 'daily tasks of life', like getting up, washing and dressing, to being better able to negotiate mainstream life through improved access and assistance. Such support is not understood as compensating for disabled people's 'inadequacies' but as *enabling* them to do things for themselves, like having a job and a home, being a parent and contributing to their communities like anyone else (Campbell and Oliver, 1996).

This is a very different notion of support from traditional ideas of 'caring for' disabled people; a different understanding of what is needed and what they can do. It means that while disabled people and other service users have traditionally been seen as needing to be 'taken care of', institutionalised or subsidised because they could not live 'independently', with the right kind of support, many can live independently. Service users have demonstrated that with such personal and social support they could live in their own homes, gain skills, have families, be active citizens, take part in voluntary action and often get jobs. This is seen to apply to all groups of service users. Thus two very different interpretations of living independently have developed here.

While the philosophy of independent living has made some impact on policymakers internationally, 'in a service-led and grossly under-resourced system of social care' like that operating in the UK, independent living opportunities for many disabled people have so far been limited and further restricted by severe cuts in welfare benefits (Pearson, 2012, p 240). As Townsley et al's research has also shown (2009), independent living across Europe has been seen by governments as an unwelcome expense in a difficult economic climate, as underlined, for example, by serious cuts in personal budgets in the Netherlands.

However, independent living is now enshrined in the UN Convention on the Rights of Persons with Disabilities (UNCRPD), and while neoliberal politics has qualified independent living's impact in the West, it has become increasingly important as a policy goal in the Global South, given force by the UNCRPD, and is having an increasing effect in disabled people's lives (Grech and Soldatic, 2016). Thus disabled people's challenging of traditional categories and conceptions of disability, instead identifying it as a particular form of social oppression, is now having a transformative impact globally, at individual and policy levels.

Case 2: The *General Report on Poverty* (1994)

The Belgian case is about the production process of the *General Report on Poverty* (KBF, 1994) between 1992 and 1994. It is a white paper commissioned by the Belgian government and has been framed in Belgian history as the first policy document to be produced while embracing the voices of people in poverty (Degerickx et al, 2020). Its 431 pages are infused with oral testimonies of people in poverty on diverse life domains, while a fundamental underlying argument on citizenship is made: 'If we tell about our lives, we have to be able to draw the conclusions ourselves, therefore we have to be enabled to take part in societal debates on poverty from which we are excluded at the present time.' (KBF, 1994, p 18).

The report was ordered in the aftermath of Black Sunday, 24 November 1991, the elections which marked the federal breakthrough of the far-right populist political party Vlaams Blok. In response, the traditional political parties formed a coalition government and commissioned the report as part of 'an urgency program' to address 'new societal needs and challenges' (Dehaene, 1992, p 11). The idea of the report was inspired by the French poverty report published in 1987, written by the founder of the French ATD Fourth World, Joseph Wresinski. ATD Fourth World redefined poverty as a violation of human dignity and human rights, which was groundbreaking at that time and challenged the individualist and pejorative discourse on the 'deserving and undeserving poor' (Dean, 2015).

The General Report on Poverty was produced through close collaboration between three major societal stakeholders: ATD Fourth World (ATD), an international (self-)advocacy movement on poverty, the Local Public Welfare Agencies (LPWA), representing professional social work, and the King Baudouin Foundation (KBF), a philanthropic high society organisation which had already published several poverty reports in the 1980s in Belgium. The report encompassed a two-year process in which 26 thematic group gatherings (13 in Dutch and 13 in French) across the country were set up, concerning all aspects of life. It embraced a grassroots approach in which the practical knowledge of frontline social workers (courtesy of the LPWA) was merged with the lived and experiential knowledge of self-advocates and advocates (through the ATD and similar NGO's).

The report had an institutional impact on anti-poverty policymaking in Belgium: it spurred the foundation of the federal Combat Poverty, Insecurity and Social Exclusion Service in 1999, as well as the Flemish Poverty Decree of 2003, which recognises the so-called 'organisations where people in poverty take the floor'. Today 59 of these local NGOs are active.[2] The report also aligned with other European participatory ventures on policymaking, such as the work of the Child Poverty Action Group in the UK, the Poverty Alliance in Scotland and the Welfare Alliance in Norway, which were all interconnected within the European Anti-Poverty Network (EAPN).

Methodologically, this case study is based on archival research and oral history. We analysed the archival records from ATD and the KBF on the report's production process and interviewed 17 key figures who were all closely involved from the different stakeholder perspectives: four politicians, two academics, six representatives of (self-) advocacy organisations, three social workers and the two project leaders of the report.

Our analysis reveals how the making of *The General Report on Poverty* was a highly conflictual and rhetorical process in which the participation concept understood as 'voice of and by the poor' was introduced by ATD's advocates as a means to question the dominant status quo and open up new ways to conceptualise the poverty problem as a structural problem, as a violation of human rights, instead of as an individual problem of deviant persons. However, this was a problematic process, as at least four different understandings of the participation concept arose in the power struggle between the stakeholders: participation as 'mobilisation', as 'consultation', as 'confrontation' and as 'social inclusion'.

Participation as mobilisation

From the beginning of the negotiations, ATD underlined the importance of *The General Report on Poverty* as an instrument whereby people in poverty could speak for themselves. Meetings were held in French and the word 'démarche' was used frequently by ATD to stress that giving voice was a political act, aimed at the recognition of people in poverty as full citizens: 'This report is a démarche, completely different than all former poverty reports. This report has to be about the opportunity for the affected people to publicly take the floor about their ideas, their aspirations and their struggles' (Degerickx et al, 2020).

ATD also coined the term 'partnership with the poor' because 'people in poverty, AND those engaged at their side, had to be given voice' (Degerickx et al, 2020, original emphasis). In sum, they claimed that 'everyone who can move things forward from a standpoint of partnership' should be given a voice. The report had to be an instrument of profound social change, and therefore an overall mobilisation process of poor as well as non-poor citizens was needed. This understanding of participation 'stood at odds with the logic of concrete and short-term solutions; which was, so they argued, the approach of the government and the other stakeholders (Degerickx et al, 2020). However, in their in their eagerness to label the non-participation of people in poverty as politically wrong, they spoke *for* people in poverty, who were not included in the negotiations.

Participation as consultation

The representatives of the welfare agencies perceived *The General Report on Poverty* initiative as "a political momentum" because policymakers seemed "very much willing to mobilise themselves against poverty" (Degerickx et al, 2020). They therefore believed that it was "of utmost importance to write very concrete policy proposals" into the report. Although they considered the idea of a nationwide participatory dialogue with people in poverty somewhat "out of the ordinary", they stressed the importance of "the harvest of testimonies" for keeping the political momentum going (Degerickx et al, 2020). This idea, however, was challenged by the KBF, which appeared at the table after six months of lingering preliminary negotiations. The KBF even questioned the necessity of participation as consultation: "What do you want this report to be, a scientific work or a journalistic work? I think it is not that interesting to consult again a lot of people, neither the poor nor social workers" (Degerickx et al, 2020).

In response to this derogation, the representatives of the welfare agencies and ATD jointly asserted 'that this consultation [of both people in poverty and social workers] was the only novelty in the démarche and thus had to be retained' (Degerickx et al, 2020). The Cabinet agreed with them and even insisted on the production of 'raw material' that 'did not deform the voice of the involved people' (Degerickx et al, 2020). For the government, the report had to become the ultimate proof of democracy through testimonies of the most marginalised groups in society. As such, the report needed to legitimise their policies.

Participation as confrontation

Furthermore, the Cabinet emphasised 'the importance of confrontation of knowledges' (notes KBF, 20 November 1992, pp 2–3). Through a dialogue process, the practical knowledge from professional social workers and the experiential knowledge of self-advocates had to be merged. ATD was at first reluctant about this idea of participation as confrontation because of the power imbalance. They argued that people in poverty were not used to raising their voices or trained to do so in a context of formal meetings and hearings, especially not with professional social workers at the table, who, at the end of the day, still decided on their welfare benefits (notes KBF, 20 November 1992, pp 1–2). However, the other stakeholders found this a rather paternalistic reflex and the direct dialogue method would become the heart of the report process. For this purpose, ATD organised intense preparations throughout the country for people in poverty to speak up as self-advocates. It can be seen as a real tipping moment in Belgium as ATD and like NGOs then shifted from being predominantly advocacy organisations to embracing processes of self-advocacy at the heart of their organisations.

Participation as social inclusion

> The report has to be an instrument to promote the participation as well as the inclusion of the poorest, with the involvement of the social workers.
> (The Cabinet, 20 November 1992, p 2)

Once the participatory process started, the Cabinet chaired the management committee and reframed participation as a process of social inclusion. By doing so, the government aimed to kill two birds with one stone: the participation of people in poverty would contribute to democratic social policymaking and enhance poor people's inclusion in society, thus remedying their state of being poor (since poverty was understood as social exclusion). In this understanding of participation as social inclusion, participation of people in poverty became a social intervention strategy in the struggle against poverty.

Towards the end of the report process, the competing participation discourses crystallised into a dominant policy rhetoric because of the highly mediated public launch of *The General Report on Poverty* on 17 October 1994, the first World Day Against Poverty. A small revolt occurred as several people simply stood up to speak unannounced: self-advocates, advocates and social workers. This symbolism enshrined the report as a milestone for participation and self-advocacy in Belgian social policymaking.

This case study shows how people in poverty became entitled to speak up but were also were held responsible and obliged to do so. Marginalised citizens were obliged to identify as 'poor' and as 'self-advocates' – identities which possibly can inflict restigmatising processes.

Notwithstanding the reality that *The General Report on Poverty* was written and composed by advocates, social workers and academics, it was framed in Belgian history as a report *of* people in poverty. As a counterproductive effect of this framing, we might witness the historical birth and rise of identity politics among people in poverty in Belgium as a conceptual shift and a new regime, under which they are expected to be proud and to advocate for social change while making claims for recognition 'as self-advocates in poverty' in the public realm (Dean, 2015; Degerickx et al, 2017; Degerickx et al, 2020), with their non-poor allies being addressed predominantly as facilitators of empowerment processes (Boone et al, 2018).

Conclusion

Both case studies highlight clashes between organisations operating on the basis of different ideologies and attitudes *towards*, and understandings *of*, participation and empowerment. Both accentuate significant power differentials between traditional and more grassroots approaches to involvement, and demonstrate a gap between participation's rhetoric and reality. However, both also show how rhetorical processes not only contribute to silencing marginalised groups but equally can challenge dominant understandings and thus facilitate new realities and understandings of poverty and disability. Both demonstrate that moving to more participatory approaches in policymaking is – and will continue to be – a work in progress rather than a readily achieved goal and commonplace reality. In the constant struggle, the democratic potential is encapsulated but not at all guaranteed.

Much has happened in the UK since the publication of *The Fundamental Principles of Disability*. Popular and cultural understandings of disability and disabled people have changed to become more in line with the demands of UPIAS and disabled people's organisations. Where once parents with disabled children might have acquiesced to professional assumptions that they would be dependent and need to be institutionalised, now parents are much more likely to fight determinedly for them to be educated and live in the mainstream and have the support to live equal lives. Now disabled people can expect to be presented in the media in much less stereotypical terms and influence their portrayal and public roles. However, ideological and political shifts have exerted immensely powerful counterforces.

Perhaps most significant has been the war against disabled people, portrayed as 'welfare reform', based on severe cuts and rationing of disability benefits. This has been associated with a massive loss of income among disabled people, resulting in loss of rights and opportunities, increased impoverishment and also significant loss of life through the resulting harsh conditions and evidenced suicides (Clifford, 2020). As a result of these major political changes, and while, as we have seen, disabled people from the 1970s argued against their crude association with poverty, increasingly this association has become more dominant and damaging, to the detriment of both disabled and non-disabled people, challenging our understanding of each other and increasing social fragmentation.

Since *The General Report on Poverty* was published, the expectation that people in poverty address their own claims for recognition and change still tends to dominate contemporary anti-poverty policymaking in Belgium (Roets et al, 2012) and to 'decenter, if not to extinguish, claims for egalitarian redistribution' (Fraser, 1996, p 4).

The fundamentalist idea that poverty will be intrinsically eradicated by involving and embracing the viewpoints and experiences of people in poverty themselves through self-advocacy becomes vital. As such, anti-poverty policymaking might be committed to an identity politics that operates for people in poverty in the name of their making social change on their own

(Baistow, 2000), while leaving the agenda to be set by people whose power has been taken for granted (Phillips, 2004). However, our findings also support Rancière's (1999, p 36) conceptualisation of subjectification whereby participation and self-advocacy are about a process of dis-identification, the progressive 'opening up of a subject space where anyone can be counted since it is the space where those of no account are counted'.

Notes
[1] We predominantly refer to 'people in poverty' as the English translation of the Dutch concept 'mensen in armoede' which was used in Flanders, Belgium, since the 1990s. The term was introduced to break away from more reifying terms like 'the poor'.
[2] http://www.netwerktegenarmoede.be

References

Adams, R. (2008) *Empowerment, Participation and Social Work*, 4th edn, New York: Palgrave Macmillan.

Baistow, K. (2000) 'Problems of powerlessness: psychological explanations of social inequality and civil unrest in post-war America', *History of the Human Sciences*, 13(3): 95–116.

Beresford, P. (2000) 'Service users' knowledges and social work theory: conflict or collaboration?', *British Journal of Social Work*, 30(4): 489–503.

Beresford, P. (2001) 'Service users, social policy and the future of welfare', *Critical Social Policy*, 21(4): 494–512.

Beresford, P. (2010) 'Public partnerships, governance and user involvement: a service user perspective', *International Journal of Consumer Studies*, 34(5): 495–502.

Beresford, P. (2016) *All Our Welfare: Towards Participatory Social Policy*, Bristol: Policy Press.

Boone, K., Roets, G. and Roose, R. (2018) 'Social work, participation and poverty', *Journal of Social Work*, 19(3): 309–26, DOI:10.1177/1468017318760789.

Campbell, J. and Oliver, M. (1996) *Disability Politics: Understanding Our Past, Changing Our Future*, London: Routledge.

Carr, S. (2007) 'Participation, power, conflict and change: theorizing dynamics of service user participation in the social care system of England and Wales', *Critical Social Policy*, 27(2): 266–76.

Clifford, E. (2020) *The War On Disabled People: Capitalism, Welfare and the Making of a Human Catastrophe*, London: Zed Books.

Cornwall, A. and Brock, K. (2005) 'What do buzzwords do for development policy? A critical look at "participation", "empowerment" and "poverty reduction"', *Third World Quarterly*, 26(7): 1043–60.

Dean, H. (2015) *Social Rights and Human Welfare*, Oxford: Routledge.

Degerickx, H., Roets, G. and Van Gorp, A. (2017) 'The visual rhetoric of self-advocacy organisations on poverty: all about courage?', *Social and Education History*, 6(1): 53–77.

Degerickx, H., Rutten, K., Van Gorp, A. and Roets, G. (2020) 'Proud to be poor? Untangling identity politics with the families portrayed in the photobook *Courage* (1998)', *Visual Studies*, 35(2–3): 285–98, DOI: 10.1080/1472586X.2020.1788981.

Degerickx, H., Van Gorp, A., De Wilde, L. and Roets, G. (2020) 'Giving voice to people in poverty in Belgian social policy-making since the 1990s: a window of opportunity for a political demarche?', *Journal of Belgian History*, L: 3–4.

Dehaene, J.-L. (1992) *Regeringsverklaring uitgesproken voor het parlement op 9 maart 1992 door de Eerste minister, de heer Jean-Luc Dehaene en regeerakkoord*, Brussels: INBEL.

Grech, S. and Soldatic, K. (eds) (2016) *Disability in the Global South: The Critical Handbook*, New York: Springer.

KBF (King Baudouin Foundation), in collaboration with ATD Fourth World and Belgian Association of Cities and Municipalities (1994) *General Report on Poverty*, Brussels: KBF.

Krumer-Nevo, M. (2005) 'Listening to "life knowledge": a new research direction in poverty studies', *International Journal of Social Welfare*, 14(2): 99–106.

Krumer-Nevo, M. (2008) 'From noise to voice: how social work can benefit from the knowledge of people living in poverty', *International Social Work*, 51(4): 556–65.

Lent, A. (2002) *British Social Movements since 1945: Sex, Colour, Peace and Power*, Basingstoke: Palgrave Macmillan.

Lister, R. (2002) 'A politics of recognition and respect: involving people with experience of poverty in decision making that affects their lives', *Social Policy and Society*, 1(01): 37–46.

MHF (Mental Health Foundation) (2015) 'Rights, dementia and the social model of disability: a new direction for policy and practice?', draft policy discussion paper, London: Mental Health Foundation.

Oliver, M. (1983) *Social Work and Disabled People*, Basingstoke: Macmillan.

Oliver, M. (1990) *The Politics Of Disablement*, Basingstoke: Macmillan and St Martin's Press.

Oliver, M. (2013) 'The social model of disability: thirty years on', *Disability & Society*, 28(7): 1024–26.

Pearson, C. (2012) 'Independent living', in N. Watson, A. Roulstone and C. Thomas (eds), *Routledge Handbook of Disability Studies*, London: Routledge, pp 240–52.

Phillips, A. (2004) 'Identity politics: have we now had enough?', in J. Andersen and B. Sim (eds), *The Politics of Inclusion and Empowerment: Gender, Class and Citizenship*, New York: Palgrave Macmillan, pp 36–48.

Rancière, J. (1999) *Disagreement: Politics and Philosophy*, Minnesota: University of Minnesota Press.

Roets, G., Roose, R., De Bie, M., Claes, L. and van Hove, G. (2012) 'Pawns or pioneers? The logic of user participation in anti-poverty policy-making in public policy units in Belgium', *Social Policy & Administration*, 46(7): 807–22.

Shakespeare, T. (2002) 'The social model of disability: an outdated ideology?', *Social Science and Disability*, 2: 9–28.

Thomas, C. (2007) *Sociologies of Disability and Illness: Contested Ideas in Disability Studies and Medical Sociology*, Basingstoke: Palgrave Macmillan.

Townsley, R., Ward, L., Abbott, O. and Williams, V. (2009) *The Implementation of Policies Supporting Independent Living for Disabled People in Europe: Synthesis Report*, Utrecht: Academic Network of European Disability Experts.

UPIAS (Union of the Physically Impaired Against Segregation)/Disability Alliance (1976) *Fundamental Principles Of Disability: Being a Summary of the Discussion Held on 22nd November, 1975 and Containing Commentaries from Each Organization*, London: The Union of the Physically Impaired Against Segregation and the Disability Alliance.

16

Experiential knowledge as a driver of change

Har Tortike and Vicky Lyssens-Danneboom

Introduction

Domestic violence, child abuse and violence against women are deep-rooted problems in our society with a far-reaching impact on the lives of all those affected by them. In addition to feelings of shame and/or guilt, many victims encounter taboos in their search for safety, legal support and assistance. User involvement against these types of oppression can take many forms, as the projects of the author of this chapter, Har Tortike, prove. Since 2005, Har has been involved in numerous creative projects in cooperation with young people and women who have experienced oppression, domestic violence and violation of their rights. Besides videos, books, curricula, blogs and television broadcasting, they organise forum theatre and workshops. All projects are intended to make people realise that they are allowed to throw off the 'blanket of shame', to speak openly about oppression and to organise new ways of living without it.

Since the voices of the experts by experience have a strong impact on practitioners, policymakers, teachers and students, Har and his groups are always looking for opportunities to influence the policies of civil society organisations and governments.

Three sources of knowledge

After being a Dutch cameraman and documentary filmmaker for 25 years, in 2005 Har started working with young people and women who experienced oppression. In this work, he combines three sources of knowledge: an academic expertise in psychology, which he studied for four years, a 'professional' expertise in film and theatre developed at the Psychopolis Free Art Academy and an 'experiential' expertise through his experiences of forms of child abuse as a child of parents traumatised by Japanese imprisonment during World War II. In later life, Har managed to refer to his childhood experiences as 'trans-generational traumatisation', and wondered why 'no one had ever told him this before'. This question became the foundation of his later creative work.

School dropouts as experiential experts

In 2005, Har supervised a 'camera-acting' training course for young school dropouts, aged 12 to 18 years. Because of his openness about his own struggles, the youngsters felt safe and free to speak. They took the initiative of creating a theatre performance about their experiences with child abuse. The performance, using dance, raps, circus acts and shadow theatre, ended with the question to the audience: "What can we do about this?"

The group was invited to Amsterdam and Antwerp to give performances for secondary school children; with great success, as it turned out. Most of the young audiences that visited the 30 performances stayed for up to one hour after the event to share their own experiences of child abuse.

Later, the theatre youngsters gave ten performances for youth care professionals in the Netherlands. In contrast to the peer group audiences, fierce discussions arose. There was an urgent demand from the young people to address the professionals' lack of training in dealing with this issue. The diversity of the audiences was an eye-opener. Was it that simple: finding a way to speak honestly, giving the audience the freedom to talk about it and looking for change together?

For the youth actors themselves, the theatre performances turned out to be a turning point in their personal lives as they succeeded in making their way of surviving experiences of mistreatment, neglect or abuse useful to others.

> 'I want the young people in the audience to feel safe to share their experiences. Being a child and having the childhood I had was very difficult for me. In this group I can be myself and develop myself in my own rhythm. It was the best therapy I had.' (Experiential expert)

While many members of this first group went back to school and became professional actors, theatre teachers or journalists, new young people joined the group. In 2008 the Dutch foundation Kinderpostzegels (Children's Stamps) invited Har to assist secondary school pupils in making video films; in 2012 the Belgian BZN Atlas asked him to start a forum theatre group with youngsters; and in 2014 he was invited by the Brussels women of Citizenne Vormingplus to start a forum theatre group with mothers from the Brussels district of St Jans-Molenbeek. All three initiatives were based on the main topics of child abuse and the violation of rights. These projects have influenced the policies of civil society organisations, governments and the curricula of educational institutions.

Methodology

The participants take part in the creative projects on a voluntary basis. They are free to decide how long they participate and what experiences they want to share. It is psychologically liberating form of creativity and it can be therapeutic, but the shared stories are basically considered as being material for videos, theatre scenes. Participants work on projects in an improvisitory way while learning to trust their own intuition, and they have the responsibility to be as committed as possible while respecting their boundaries and those of the other participants. Everyone is involved in (after) caring for each other: "We all know what it is like to have adults above you who are incapable of lovingly raising you. But everyone has different experiences. That is the strength of our group. Being equal in sharing and at the same time recognising and respecting the differences in experience" (Experiential expert).

Har supervises the projects, offers safety, shows enthusiasm and provides practical advice in the media used, but it is always the participants who take action, determine which topics are discussed and choose the form in which these are shared with the public.

> 'I take the responsibility to challenge participants to come up with personal experiences to help other people. But I am limited, being an older, white, Western European Dutchmen. It is therefore of the utmost importance that I do not take others by the hand, but invite them to do so themselves. I want to be very clear about this and at the same time ensure safety in the group.' (The author)

All projects follow more or less the same structure. The participants meet over several weeks for a few hours each time. Meetings start with a communal meal, some of which is brought by the participants themselves. During the meal, the participants exchange their daily experiences and let off steam. Afterwards, theatrical improvisation games are played and then the participants, alone or in small groups, work on their stories. After a short time, 20 minutes, everyone presents her or his progress to the others. Everyone can give feedback. The meetings end with confidence exercises for the whole group. At the end of the process, results are presented during try-outs. First with 'safe' audiences chosen by the participants themselves, later with open try-outs for the target group. All performances are interactive.

The participants receive a maximum volunteer fee for their performances, and are also insured during rehearsals and performances. All expenses incurred are reimbursed. The operation costs are financed through a buy-out sum for one or more workshops or through a subsidy received for giving free performances. The STUK Foundation provides support for all Dutch projects through financial management and consultancy. Jeugdzorg Emmaüs Antwerpen (JEA) provides the same support for the young people's forum theatre projects, and Citizenne Vormingplus arranges this support for the women's forum theatre group in Brussels.

Case 1: The Dutch follow-up – the Netherlands, 2008–2020

In 2008, the Stichting Kinderpostzegels (Children's Stamps Foundation) started to financially support projects guided by Har Tortike. This has led to numerous projects from experts by experience that have influenced Dutch society.

Videos for YouTube

An initiative to produce videos on child abuse and domestic violence for YouTube was extremely necessary, since previously there was a lack of open and honest testimonies on the subject on YouTube. Har started with video workshops in secondary schools. Young people aged 12 to 18 have made their own videos and uploaded them to YouTube. Subsequently, the youngsters initiated a website where they provide more background information about the videos.[1] More than 80 videos on the topic were uploaded, accounting for more than 300,000 hits. The videos are used in all kinds of training courses for both students and professionals.

Workshops

The youngsters were invited to give workshops with their videos. On the basis of a quiz they developed themselves, they discussed themes like: 'What is child abuse?' and 'What can you do?' The message 'Doing nothing is not an option' was strongly highlighted everywhere. Over the past 12 years, more than two hundred video workshops took place, for an audience of about fifteen to forty people each time, in secondary schools, universities of applied sciences, universities and youth care institutions. They visited secondary schools 38 times, universities of applied sciences eight times, five universities and youth care institutions 24 times. They were also invited 26 times to a governmental or NGO conference, for audiences up to 600 professionals.

In 2010 and 2016, the STUK foundation was awarded the Dutch Jan Brouwer Prize for the prevention of child abuse for the video project and workshops. The prize, which involved a considerable amount of money, had to be spent on the development of a new project.

STUKboek

A new initiative, funded by the Jan Brouwer Prize, was the creation of STUKboek (STUKbook), with the aim of making the previously made videos available to young people in youth care institutions with little or no access to the internet. A class of students of fine art and design in education from Utrecht University of Applied Sciences presents a collection of the videos in book form. The book, with a circulation of 6,000 copies, was enthusiastically received in the Netherlands and Belgium. 4,000 copies were distributed to young people in youth care institutions, and 2000 STUKbooks are used as teaching material for various courses.

Actie ENTER

After attending workshops of experiential youth experts, *Action ENTER* was developed by students of the Amsterdam University of Applied Sciences out of dissatisfaction with the information about child abuse and domestic violence at their educational institution. The project, which lasted two years, brought about a successful change in the curriculum of five universities of applied sciences as well as in the orthopedagogy programme of the University of Groningen. Thanks to *Action ENTER*, the students and their university management started to attach great importance to the involvement of experiential experts in the training of social workers, physiotherapists, educators and legal aid workers.

'How to'

In the Netherlands, nine young people with experience in foster care made a series of five videos entitled 'How to survive foster care'. They have already given 28 workshops in six different foster care institutions, not only for young people in the same situation but also for foster parents and foster care workers. Three foster care institutions are currently working with experienced young people to influence youth care policy in their region. And every year, the orthopedagogy programme of the University of Groningen also invites experienced young people to give workshops to all third-year students.

> 'In various places countrywide these projects have contributed greatly to an open dialogue about violence in upbringing and relationships. It is striking that it is the adults who – in contact with the young people – discover that they have inner resistance to talk about it.' (Former project leader Stichting Kinderpostzegels – Children's Stamps Foundation)

Case 2: Forum theatre in Antwerp and Brussels

Forum theatre is one of the techniques of the theatre of the oppressed (TO), developed in the sixties of the last century by pedagogy professor Paulo Freire (1972, 1974) and theatre director Augusto Boal (1979). TO explores social (in)justice and promotes social change through the use of interactive theatre techniques, while supporting the oppressed. TO is designed to reach a conclusion in a dialectical way, by considering opposing arguments, rather than a didactic way, where the moral argument is one-sided and pushed by the actors.[2]

In Boal's forum theatre a play is performed with a scripted core, about an oppression relevant to the audience. After reaching the conclusion, in which the oppressed characters fail to undo their oppression, the actors re-enact their performance. Now each spectator may call out 'Stop!', replace the actor portraying the oppressed and try to 'break through the oppression'. The actors improvise against the spectator's attempts to change the story so that the difficulties in making a change are acknowledged.

Participants who have experienced forum theatre will ideally desire to be proactive and have the courage to break through oppressive situations in real life because they feel much better prepared and more confident in resolving the conflict.[3]

It is the joker who invites the audience to react and participate. After each replacement, the joker asks the audience what they think about the alternative in an ongoing dialogue between the audience and the actors. The joker does not take a position on the alternatives proposed by the spectators but ensures that the process remains a dialogical and non-judgmental search for alternatives, not dominated by those who take advantage of the existing unequal balance of power within the community.[4]

Forum theatre as developed by Antwerp youngsters

In 2012, BZN Atlas, an organisation for the prevention of child abuse, asked Har to set up a forum theatre group with young people. They developed their own specific form of forum theatre: no involvement of professional actors; no involvement of actors without experiential knowledge; no use of costumes, sets, special lightning, props and make-up so as to be able to play anywhere and anytime; rehearsals take place at schools, instead of theatres, to make it easier for students to become part of the group; they perform various short scenes instead of an entire play; and each scene is based on the group members' own experiences.

> 'As a child I experienced violence and neglect and I can use this directly in my contact with the audience. I feel safe in Har's way of working.

> There are no supervisors, teachers or other adults between what I want to say and the people in the audience.' (Experiential expert)

Every youth actor should be able to improvise on every role.

> 'You hear the stories of the others in the group and you can just talk about it without being ashamed. So I can play my stepmother, I know her techniques of humiliation, and someone else in the group is playing me. Or we change roles and I teach her how I reacted. After a rehearsal I always go to sleep with peace of mind. I'm not the abused one, it's part of our history.' (Experiential expert)

In contrast to Boal's forum theatre, in the Antwerp forum theatre youth group it is not only the joker who enters into dialogue with the audience but also the youth actors. After every separate scene the audience can react to four questions:

1. What did you see?
2. Is it realistic?
3. Is it recognisable?
4. What can we do to improve the fate of the protagonist?

Finally, and perhaps the most important difference with Boal's forum theatre, no scripted scenarios are used. All performances are based on improvisation as well. The youngsters found this important because they play their own experiences with child abuse.

> 'In order to enter that area, participants must be free to decide how far they want to go into it, every time again. Dealing with child abuse is never really finished. It is no good if you have to play one scripted solution over and over again. Life is improvisation and during rehearsals and performances new insights arise that can be applied directly in the scene being played without changing the plot. In this way the participants can develop their own courage to change things in real life. And this sincerity and originality is what really appeals to the audience.' (Har Tortike)

Invitation from the Province of Antwerp

The Forum Theatre Group was invited by the Domestic Violence Department of the Province of Antwerp to give two performances each day for a week for secondary school students once every year. Over a period of six years, 50 different youth actors performed with 2160 secondary school pupils. After each performance, the Province of Antwerp organised additional conversations in small groups, under the supervision of professional social work moderators. The youth actors joined the different groups to participate in the conversations. Teachers also participated in a separate group for teachers. The secondary school students could voluntarily take the opportunity to talk openly about the violence they experienced at home or at school. Professional counsellors were present for a direct follow-up. In the two weeks after each performance, extra lessons were given at each school.

> 'There were people my age in front of me. They played exactly what happens at my home. It was the first time I had my own opinion about this. I dared to talk about it with a care coordinator from school. This changed everything at home. Later my mother came to thank the group. We all cried, out of relief.' (Participant from the audience)

The Antwerp forum theatre group of youngsters also began to produce short scenes about their experiences with violence in young relationships, peer pressure, the rights of young people in special youth care or juvenile detention, discrimination, racism, bullying and gender inequality.

Forum theatre by women of Vormingplus-citizenne

In Molenbeek (Brussels) a group of mothers and grandmothers were inspired by the Antwerp forum group of youngsters and invited Har to work with them on a weekly basis at Citizenne Vormingplus. The group, consisting of women from non-Western-European countries but mostly born in Brussels, performed forum theatre on the themes of violence – at home and outside – and later fear of parents losing their child to radical Islamic groups. Currently, the group focuses on gender inequality, education and modern life: "People react very emotionally to our performances and they touch us with their feedback. I got a hug from a woman without saying anything. People are more than willing to talk about injustice, especially when you see that we as a group want to oppose this" (Trainer, Vormingplus Citizenne).

The women play their scenes in Belgium, the Netherlands and France in front of audiences of other women in the same position. The performances often turn out to lead to the emergence of new temporary women's groups in which women support each other in converting powerlessness in the face of violence, poverty and exclusion into joint actions for change. The group won the 2016 Ultima Flemish Cultural Prize for Amateur Arts for, as the jury wrote, 'their valuable voice in the debate and their artistic performance as (amateur) theatre makers'.

Case 3: Experiential experts in youth care in Antwerp/ Belgium

Youth Care Antwerp Emmaüs (JEA) is one of the Flemish government institutions providing shelter, support, mediation and guidance to young people and their families. The expertise of the client and their network, the expertise of the people working at JEA and the expertise of the scientific literature/research are regarded as equally important. Together with the Catholic University of Leuven, JEA has set up an academic workplace. Experiential experts are involved from the outset in formulating the research questions and setting up a methodology. Experiential experts are also questioned via in-depth interviews, focus groups and the outcomes of creative workshops like forum theatre and the Open Mind Weeks (projectweken) led by Har: 'We have changed our way of doing research by adding a methodology based more on the way Har works with the youngsters. In the beginning we felt uncomfortable. We were made aware of blind spots that we had not discovered before.'[5]

Forum theatre in youth care – the essentials of experiential expertise

In 2015, JEA took the initiative to cooperate with the forum theatre group. JEA offered to provide rehearsal space and take on production tasks. In return, they wanted the forum group to allow JEA youngsters to join and give performances for young people of the institution and the institution's staff. The forum theatre group was completely free to determine the topics of the scenes. The group of young people expanded and scenes were made about living in youth care institutions, including the legal rights of young people in special youth care.

During their performances for supervisors and staff of JEA, one of the essentials of experiential expertise came to the surface. The youngsters started to play scenes that happened recently in their youth care institutions. They played the roles based on their own experiences, and in doing so they played the roles of the counsellors, parents, staff-members and juvenile judges. Supervisors and staff were invited to respond: 'Everyone steps out, for a moment, of their daily role of counsellor, staff member, psychologist or young person in special youth care, to question and inform each other as equals. Afterwards, everyone returns safely to their own role in real life, but something has changed' (the author).

Young people whose confidence in adults has been seriously affected by previous negative experiences notice that quite a lot of adults are willing to have an open conversation. The adults, on the other hand, discover that young people have a lot of experience that is worth sharing and that they are willing to engage in dialogue.

Fruitful cooperation

Outside the institution, cooperation between the forum theatre group and JEA led to performances for secondary schools, colleges and universities, and training days for youth care staff, government institutions and social organisations. Since 2015, more than 120 performances have been realised, involving 80 youth actors and more than 2000 spectators/participants.

> 'They can tell their stories in a way that I as a teacher can never do in such a haunting way I never will never be able to. For three years now I have been using the forum theatre group within a course for third-year students in the Bachelor of orthopedagogy [oropedagogy].'
> (Lecturer, University of Applied Sciences, Odisee)

Another way of using the same method – the Open Mind Week

Within JEA, Open Mind weeks (project weken) are organised twice a year. During such a week, a group of ten young people residing in the institution use the opportunity to work together intensively for four days on media such as video, songs, rap, images, theatre, lectures, games and so on. The basic question is: What should be changed and what is well organised?

The products of the Open Mind Week are used in meetings with the staff. Every year, JEA organises a two-day 'in the woods' event wherein they look at the past period and think together about the future. The whole last afternoon is available for the young people to discuss with 60 employees the things they find most important. Examples of topics presented are: the basic rights of young people in youth care; the desired professional proximity instead of professional distance; privacy; the possibility of viewing their own files; promises made by youth care workers that are not kept; the quality of the food; the possibility and right to be hugged; being recognised as someone with a lot of experience instead of as a problem case; the shortage of pocket money while they're being asked to become more independent; the preparation for becoming 18, and so on.

Young people participating in the Open Mind weeks do not receive a volunteer allowance, instead they are supported in their search for follow-up courses in line with their interests or talents.

Special results of Open Mind weeks

Sometimes the results of the Open Mind Week lead to actions outside the youth care institution. One of the noteworthy actions was a letter to the juvenile judges.

During an open mind week in 2015, one of the young participants got angry because of a measure imposed by his juvenile judge. The youngsters wrote an open letter to all juvenile judges in the nearby districts. It was an invitation to discuss nine topics and they promised to bring homemade biscuits. Their letter was picked up by the media, and the juvenile judges responded positively to the invitation. They promised to bring soft drinks in return.

The first meeting with the juvenile judges was uncomfortable for everyone. The young people could not resist speaking almost aggressively, the invited adults listened and took notes and the press waited outside. But at a third meeting, everyone worked together and a common schedule was drawn up for changes by the juvenile judges, by the government and by the youth care institution in collaboration with the young people. Over the next two years the juvenile judges visited the youngsters more often in the institution, had normal conversations with them before the trials started, and spoke with them in normal clothes, and a serious effort was made to have the same juvenile judge deal with the young person's case every time.

And moreover, together with the young people who wrote the letter to the juvenile judges and design students from the Karel de Grote University of Applied Sciences, JEA produced new information flyers about juvenile judges for the young people and their families, in an understandable language.

During the next Open Mind week, videos were made by youngsters with advice for juvenile judges, counsellors and lawyers. One of the youngsters in this project was asked to decorate the cells of the police station, using her homemade tarot cards as an example.

Lessons for social work students

In 2019, during an Open Mind week, young people put together a lesson intended for students of universities of applied sciences and universities, that is, for future counsellors, psychologists and social workers. JEA and the Karel de Grote University of Applied Sciences reacted enthusiastically, and the Ghent University and the AP University of Applied Sciences also joined this project.

This is what happened: One month before the lessons, the students received an online link to 'the Reader'. This included a selection of topics compiled by the youngsters during the Open Mind week:

- What makes a person a good youth care counsellor?
- Who makes decisions: your counsellor, your consultant, your juvenile judge, your parents or you?

- The counsellors are usually educated, middle-class white people, while young people in youth care come from all classes and from all over the world. What goes right and wrong in this dynamic?
- What do you think about the need for touch and cuddling and professional distance versus professional proximity?
- Is privacy respected?
- Who is important to me? Respect my network!

The lessons are given by three to five young people, supervised by Har, for a maximum of 20 students online and a maximum of 40 students offline. The workshops last two hours and three of the six topics can be discussed. The last half hour is for open conversation wherein all attendees can ask each other questions.

Conclusion

When people with experiences of oppression and violation of rights are brought together and offered the freedom and security to speak about their experiences, it gives them the possibility to pick up their lives again. The realisation that the oppression is not their own fault and that they are not the only ones affected allows them to throw off their 'blanket of shame'. Moreover they start to realise that they are not 'the abused' but that this experience is part of their history, and this gives them the opportunity to positively appreciate the survival techniques they have learned during the oppression and apply them in a useful way for themselves and for others.

The use of creative techniques, such as forum theatre or video, and the way in which these practices have been developed by the young people and women in collaboration with Har Tortike gives them freedom to share their own experiences through a creative model.

It is amazing how this way of working appeals to all kinds of audiences and is useful for different forms of conversation and education about so-called difficult subjects. It has even influenced the public debate in both Belgium and the Netherlands. This can be explained by the sincerity of the work of the experiential experts and the joy with which the liberating new possibilities are propagated.

It is remarkable that as a result of the performances and workshops, people often feel inspired to start new groups with the aim of supporting each other against powerlessness in the face of violence, poverty and exclusion.

At least as important and noteworthy for a real change of policy is the fact that organisations such as educational and youth care institutions dare to support this form of work in their practice and policy. The projects with experiential experts have proven to be a driver of social change in many places in both Belgium and the Netherlands.

Notes

1. STUKonline.com
2. Wardrip-Fruin, N. and Montfort, N. (2003) 'From theatre of the oppressed', in N. Wardrip and N. Montfort (eds), *The New Media Reader*, Cambridge, MA: MIT Press, pp 339–52.
3. Ceulemans, A., Wyckaert, V. and Makine, A. (2011) *Onderzoek naar veranderingen bij jongeren na hun deelname aan forumstuk*, Antwerp: BZN Atlas.
4. Miramonti, A. (2016) 'Factsheet: exploring transformative actions through forum theatre'. Available from: http://www.braced.org/fr/resources/i/?id=865709a4-a07e-4bd7-bc39-547e55e4b85f
5. Steens, R. (2019) 'Wat vinden een jongere en zijn gezin echt van je werking?', social.net, 19 August. Available from: https://sociaal.net/achtergrond/jeugdhulp-clientenfeedback/

References

Boal, A. (1979) *Theatre of the Oppressed*, London: Urizin Books.

Ceulemans, A., Wyckaert, V. and Makine, A. (2011) *Onderzoek naar veranderingen bij jongeren na hun deelname aan forumstuk*, Antwerp: BZN Atlas.

Freire, P. (1972) *Pedagogie van de onderdrukten*, Baarn: Uitgeverij In den Toren.

Freire, P. (1974) *Culturele actie voor de vrijheid*, Baarn: Uitgeverij In den Toren.

Miramonti, A. (2016) 'Factsheet: exploring transformative actions through forum theatre'. Available from: http://www.braced.org/fr/resources/i/?id=865709a4-a07e-4bd7-bc39-547e55e4b85f

Steens, R. (2019) 'Wat vinden een jongere en zijn gezin echt van je werking?', social.net, 19 August. Available from: https://sociaal.net/achtergrond/jeugdhulp-clientenfeedback/

Tortike, H. (2018) De wind leren lezen op het water. Projecten met kunst in de jeugdzorg, kan dat? Handboek integrale jeugdhulp - Kunst en hulpverlening (10). Leuven: Politeia.

Wardrip-Fruin, N. and Montfort, N. (2003) 'From Theatre of the Oppressed', in N. Wardrip and N. Montfort (eds), *The New Media Reader*, Cambridge, MA: MIT Press, pp 339–52.

PART III

Reflective chapters

17

Experiences matter equally

Henrike Kowalk and Jenny Wetterling

Introduction

In March 2018, the Karel de Grote University College in Antwerp initiated an international dialogue between social work lecturers, researchers and experts by experience (EBE) about the benefits and obstacles of service-user involvement in social work education and research. Approximately 20 EBE with different sociodemographic characteristics and backgrounds from the UK, Poland, Sweden, the Netherlands, Belgium and Italy participated and discussed the involvement of people with lived experiences in many different contexts. Among the participants there was an overall agreement regarding the benefits, but we also identified a number of factors that hinder the integration of EBE in education and research. These factors are linked to cultural and societal structures, which is why we think that they need to be made more explicit. Before elaborating the obstacles that EBE encounter in their activities, we elaborate on two important beneficial factors.

Terminology

Each country uses a specific term to refer to people with lived experiences in the social service and mental healthcare system, for example: service users, experiential experts, experts by experience, peers or service users. For the purpose of this chapter, we stick with the term experts by experience because it stresses the expertise that people with lived experiences have, and it encompasses a greater variety of people. After all, not every EBE is still a service user. An EBE is understood as a person with lived experiences in social and mental healthcare services from which he or she has developed insights which they use as a resource to support others or to inform the broader services and institutions in general (for example, Sedney et al, 2016; Videmšek, 2017).

Vision social change

Facilitating service-user participation and co-production in social work education and research, as well as in the practice of social work, is considered an integral component of today's policies and guidelines for social work in several European countries (Beresford and Carr, 2018). Developments in social work practices and policies have a direct impact on education. In order to adequately prepare students for their future fieldwork and their role and position as care providers, establishing a connection with what is happening in the field and with citizens is crucial. This connection can especially be established by giving the knowledge and experiences derived in the field a structural place in education, which is something EBE, teachers and researchers agree on. Furthermore, we think that it is important to stay aware of the fact that social work education, research and practice exist because of structural imbalances, social injustice and divisions in our societies (Stuart, 2013). People with physical and mental health problems, people who are 'different', are being systematically stigmatised and socially excluded. Dissatisfaction with social and mental healthcare services has also not disappeared since the beginning of the client movement. This means that the benefit of involving EBE exceeds the benefits specific to the classroom. Therefore, we also need to attend more directly to how the involvement of EBE can benefit people in need, clients and service users. The EBE that participated in the dialogue in Antwerp consider their knowledge vital to the creation of social and mental healthcare that is truly at the service of the people and not at the service of the conditions and control of the system.

Beneficial factors

Something as fundamental as lived experience needs to be heard, seen and valued in the process of developing social work education, practice and research. This is something EBE and teachers and researchers agree on, but some EBE have shared experiences with professionals who were so focused on rules, diagnoses, procedures and labels that they seemed to struggle with establishing a human and equal connection. There is a strong wish to create programmes in which such experiences can be safely explored in order to learn from them. The two most important beneficial aspects of involving EBE that have been highlighted during the meeting in Antwerp are the sharing of knowledge and respect.

Sharing knowledge

The involvement of EBE is about integrating different knowledge and perspectives and providing students, academics, social workers and EBE the opportunity to ask questions they would otherwise avoid or be too cautious to ask in practical settings. Hearing about lived experiences helps professionals reflect on their studies and research programmes and on their own role in an educational or organisational system that is influenced by political agendas. In addition, it helps students to reflect on their future role as social workers or as mental healthcare professionals in a broader context (Skilton, 2011). By discussing loopholes in the welfare and healthcare system and the harmful effects of rules and regulations, students learn that supporting clients is not only about supporting people but also about advocating for people's rights. This is an area where much can be gained by bringing in EBE, because for 'outsiders', the violation of rights is often invisible. As Ahmed (2016) points out, people who are part of an institution do not always see or come up against 'the [institutional] walls', and certain problems that tend to be treated as individual problems are in fact structural and organisational issues that need to be addressed by professionals. People in need are usually not in a position to insist on their rights. The input of EBE can help to make students and professionals more aware of such dynamics. Students benefit from a 'taste of reality', and personal stories help them to understand how important it is to see the whole person and not just the problem or diagnosis (Bates, 2020). Hearing about helpful and harmful aspects of social and mental healthcare services causes them to feel better equipped in practical situations. EBE can raise awareness of alternative solutions and approaches to the methods students are being taught. Our experience in Amsterdam and Sweden suggests that hearing many individual stories also stimulates and encourages students to explore their own lived experiences in relation to their profession, which helps with breaking stigma, learning from each other and gaining a better understanding of the difficulties in the field.

Respect

Participants in the dialogue in Antwerp noted that genuine integration makes EBE feel respected. Respect is about being seen and acknowledged as a competent, credible and equal person. In practice it means turning rhetoric into meaningful action in which all parties involved feel taken seriously and are not overruled. EBE are people who have often been silenced, and many have lost dignity and confidence in their abilities. Being able to use their lived experiences can help to restore both, and it can also offer hope to other former service users who are still struggling with particular issues and who have little future prospects. Most EBE who participated in the dialogue started using their experiences on a voluntary basis. It is a collective experience for EBE that being offered a paid position (which we will discuss more in the next section) not only increases their sense of being of equal value but also seems to have a positive effect on their self-development.

Obstacles

The integration of EBE in education, practice and research has proven a challenge (Sedney et al, 2014; Videmšek, 2017). Projects that deal with the integration of EBE in education and research tend to be developed on ad hoc and inconsistent bases, and knowledge about the effects of these efforts is still limited (Schön, 2016). The involvement of EBE cannot be understood as something that is inherently good. On the contrary, the results present a rather complex picture associated with changing and contested views on the role of the social worker, the academic world and the EBE themselves. Since the 1960s, greater service-user involvement in healthcare has been advocated. However, tracing the development of this involvement reminds us that the road ahead can still seem unclear, fraught with difficulties, and has not really achieved what it is set out to do (Clews, 2014). The four major themes we identified as hindering involvement are tokenism, lack of capacity, economy and power.

Tokenism

Tokenism is closely related to the concept of exerting influence, as it is about the *appearance* of facilitating participation (Arnstein, 1969), and is one of the main concerns that emerged from our discussions in Antwerp. EBE are still mainly invited to 'tell their story' and to present a different narrative, or they are asked to join in because their views are in line with the perspective of the professionals. Such practices are also common in research settings. We observe that not all professionals are able to accommodate different perspectives and critical viewpoints with the same courtesy they do academic and scientific knowledge (Desain et al, 2013). EBE report witnessing a tendency among professionals to exclude them from holding 'real' power, such as by allowing them to make decisions about service development or in regard to the educational or research agenda. The conditions for genuine involvement will never be satisfied as long as EBE can expect to be treated as an afterthought, involved only after the main decisions and activities have already been fixed.

In addition, it has been noted that the focus of professionals is usually on whether EBE have the 'necessary skills' to work within an educational or research setting, while little attention is paid to whether teachers and researchers have the skills to work with EBE. An equal integration of EBE will mean being critical about the competencies of professionals. Our experiences as EBE in education reveal that it is crucial that academic staff and EBE prepare programmes and classes together to ensure that EBE are not seen and treated merely as tokenistic, and integration and involvement as being only about maintaining the semblance of equality. How experiential expertise is being represented and by whom, thus talked and written about, can have an impact on whether it is truly treated as an autonomous and different but equal source of knowledge or made to fit into the existing dominant knowledge, language and structures, for instance regarding to scientific knowledge and academic and the standard language. Last but not least, another question regarding tokenism is how people with greater cultural capital become the privileged voice of service users, excluding disadvantaged and marginalised subgroups?

Lacking capacity

A major element in the history of social work is its paternalistic character, partly due to a philanthropic tradition and the importing of an individualistic and medicalised 'expert model' into the practice of social work. As a result, service users are mainly seen as people with deficiencies and problems, and these attitudes are transferred to social work students. Reports from service users show that they often feel humiliated and oppressed as a result of their contact with the people employed to help them. Contrary to this paradigm, there is a model based on reciprocal relationships and co-production of knowledge. This participatory model suggests that social workers should see vulnerable and disadvantaged groups as their allies in mutual efforts to change and improve society (Beresford and Croft, 2001). The inclusion of EBE in the development of society and its services is both a political issue and an issue of human rights.

There are also organisational issues that hamper involvement, such as inaccessibility of universities, bureaucratic paperwork and inflexibility of working hours and work structures. Although personal experience is a prerequisite for EBE, it is sometimes described as insufficient for the transfer of knowledge and skills to students or staff. Also, there is a concern that the new partnerships are university driven and that some agency partners are left unclear about what is happening and why. This may exacerbate inequalities in power positions between EBE and professionals. Those whose expertise comes from personal experience may not identify themselves as users, yet students and lecturers may, consciously or unconsciously, treat them as such. To ensure meaningful involvement, we think that EBE and academic staff should receive appropriate training and intervision. Other facilitating factors for successful and effective participation and good relationships between EBE and staff include the provision of information and support, the sensitivity of staff to people's circumstances, the allowing of EBE to work at their own pace and the ensuring of regular communication.

Economy

Lack of money and resources is a key and potentially harmful barrier to meaningful and respectful involvement of EBE. During a work conference in Antwerp (in March 2018) for social work professionals and EBE in order to prepare the content of this book on service user involvement, the group of EBE often stressed the need to create proper economic conditions for continuity. Our experience is that the involvement of EBE in social work education and practice is not yet seen – by people on management levels of universities and organizations – as a permanent valuable resource and therefore does not have permanent funding. Sufficient resources, both social and economic, are a vital factor in the successful involvement of EBE. So far, very limited resources are being committed to realise participation. Paid positions in the field are slowly increasing in number, but paid positions in higher education and research for EBE remain scarce. Much of the existing involvement is based on individual projects and is not implemented as a compulsory part of social work education and research. EBE are still frequently asked (and expected) to work on a voluntary basis and without proper contracts. What is absolutely non-negotiable, though, is that EBE must be paid for the work they do (volunteers can also be reimbursed financially).

However, another obstacle for EBE regarding payments is the poverty trap. A number of EBE are unable to work full time and receive disability and housing benefits. In most countries, the rules and regulations regarding social benefits are so strict that the standard payments for part-time involvement can ultimately lead to people having less overall income when they start working as an EBE. Experiences show that staff members at universities and research centers can forget about these difficulties and do not get involved in the question of how the poverty trap can be avoided through creative and flexible contracting and reimbursements (for instance through financial support for further education).

Power

Could EBE positively challenge and develop social services if their influence was to be sufficiently accepted in positions where they hold real power and can affect organisational changes? Idealistically, they should be able to. One major factors that hinders the equal integration of EBE is power imbalances. These imbalances relate not only to the real differences between tenured and non-tenured positions but also to issues such as language, certain knowledge, sense of self-worth, lack of confidence and financial, mental and emotional security (Clews, 2014). Teachers and researchers, for instance, express themselves linguistically in ways that leave little room for people who are less strong verbally and who can therefore easily be overpowered by professionals. In accordance with previous observations, professionals also need to investigate and release prejudices and seek human and equal contact (Beresford and

Croft, 2001). The integration of EBE has the potential to contribute to the reduction of power differences and the promotion of collaborative partnerships through the recognition of the knowledge of EBE in social work. This recognition should be achieved through dialogue and through sharing knowledge about how people experience functioning in an academic setting. However, while EBE represent the interests of people who are mostly excluded, they also still belong to a minority in the work field. What we have seen in our group in Antwerp is that EBE usually stand alone in a team, which puts them automatically in a less powerful position. Service representatives and providers are the controllers of services and lecturers, and researchers are the controllers of academic views. They operate in a management-like model and in a setting where there is little variation in perspectives, which makes it unlikely that EBE will have any real power in the purchase and provision of services or the design of education and research (Clews, 2014). We cannot assume that the social work academics will be keen to share their power with EBE, but we must continue to work in that way. The goal is to break down or through these invisible hierarchies and to replace them with connectedness and togetherness and welcome variety and diversity on an equal level. By developing new forms of professional knowledge and collaboration, we can challenge traditional power structures. Cultural changes are required in order to achieve this, and there is a need for reciprocal relationships and recognition of each other's knowledge and experiences (Sedney et al, 2016; van Erp, 2012).

In recent decades, the involvement of EBE has gone from being a marginal activity to occupying the mainstream of social work education and research. Policy intervention can be identified as a primary catalyst for this change. However, the work of the disability movement and disability theory cannot be overlooked when laying the foundations for challenging expert knowledge and valuing other knowledge. This goes hand in hand with framing social work education within a discourse of social justice, inclusion and anti-oppressive practice. In contrast to practice and research in social work, a consumerist approach prevails in service user organizations and mental health care institutions. The consumerist approach is embedded in the prevailing neoliberal discourse that has reshaped social work in recent decades. It has utilised user involvement and partnership working as a means to sustain structures of oppression and marginalisation at the same time as it cuts costs through austerity. Involvement framed within neoliberalism has failed to achieve meaningful redistribution of power, as the scope for individual service users to achieve a voice and responsibility in decision-making has been given narrowly defined boundaries. Involvement has been understood as a bureaucratic requirement rather than a meaningful redistribution of power (Beresford and Croft, 2001). As mentioned in *Tokenism*, the act of involving EBE has come to be seen as more important than providing more effective services. Within social work education, a critical lens is beginning to problematise this, and attempts are being made to create space for a new discourse on involvement that focuses on whether it is meaningful and effective.

Conclusion

By involving EBE in social work education (and research and practice), we are taking a step towards recognising the importance of the lived experiences of marginalised people. A prerequisite for the integration of EBE is the awareness that their involvement is not intended or meant to replace lecturers or researchers but to contribute to the improvement of the quality of education and research. It must be clear what is expected of EBE and what the purpose is of including experiential expertise in specific educational programs or courses. This is important to avoid wrong expectations on all sides, students, EBE and lecturers. Randomly integrating EBE in all programmes is not a sound strategy and is likely to be counterproductive. Creating equal positions for EBE in educational institutions and social work practices turns out to be very challenging for all parties involved, because tenacious system structures have to be dealt with. However, experiences at the universities that joined in the discussion in Antwerp show that it is not impossible as long as the knowledge of EBE is given the same courtesy as academic knowledge and the hegemonic ownership of knowledge and knowledge creation is consciously and continuously questioned.

Our ultimate goal is that the involvement of EBE comes to be outcome oriented and based on social justice, and that it operates where the voices of EBE and research and social work students interconnect to develop meaningful and sustainable projects. We believe that without the involvement of EBE, the values and goals of social work are at risk of being undermined by the paternalistic traditions of social work. By choosing to involve EBE, universities take a stand in the local, national and international social debate and play an active role in shaping an inclusive society and future social workers and mental healthcare professionals. The involvement of experiential knowledge should be integrated into daily educational and research practices rather than merely added as something separate or 'exotic'.

Future

Our vision for future integration of EBE requires that instigators at universities and in the field formulate clear goals and expectations, that there is a collective effort towards a cultural change in academia, research and practice and that there is a long-term approach to the integration of

EBE. Furthermore, we think it is important to ensure adequate training for everyone involved and to keep stimulating awareness of, and strategies to deal with, power imbalances. This will require a greater involvement and inclusion of rarely heard groups, robust research exploring the benefits and effects of EBE involvement, a re-evaluation of the dominant cultural and power-knowledge discourse, a more critical and reflexive interpretation of the integration of EBE and the ambivalence towards power-sharing that poses challenges to partnerships and that the deep-rooted flaws in involvement and its emancipatory claims are constantly addressed.

References

Ahmed, S. (2016) 'How not to do things with words', *Wagadu: A Journal of Transnational Women's and Gender Studies*, 16: 1–10. Available from: http://sites.cortland.edu/wagadu/wp-content/uploads/sites/3/2017/02/v16-how-not-to-do-ahmed.pdf

Arnstein, S.R. (1969) 'A ladder of citizen participation', *Journal of the American Institute of Planners*, 35(4): 216–24.

Bates, P. (2020) 'The benefits of involving service users and carers', peterbates.org. Available from: https://peterbates.org.uk/home/service-user-and-carer-involvement-in-nurse-education/the-benefits-of-involving-service-users-and-carers

Beresford, P. and Carr, S. (2018) *Social Policy First Hand*, Amsterdam: Amsterdam University Press.

Beresford, P. and Croft, S. (2001) 'Service users' knowledges and the social construction of social work', *Journal of Social Work*, 1(3): 295–316. Available from: https://doi.org/10.1177/146801730100100304

Clews, J. (2014) 'Could experts by experience gain positions of power', *Mental Health Today*, November/December: 24–27.

Desain, L., Driessen, E., Graaf, W., van de, Holten, J., Huber, M., Jansen, M., Metze, R. and Sedney, P. (2013) *Ervaringen met de inzet van ervaringsdeskundigheid*, Amsterdam: Amsterdam University of Applied Social Sciences.

Schön, U.K. (2016) 'User involvement in social work and education – a matter of participation?', *Journal of Evidence-Informed Social Work*, 13(1): 21–33, DOI: 10.1080/15433714.2014.939382.

Sedney, P., Huber, M. and Holten, J. (2014) *Werken met ervaringsdeskundigen vereist cultuuromslag*, Sociale Vraagstukken. Available from: https://www.socialevraagstukken.nl/sociale-praktijk/werken-met-ervaringsdeskundigen-vereist-cultuuromslag/

Skilton, C.J. (2011) 'Involving experts by experience in assessing students' readiness to practise: the value of experiential learning in student reflection and preparation for practice', *Social Work Education*, 30(3): 299–311, DOI: 10.1080/02615479.2010.482982.

Stuart, P.H. (2013) 'Social work profession: history', *Encyclopaedia Social Work*, DOI: 10.1093/acrefore/9780199975839.013.623.

van Erp, N., Rijkaart, A.M., Boertien, D., van Bakel, M. and van Rooijen, S. (2012) *Vernieuwde inzet van ervaringsdeskundigheid*, Utrecht: Trimbos instituut.

Videmšek, P. (2017) 'Expert by experience research as grounding for social work education', *Social Work Education*, 36: 1–16, DOI: 10.1080/02615479.2017.1280013.12.

18

Ethical issues in the meaningful involvement of service users as co-researchers

Hugh McLaughlin

Introduction

This chapter seeks to identify and discuss ethical issues in the meaningful involvement of service users as co-researchers. Just because a researcher says that they are involving service users as co-researchers, it does not follow that this is how it is experienced by service users. It is also worth stating that I believe such involvement of service users will not only enhance the quality of the research but is more likely to lead to better outcomes for service users. While there is a growing evidence base for this (Brady, 2020; Lovell-Norton et al, 2020; Moulam et al, 2020), there are also examples of when such research set out with good intentions but became unstuck as the partnership between service users, practitioners and academics broke down (Natland, 2020).

All researchers, including service user co-researchers, possess a moral perspective about what is right and what is wrong. These views may be influenced by their life experiences and interactions with others, resulting in individualised moral beliefs set within a socio-historical context. While there is large amount of agreement about what is right and wrong, and in social work we would particularly point to principles like human rights and social justice, the application of such principles in particular situations is both contested and contestable. This chapter begins by identifying key ethical research frameworks, and then considers potential ethical issues that can arise during the research process.

Ethical perspectives in research

Contemporary discussions on research ethics usually begin with the trial of Nazi doctors after the Second World War that led to the Nuremberg Code (1947), which identified ten ethical key principles including consent and avoidance of risk to research participants. However, the mere existence of ethical codes has not prevented further examples of unethical research. One of the best known of these is the Tuskegee Syphilis Study of 1932–1972 (Brandt, 1978), wherein 400 African American men were not treated for syphilis even though a treatment was available. Instead, they were studied over a prolonged period to track the progression of the disease. More recently, in the UK, there was also the removal and retention of human tissue, including children's organs, for research at the Alder Hey Hospital (Redfern, 2001) without the parent's consent. The researchers in both these studies could claim that their research increased our knowledge of individual conditions and helped us to develop treatments. Such a position could be argued from the normative utilitarian perspective whereby the harm inflicted on a minority can be offset by the greater good for the many (McIntyre, 1987).

In this perspective, research participants are treated as a means to an end and not as ends in themselves. What this form of moral calculus does not do is advise us who is to decide whose life chances should be sacrificed? This brings us to questions of power. It is not hard to see that the Tuskegee African Americans or grieving parents in the UK were not members of powerful groups.

Deontology

Earlier ethical scandals led to Beauchamp and Childress's (1979) classic ethical framework of the key research principles of respect for persons, beneficence, non-maleficence and justice. This is often referred to as a deontological approach and is associated with Immanuel Kant. As Banks (2012) notes, it is based on rational thought whereby researchers must logically work out what to do in any particular circumstance and should only do what they believe should be a universal law.

The work of Beauchamp and Childress informed Butler's (2002) ethical code for social work researchers in which he also included 'scope' as an ethical principle. Respect for autonomy, as identified by Butler (2002), is like respect for persons in that it highlights the need to treat people as ends in themselves and to respect their autonomy as long as it doesn't interfere with the autonomy of others. As such, this highlights the need to secure informed consent of research participants, which should be freely given. It also requires researchers to preserve confidentiality and to act in such a way as to avoid wilful deceit. Beneficence and non-maleficence can be considered as the imperative to do good and to avoid doing harm. Justice refers to the need to deal fairly in the face of competing claims. This requires researchers not to further their own interests at the expense of others' legitimate interests. This is particularly important when considering the involvement of service user co-researchers as part of a research team. The application of these principles identifies the scope in which individual researchers can act in accordance with their own moral conscience. It is quite possible for each of these principles to be in conflict, and in such cases the researcher will have to present a defensible argument as to why they have chosen one principle over the others.

Both utilitarianism and deontology can be viewed as principal-based approaches to ethics in that they are more concerned with the principles of any action than with the moral qualities of the actor. Fenton (2016) claims they are too blunt and too absolutist for social work practice, and I would also suggest for social work research. Softer features such as empathy, emotion and responsiveness are important when interviewing service users in relation to sensitive subjects like domestic violence or child sexual abuse. Banks and Gallacher also claim that they are reductionist in their approach and tend to 'compartmentalise morality or reduce it to specific actions or decisions rather than acknowledging the ongoing and integrated nature of moral life' (Banks and Gallacher, 2009, p 33).

Virtue ethics

In contrast, virtue ethics emphasises the qualities of the researcher's moral character rather than their principles, rules or the consequences of any particular action. Its focus is not on what constitutes good research but what is a good researcher? Within virtue ethics, different writers have identified differing sets of virtues that enable people to flourish. Carey and Green (2013) argue that virtue ethics can be captured in the virtues of integrity, honesty, loyalty, wisdom and kindness. Pinar and Ayerbe (2017) identify virtues in terms of undertaking excellent research, highlighting the importance of honesty, compassion, self-effacement and prudence to close the gap between cognition of the good and the motivation to do good. In so doing, they recognise the need for virtues to go beyond technical competence.

It is difficult to argue against the view that researchers should aspire to be virtuous. However, as with the principle-based approaches, the question remains what one is to do when the virtues conflict, which virtue holds sway and why. Clifford (2013) also critiques this approach for its emphasis upon individualism and its negating of the impact of social forces on behaviours under the dominant narrative of neoliberalism. He also challenges virtue ethics for its tendency to focus on self-absorption and flourishing. This neglects that the flourishing of academic researchers may be different from that of service user co-researchers and research participants. This lack of criticality can be seen as problematic, and potentially leaves the virtuous social worker in danger of just accepting common sense views. As Everitt et al, (1992, p 22) wrote: 'Common sense constitutes predominant views in society. And in an unequal society divided by race, class, gender, sexuality, age, and able-bodiedness, these views will in themselves be imbued with discriminatory notions. Common sense views need to be analysed and deconstructed.'

Everitt et al (1992) remind us that research is not value free, it is political. In adopting a virtue-based ethical stance in response to social work research and what it means to be good, we also need to consider issues of power, the promotion of social justice and the reduction of inequalities within societies which are arguably now more unequal and unjust (Dorling, 2018).

Ethics of care

Carol Gilligan (1982) is often credited with developing ethics of care emphasising relationality, compassion and partial perspectives. Fenton (2016, p 70) claims that 'in essence, the ethics of care is about the person in the context of their relatedness to others'. The ethics of care critiques traditional liberal ethics, whether utilitarian, deontological or of virtue, in portraying individuals as if they were isolated individuals, neglecting the social. The ethics of care is an approach used in much feminist and participatory research where researchers may develop close relationships with their participants.

The ethics of care, with its focus on the morality of close relationships, can be problematic in research where a degree of social distance is desirable. Hugman (2010) notes that a researcher in a long-term participant-observation study should, from time to time, remind participants of their identity as a researcher so that they do not confuse the researcher as a work colleague or 'friend', thereby reintroducing a degree of social distance.

The ethics of care, though, speaks to the relationship between a principal researcher and their co-researchers. It is to be hoped that the relationship between the researcher and their co-researchers is one of a duty of care marked by reciprocity, compassion, attentiveness, responsiveness, responsibility and competence (Tronto, 1993).

Moral pluralism

From this analysis of the key ethical research frameworks, we are left to agree with Banks (2006, p 66) that 'none seems complete on its own'. One potential solution to this is 'moral pluralism'. This is not to claim that anything goes, but to suggest that there is no single over-arching ethical framework that subsumes all the others. Moral pluralism recognises that in every situation there may be competing values, each of which needs considering when making a decision to act. Moral pluralism is an approach in which 'the various factors in any given situation are weighed in terms of duties (including rights and responsibilities), utilitarian objectives, ideals (which could include religious values), caring for relationships, personal obligations and commitments (which could include ideas of virtue)' (Banks, 2006, p 67 as cited in Hugman, 2010, p159).

Moral pluralism allows us to address situations in which values cannot be simultaneously satisfied. In doing this, we are not making a claim for more formal processes for quantitative studies or an ethics of care approach for qualitative studies. Moral pluralism still requires research studies to address what is good in terms of rights, responsibilities and social justice. Also, we cannot forget that certain aspects of qualitative research can be identified beforehand, including issues of informed consent. Similarly, an ethics of care may be appropriate for quantitative approaches when dealing with topics such as marginalisation, exclusion, oppression or discrimination. Attentiveness, responsiveness, responsibility and competence are just as important in developing and interpreting questionnaire data as in qualitative studies (Hugman, 2010). Thus, with a pluralist perspective it can be seen that an ethics of care approach adds to the tools available to a researcher, and does not replace the other tools in the toolbox. In all of this it is clear that ethical research is a challenge, not a right. Husband's (1995, p 87) account of 'the morally active practitioner' is helpful for recognising that ethics is not reducible to routinised processes and that researchers cannot hide 'within professional ethical anaesthesia' but retain responsibility for their own decisions and actions.

Ethical considerations inhabit every phase of the research process. In order to examine this I am going to focus on the different stages of the research process, looking at ethical issues before the research begins, ethical issues during the research process and ethical issues after the research has been completed.

Ethical issues before the research has begun

Involvement of service user co-researchers

Prior to involving service users as co-researchers, consideration should be given to who is to be involved and how they are to be involved and recruited. What data is to be given legitimacy? Does this include service-user knowledge? What or whose interests does the research serve? Is it just to help the researcher develop their career or is it aligned with service user co-researchers aspirations for change and/or social work's mission to promote human rights and social justice in solidarity with service users (IFSW, 2014)?

Most requests to involve service users in research are made after the research problem has been identified and the research funding secured. This perspective is increasingly being challenged, and Moulam et al (2020) have usefully distinguished between co-creation and co-production in research. In this they identify co-creation as 'activities where members of the research team worked together to create the project from the concept, writing the funding bid, the full research cycle and even through to evaluation' (Moulam et al, 2020, p 432).

This can be seen as an immersing of service user co-researchers within the research team where they are accepted as integral members from the beginning to the end. As such, they are entitled to all the benefits of being a team member, including being heard and contributing ideas and their skills for the successful achievement of the project. Co-production, on the other hand, refers to ad hoc or specific activities which service user co-researchers may undertake post-research-award. These can either be paid or voluntary roles to help develop research tools, engage in data collection and/or analysis or become a member of advisory meetings. The important distinction here is between being involved in developing and conducting the research from the initial idea to completion and joining a research team post-award that the service user co-researcher had not contributed to beforehand.

While co-creation would be the gold standard, it may not always be possible or desirable. Service-user involvement in research teams remains mostly co-production. However, this does not mean it is not valuable for the research team, the research itself or the service users involved. Research councils and funding bodies are increasingly asking for research bids to evidence how service users have been involved in developing bids, and this is to be commended, but it is not always followed up with the resources to support this to happen.

Research governance and research ethics committees

Once funding has been secured for a research project, and before any data can be collected, ethical approval will be required. Research ethics review committees represent a form of procedural ethics whereby the completion of the form(s) is a hurdle that must be surmounted before the research can commence. Carey (2019, p 150) has claimed that the process of procedural ethics review is now so complicated that researchers are 'avoiding important topics of investigation, co-production or methodologies identified as sensitive or too difficult to navigate through over-zealous committees'. Furedi (2002) goes even further and suggests that such paternally protective committees act to protect risk adverse institutions, using ethics as the new managerial ideology controlling which types of research are acceptable.

Guillemin and Gillam (2004), like many other qualitative researchers, accept that research ethics approval is an onerous task in which they complete the form(s) diligently using the language the committee wants to hear even though all the questions may be irrelevant to their research. Research ethics committees have an anticipatory aspect whereby researchers are expected to consider ethical issues that might arise and how those risks might be mitigated. Researchers are also required to seek regulatory approval for their actions to mitigate risks and protect their research subjects from harm, including secure data storage, breaches of confidentiality and anonymity (although, depending on the subject matter, confidentiality may not be sacrosanct). If issues of child or adult abuse should be identified, this may require details being passed onto safeguarding agencies. Such possibilities should be included within the informed consent form along with details of how such issues will be managed (McLaughlin, 2018).

Gaining ethical approval has, in many cases, become an end in itself rather than part of an ongoing ethical process. It can never be certain that all potential ethical risks will, or could be, identified prior to any research commencing (Mclaughlin, 2009). Gaining ethical approval from a research ethics committee is not the same as acting ethically. Acting ethically begins when choosing the topic for research and extends to the end of the research project and potentially beyond. This is why we need to adopt the perspective of the morally active researcher, and in research projects this will concern research subjects and co-researchers as well.

I would argue that informed consent is not only a matter for research participants but also for service user co-researchers, especially when they are new to research. When asking service users to be involved as co-researchers, it is important that they are aware of what roles and tasks they are being expected to fulfil. This should be discussed early on in the research process and needs to be revisited as the research develops and progresses through the different stage of the process. This requires an attitude of informing for research. Service user co-researchers should have the opportunity to opt in or out at each stage without prejudice. While it is hoped that most will stay engaged, it does make sense to recruit more service user co-researchers than might initially be considered necessary.

Which service users get asked to be involved?

It is important to ask which service users get asked to be part of a research team. This may be constricted by the nature of the research; for example, research on those leaving care services should include care leavers. However, which care leavers should be included? In the first instance, there is a need to develop equitable access to opportunities for involvement. To be able to do this, an accessible job description should be developed outlining the tasks of the co-researchers and the demands on their time the role will require. This should be provided in accessible English and with picture communication systems, tactile systems, braille or sign language depending on the co-researchers being recruited. It should then be discussed to ensure the service user co-researcher has the opportunity to ask questions or request any changes before being asked if they wish to be part of the team.

There is also a risk that principal investigators will recruit those who represent the acceptable face of a given service-user group, or the 'usual suspects'. This is an abuse of power and unethical. Researchers need to have clear criteria to decide who should become a member of a research team and who should not. Exclusion of people should be based on the needs of the research project and not on any unconscious biases or prejudices.

Service user co-researchers are not clients

It may sound obvious, but social work researchers are not there to provide counselling or therapy to service user co-researchers. The researcher may also be a registered social worker, however, their relationship with service user co-researchers is not one of social worker and client. Research has similarities to social work (McLaughlin, 2012), but it is not social work. While both are based on the importance of relationships, it is imperative that social worker researchers do not slip into a practice-type relationship. Principal investigators have a duty of care, as do all the members of the research team. If a service user applies to be a co-researcher and it is clear they are racist and view women as sex objects, it would not be acceptable to recruit them. This is different from social work practice, in which the social worker would be expected to continue to work with them, challenging such unacceptable attitudes.

Part of the duty of care suggests that if service user co-researchers are having difficulties and problems, a principal investigator should listen to them. If it is a general issue that the principal investigator can resolves as they would do for any other member of the team, they should do. Clearly, it is not up to them to resolve a social work issue but to signpost or even refer the co-researcher to where help can be accessed.

Service user co-researcher ground rules, remuneration and informed consent

The involvement of service users as co-researchers is not without its difficulties. This may be due to the competing interests of researchers and service users and the different agendas and expectations that each of them bring to the research project. 'Membership of different social divisions, values, beliefs and ethical positions may cloud understanding of the 'others' [sic] position in the relationship' (Burke and Newman, 2020, p 57). This suggests the need to develop safe spaces in order to build meaningful relationships and an awareness and acknowledgement of power differentials, as well as the need to reflect on personal and social histories. This should also include the development of ground rules as to how the team will work together, including for resolving ethical issues. These should include expectations as to how the team will listen to each other's perspectives, valuing experiential and research knowledge and clarifying how disputes will be resolved. Natland (2020) provides an example of conflicts in collaborative research and how they can be transformed into productive action.

This information should also identify what expenses and remuneration the co-researchers will receive for their involvement and how it will be paid. Expenses should preferably be paid upfront or at a meeting. It is not ethical that service user co-researchers should be out of pocket in engaging in a research project when the other members are being paid.

This leads onto the contested question of whether service user co-researchers should be paid for their time and expertise. Steel (2006, p 5) has usefully identified key reasons why they should be paid, which include:

- as an incentive to engage in a research project;
- to allow a broader range of people to be involved;
- to support equity of power in research relationships;
- to support inclusion by offering payments those who are usually excluded so that they may be able to get involved in research;
- to allow more effective and equitable involvement of people who use services by easing financial constraints; and
- to reduce barriers to involvement.

Steel (2006, p 5) goes on to say that 'people who use services should be paid for their time and expertise to a level consistent with the other members of the research team.' If they are being asked to act as research assistants, they should be paid as such. However, it should be remembered that once any person is paid for a task, this will subtly change the relationship. This is particularly the case when one co-researcher may feel another one is not 'pulling their weight', and can lead to dissatisfaction in the team.

Alongside this we need to consider employment law, national insurance, tax and in particular whether state allowances or benefits may be affected by service user co-researcher payment. Turner and Beresford (2005) identify a tension between the government's desire that citizens should get involved within their communities and the day-to-day operations of the state's benefits system. INVOLVE (2010), who are funded by the National Institute for Health Research in England, provide guidance for researchers on payment for active involvement in research while also considering the impact on service user co-researchers' welfare benefits. In some situations, service users may not wish to be paid beyond a certain point in order to protect their benefits.

Research ethics committees have the responsibility to veto applications when the committee ascertain that the application is unethical. One reason for doing so is when the researcher or research team have not evidenced the skills or competence to undertake the research (Haigh, 2007). It is thus important that service user co-researchers are provided with the training and development opportunities to understand the nature of the research project and to develop the necessary skills that they are being recruited to perform. It is also important that if individual members do not evidence these skills, they should not be asked to undertake tasks where such skills are required. It would be unethical to expose research participants to any researcher who was not competent. This may require some difficult conversations, but in such situations the principal researcher should also consider whether there are other roles within the service user co-researcher's competence that would benefit the research.

Ethical issues during the research

It is this part of the research process in which service user co-researchers are likely to have their closest contact with those who are being researched while interviewing or analysing research data. This is a stage in which some of the issues anticipated in the application for research ethics approval may occur, but it is also likely to be a stage in which unanticipated ethical challenges will occur.

Independent support

During the ethical approval process, it is likely that the principal investigator will have anticipated the importance of providing independent support to research respondents for whom the research questions may trigger powerful feelings. It is also possible that the situation may trigger such feelings among the research team, including service user co-researchers. It thus becomes important to consider who should take on this role. It should not be assumed that the principal researcher should do so, although they will have to use their judgement to ensure they do not blur boundaries and confuse roles. It is one thing to act as a colleague to someone who is distressed, but another thing to offer therapy. The principal investigator does, though, have the responsibility to ensure an appropriate support strategy is in place for the whole research team.

Confidentiality

It is important at this stage of the research to highlight again the importance of confidentiality. This is particularly important when the research respondents are sharing their personal stories and perspectives with service user co-researchers. Research respondents have the right to expect that such information will remain anonymous and confidential unless there are safeguarding issues or serious crime concerns as mentioned previously.

This stage of the process can become very exciting as you begin to understand the nature of your research and its findings, and it becomes imperative to ensure that service user co-researchers and other research team members do not start sharing the personal details or research responses in social situations. While the desire to do so is totally understandable, it is unethical and could lead to ridicule or harm to the research respondent, breaching the non-maleficencerequirement of Butler's (2002) code of ethics for social work researchers. Confidentiality may also refer to carers, professionals or parents who wish to know what has been happening in the research. If the co-researcher is unable to maintain the anonymity and confidentiality of the research respondents or fellow co-researchers, they may need to be asked to leave the research team.

Ethical issues following the collection and analysis of the research data

Authorship

Butler (2002, p 247) argues that, ethically, all publications from a research project 'should properly and in their proportion acknowledge the part played by all the participants'. While we can all agree with this general statement, it becomes trickier to identify what is meant by 'properly and in proportion' and who decides. Joint authorship might mean that all those acknowledged have taken an equal part in shaping the project, collecting and analysing the data and writing the report. Alternatively, different members of the research team may have led or undertaken different tasks of equal worth to complete the project successfully. Importantly, it needs to be remembered that volume and quality are not necessarily the same thing. It is more ethical that all members of the research team should be acknowledged. To leave someone off because they are a service user co-researcher is unethical and is likely to be demotivating for the future.

Having decided to include everyone, how do you decide whose name goes first? If it is clear that one or two members of the research team have done most of the work, their names should come first. This is easier to say than to obtain agreement on. In situations where this is a lack of agreement, alphabetical order maybe easiest, but if two reports are being produced, the second may consider starting from the back of the alphabet.

It is also worth considering when identifying service user co-researchers whether they would like their full name, a pseudonym or a nickname to identify them. This is not as frivolous as it first sounds. Many of the areas addressed by social work research cover sensitive research areas like domestic violence, sexual abuse or dementia. Service user co-researchers may not wish to be identified as people who have experienced domestic violence, suffered sexual abuse or lived with dementia. Having their full name on the research report or subsequent articles could run the risk of alerting others to their service-user status. Once reports or articles are in the public domain, authors have no control over who has access to them. There is no guarantee how they will be received. Service user co-researchers may experience hurt or be embarrassed by what others may say about them or the research findings.

As mentioned before, this is another example of informing for consent, whereby the principal investigator should discuss with the service user co-researchers the risks and opportunities of having their full names on the report and other publications, agreeing a way forward.

Endings

Service user co-researchers are likely to have expended a lot of their energy and time in contributing to a successful research project. It is hoped that they will have enjoyed the experience, although it may also have been frustrating! It is anticipated that they will have learned a lot from the experience, as will the traditional researchers. It is thus essential that this is acknowledged and celebrated: 'It is important to mark the end of a research project properly to allow the members to celebrate the past, their new relationships and to be able to move onto the future' (McLaughlin, 2009, p 62). This may also include some form of celebration and the awarding of certificates to the research team outlining the areas in which they contributed to the research. In my experience, most service user-co-researchers want to be involved in another research project. While this may not be difficult for lead researchers, it is likely to be so for service user co-researchers, and consideration should be given as to whether this may be possible or not.

Conclusion

This chapter has sought to identify the ethical issues in involving service users as co-researchers. It began by addressing four different ethical frameworks, but acknowledging that none of them were sufficient by themselves. As Gray and Gibbons (2007, p 220) noted in relation to teaching social work students ethics, 'There are no answers, only choices'. There are also no shortcuts to exercising good judgement.

This chapter considered the ethical challenges within a research project, and noted that this was not the same thing as gaining research ethics approval. While a potentially useful pre-research ethics exercise, it is experienced more as a form of control. This led onto the importance of informing for research and the need to adopt the stance of a morally active researcher. In relation to service users as co-researchers, we also discussed the type of ethical challenges that could occur at different points in the research process.

In so doing, it became clear that nearly all of these (except those relating to payments and welfare benefits) would equally be applicable to other research team members. Thus, while they may be highlighted by involving service users as co-researchers, I would strongly suggest these ethical challenges and the responses outlined are indicative of best practice for everyone!

References

Banks, S. (2006) *Ethics and Values in Social Work*, 3rd edn, Basingstoke: Palgrave Macmillan.

Banks, S. (2012) *Ethics and Values in Social Work*, 4th edn, Basingstoke: Palgrave Macmillan.

Banks, S. and Gallacher, A. (2009) *Ethics in Professional Life*, Basingstoke: Palgrave Macmillan.

Beauchamp, T.L. and Childress, J.F. (1979) *Principles of Biomedical Ethics*, 3rd edn, Oxford: Oxford University Press.

Brady, L.-M. (2020) 'Rhetoric to reality: challenges and opportunities for embedding young people's involvement in health research', in H. McLaughlin, P. Beresford, C. Cameron, H. Casey and J. Duffy (eds), *The Routledge Handbook of Service User Involvement in Human Services Research and Education*, Abingdon: Routledge, pp 454–67.

Brandt, A.M. (1978) *Racism, Research and the Tuskagee Syphillis Study (report no. 8)*, New York: Hastings Center.

Burke, B. and Newman, A. (2020) 'Ethical involvement of service users', in H. McLaughlin, P. Beresford, C. Cameron, H. Casey and J. Duffy (eds), *The Routledge Handbook of Service User Involvement in Human Services Research and Education*, Abingdon: Routledge, pp 54–64.

Butler, I. (2002) 'A code of ethics for social work and social work research', *British Journal of Social Work*, 32(2): 239–48.

Carey, M. (2019) 'The tyranny of ethics? Political challenges and tensions when applying ethical governance to qualitative social work research', *Ethics and Social Welfare*, 13(2): 150–62.

Carey, M. and Green, L. (2013) *Practical Social Work Ethics: Complex Dilemmas within Applied Social Care*, Farnham: Ashgate Publishing Ltd.

Clifford, D. (2013) 'Limitations of virtue ethics in the social professions', *Ethics and Social Welfare*, 8(1): 2–19.

Dorling, D. (2018) *Peak Inequality: Britain's Ticking Time Bomb*, Bristol: Policy Press.

Everitt, A., Hardiker, P., Littlewood, J. and Mullender, A. (1992) *Applied Research for Better Practice*, Basingstoke: Macmillan.

Furedi, F. (2002) 'Don't rock the research boat', *Times Higher Education Supplement*, 11 January, p 20.

Gilligan, C. (1982) *In a Different Voice*, Cambridge: Harvard University Press.

Gray, M. and Gibbons, J. (2007) 'There are no answers only choices: teaching ethical decision-making in social work', *Australian Social Work*, 60(2): 220–38.

Guillemin, M. and Gillam, L. (2004) 'Ethics, reflexivity, and "ethically important moments" in research', *Qualitative Inquiry*, 10(2): 261–80.

Haigh, C. (2007) 'Getting ethics approval', in T. Long and M. Johnson (eds), *Research Ethics in the Real World: Issues and Solutions for Health and Social Care*, London: Churchill Livingstone Elseiver, pp 123–38.

Hugman, R. (2010) 'Social work research and ethics', in I. Shaw, K. Briar-Lawson, J. Orme and R. Ruckdeschel (eds), *The Sage Handbook of Social Work Research*, London: Sage, pp 149–63.

Husband, C. (1995) 'The morally active practitioner and the ethics of anti-racist social work', in R. Hugman and D. Smith (eds), *Ethical Issues in Social Work*, London: Routledge, pp 84–103.

IFSW (2014) 'Statement of ethical principles', [online] 2 July, IFSW. Available from: http://ifsw.org/policies/statement-of-ethical-principles/

INVOLVE (2010) *Payment for Involvement: A Guide for Making Payments to Members of the Public Actively Involved in NHS, Public Health and Social Care Research*, Eastleigh: Involve. Available from: http://www.invo.org.uk/wp-content/uploads/documents/INVOLVEPayment%20Guiderev2012.pdf

Lovell-Norton, J., Poursanidou, K., Machin, K., Jeffreys, S. and Dale, H. (2020) 'How can we survive and thrive as survivor researchers?', in H. McLaughlin, P. Beresford, C. Cameron, H. Casey and J. Duffy (eds), *The Routledge Handbook of Service User Involvement in Human Services Research and Education*, Abingdon: Routledge, pp 403–19.

McIntyre, A. (1987) *After Virtue: A Study in Moral Theory*, 2nd edn, London: Duckworth.

McLaughlin, H. (2009) *Service User Research in Health and Social Care*, London: Sage.

McLaughlin, H. (2012) *Understanding Social Work Research*, London: Sage.

McLaughlin, H. Robbins, R., Bellamy, C. and Thackray, D. (2018) 'Adult social work and high-risk domestic violence cases', *Journal of Social Work*, 18(3): 288–306.

Moulam, L., Meredith, S., Whittle, H., Lynch, Y. and Murray, J. (2020) 'Augmented communication patient and public involvement in research: rhetoric and reality', in H. McLaughlin, P. Beresford, C. Cameron, H. Casey and J. Duffy (eds), *The Routledge Handbook of Service User Involvement in Human Services Research and Education*, Abingdon: Routledge, pp 427–40.

Natland, S. (2020) ' "Recently I felt like a service user again": conflicts in collaborative research, a case from Norway', in H. McLaughlin, P. Beresford, C. Cameron, H. Casey and J. Duffy (eds), *The Routledge Handbook of Service User Involvement in Human Services Research and Education*, Abingdon: Routledge, pp 467–77.

Nuremberg Code (1966) 'Nuremberg Code', *British Medical Journal*, 313: 1448. Available from: https://media.tghn.org/medialibrary/2011/04/BMJ_No_7070_Volume_313_The_Nuremberg_Code.pdf

Pinar, M.P. and Ayerbe, L. (2017) 'Value ethics of clinical research', *Perspectives in Clinical Research*, 8(2): 103–4. Available from: https://www.ncbi.nlm.nih.gov/pmc/articles/PMC5384398/

Redfern, M. (2001) *The Royal Liverpool Children's Inquiry Report*, London: HMSO.

Steel, R. (2006) *A Guide for Reimbursing and Paying Members of the Public Who Are Actively Involved in Research*, 2nd edn, Eastleigh: Involve.

Tronto, J. (1993) 'Creating caring institutions: politics, plurality and purpose', *Ethics and Social Welfare*, 4(2): 158–71.

Turner, M. and Beresford, P. (2005) *Contributing on Equal Terms: Service User Involvement and the Benefits System*, Bristol: SCIE/Policy Press.

19

Involving service users in social work education and research: is this structural social work?

Kristel Driessens and Vicky Lyssens-Danneboom

In the concluding chapter of the recently published *Routledge Handbook of Service User Involvement in Human Services Research and Education*, Cameron et al (2021) discuss whether or not service-user involvement makes a difference. They are very careful and modest in their answer: 'It can and should make a difference when it is carried out meaningfully and when it is allowed to have an impact' (Cameron et al, 2021, p 507). In this chapter, we take this discussion a bit further by connecting the collaborative models presented in this book to the social work theory of 'structural social work'. This theme was developed at a meeting in Antwerp where members of Bind-Kracht and representatives of the Mobilisation course discussed the values underlying their projects. We built on this discussion at the international meeting in Antwerp as part of our transnational European Social Fund project. During the group discussions, we discovered how the objectives, methods and results of our models are linked to the characteristics of structural social work. In other words we investigated whether cooperation with service users in education, research and policy is structural social work.

In order to answer this question in a well-founded way, we dispose the core elements of structural social work and link them to the examples and conclusions of the chapters in this book. But first we start with a brief description of our view on structural social work. Structural social work is grounded in critical social theories and is related to critical and radical social work. It emphasises emancipation and social justice and challenges the dominant social and economic structures and excluding societal processes like colonialism, capitalism, racism, heterosexism and ageism. This approach focusses on how these structures and mechanisms are the root causes of social problems and produce and reinforce oppression. This view does not ignore personal issues or individual difficulties because it also looks at human agency. Individual and structural changes are addressed at the same time because they are interrelated and influence each other. Based on the values of freedom, humanitarianism, collectivism, equality, self-determination and participation, social transformation is envisaged. Two objectives are leading: alleviating the negative effects of an exploitative and alienating social order on individuals and transforming society. In this chapter, we look for the practice of structural social work (and other radical approaches) in the models for cooperation with experts by experience. We systematically discuss four core elements of structural social work, as elaborated by Murray and Hick (2013), and analyse how these are applied in the collaboration models described in education and research. The core elements are:

- critical analyses and problematisation of unjust social, political and economic relations;
- the issue of power and forms of oppression;
- dialectical analyses of the relationship between human agency and social structures; and
- the commitment to social transformation.

Critical analyses and problematisation of unjust social, political and economic relations

Structural social work highlights issues of power and inequality. Rights, resources and rewards are allocated differently according to gender, class and race. Social, economic and political injustices suffered by different groups are critically examined to reveal how they can be dismantled.

This approach also focuses on 'materialisation'. Structural social work understands the problems of individuals as grounded in their relationship to the distribution of material resources. It takes into account the survival needs of clients, which explains the limits of self-help, mutual aid or counselling when there is no redistribution of power and resources. Thoughts, feelings and behaviour are always linked to material circumstances, and it is important to emphasise the material foundations of seemingly personal issues. It is crucial to pay attention to the material needs of the individual (including income, housing, food, necessities) and to understand that economic inequality produces differentiated access to services such as childcare, legal representation and healthcare, and to resources, including time. Facilitating access to resources, reducing barriers to access and redistributing resources are objectives of structural social work. For education, this means raising awareness in these areas.

Meaningful cooperation with service users in education and research requires attention to be paid to these topics. In all models where students enter into dialogue with service users, it becomes clear that the living situation of service users can block their chances of personal development.

Cecilia Heule, Markus Knutagård and Arne Kristiansen (Chapter 2) indicate in their chapter on the Mobilisation course that their classes focus on the community rather than on individual problems. The theoretical framework they offer students includes theories about different social structures and mechanisms, such as exclusion and inclusion.

With regard to tandem cooperation in education (Chapter 4), the authors indicate that the lectures in which service users participate focus on analyses of economic and social inequalities in society. In the Flemish universities of applied sciences which are involved in the cases described, the service users are all (certified) experts by experience in poverty and social work. They can illustrate how processes of social exclusion in different domains influence their lives and their chances of personal development. In training courses, experts by experience and students can compare their living situations, access to resources and the consequences of social and economic inequalities for them.

Also, in other collaborative models in which students enter into dialogue with service users, such as in the living libraries, during supervision by service users, in the joint workshops or through the inspiring conversations, these are topics that clarify the causes of social problems and the impact of these social structures on their individual lives. For meaningful cooperation, it is important that lecturers initiate or monitor these themes in order to address them and provide sufficient background information to feed the discussions.

A focus on power: multiple intersecting forms of oppression produced and reinforced by structures

Structural social work challenges discrimination and oppression. It seeks to uncover how contemporary social structures create structural relations of inequality, reducing access to opportunities, resources and power for certain groups, resulting in experiences of oppression in different domains. These processes affect individuals, groups and communities, and can lead to internalised oppression and the acceptance by those affected of their exploited position (Moreau, 1990; Mullaly, 2007). Producing an awareness of oppression at interconnected structural, cultural and personal levels is an important element of structural social work. In social work education it is stimulated by awareness and critical self-reflection, in which engaged students confront hidden beliefs and power issues and become more aware of processes of labelling.

Structural social work is about unmasking oppressive structures and can therefore be linked to anti-oppressive social work, in which a social worker questions his or her own actions regarding their oppressive character. To what extent do social workers consciously or unconsciously contribute to the reproduction of inequality and discrimination? How do social workers look at structural characteristics, such as ethnic background, religion and sexual preference? This micro-practice of social work critically examines the assumptions on the basis of which social workers act. This approach is based on radical humanism, which resolutely sides with vulnerable people. It is essential that awareness-raising processes are activated. Mullaly therefore links radical humanism to the critical pedagogy of Freire (1980), in which the concept of 'conscientisation', or awareness, is central (Mullally, 2007). It emphasises education and cultural action in groups, in which critical consciousness raising is developed. The aim of these awareness-raising processes is to understand how fundamentally unjust the reproduction of the balance of power is. There is also a clear link with critical social work, a theory based on the emancipating power that can emanate from the micro level. Fook (2003) focuses on critical reflection as a methodical tool in daily practice. Critical reflection by means of narrative approaches makes it possible to make one's own presuppositions explicit. It can bring to the surface the mechanisms of oppression that exist within society and that the social worker reproduces.

This core idea is present in all models of cooperation with service users. All models scrutinise and discuss the (unequal) balance of power, both in the training courses with students and in research, with the imbalance even more apparent in the structures of universities and the expectations of the academic world. Critical reflection about power issues seems a central focus in the cooperation with service users.

Floystad Kvammen and Wright Nielsen state that anti-oppressive practice and the willingness to change unequally distributed power are central to the involvement of service users in social work education, research and practice. However, not all types of involvement automatically contribute to this key idea. Meetings with service users during students' practical placements, for instance, or guest lectures in which service users tell their stories in front of a large classroom often unintendedly highlight and reinforce differences in power and status.

The Human Library method is used worldwide as an anti-oppressive tool, bringing together representatives of different minorities in society who voluntarily share their life stories and experiences to help others overcome their prejudices. The core of this method is an active dialogue based on mutual respect. Sen, Nylund, Hayward, Pardasani, Rivera and Kaila (Chapter 7) describe how they employ the Living Book approach as a tool for social work students to enable them to identify their own unconscious biases, reflect on individual blind spots and develop competence to become better professionals working with people from different social and cultural backgrounds. The Living Library model requires student 'readers' to make sense of the otherness embodied in the Living Books. To achieve deep learning by engaging with experiential knowledge, students explore how these narratives cohere with or challenge their own experiences of social work. They increase their understanding of how social work can be delivered and of how they can practice their professional strengths. The exchanges increase awareness of the different life experiences of people receiving social work services. The readers (most of them are bachelor-level students) found that the discussions with the Living Books raised human rights issues, that 'diversity was celebrated', but also that misunderstandings, prejudices and conflicting ideas were discussed. A few months after the living libraries, social work students indicated that these meetings were very meaningful, staying with them and influencing the way they deal with and interpret practice.

Cabiati and Levy (Chapter 9) analysed the reflections of students at the Catholic University of Milan on their personal meetings with experts by experience (EBE). Comparable to the living libraries, the meetings provide a safe space for dialogue and exchanges, removing barriers between the EBE and the students and bringing the students to share their own stories. The students reflected deeply on the similarities and differences in how they would behave or cope if they were in the experts' shoes. This led to their seeing the person first and not his or her disability or label, and to their respecting, valuing and being inspired by the uniqueness, courage and determination in the life experiences of the EBE. One student formulated it as follows: 'It is essential to put aside the presumption that we know what people want and need in their life.' This process was acknowledged as being unsettling, but also as being a source of deep learning.

Heidenreich and Laging (Chapter 10) also believe that contact with service users contributes to the development of interpersonal skills that are highly relevant to social work, but stress the importance of carefully considering ethical issues such as power imbalances. Their model of joint seminars is perceived by both students and service users as very meaningful and helpful. The seminars contribute to mutual respect and understanding, and enable much deeper learning for students with regard to both service users' lives and experiences and what it means to be a social professional.

The Mobilisation course also addresses the unequal roles and power relations in social work that the students often carry with them. The personal presentations are an important tool with which to problematise and transcend stereotypical roles in social work. Because all students (both the social work students and the commissioned students) have to personally introduce themselves, this exercise evens out the balance of power. The personal presentations stimulate relationship building between the students and contribute to mutual trust and equal cooperation. The method of co-teaching in tandem is based on similar principles. The lecturer and the service users act as role models for the students, demonstrating how to work together as equal partners.

At the beginning of the third-year social work training course, led by a tandem of a lecturer and an EBE, at the Karel de Grote University of Applied Sciences, both service users and students are asked to present their ecogram to each other. Here too, it is not a case of one-way traffic, with a service user telling their history, but of mutual exchange of personal narratives.

In this way, differences, similarities and the impact of the social context are analysed, and a deeper dialogue and real person-to-person connection are created. In all described cases of working in tandem, students were introduced to 'people living in another world' and were given the opportunity to feel the effects of exclusion and see how social services can lead to negative reinforcement or positive change. Although they often found it confronting, students indicated that they had to adjust their prejudices and gained more insight into the experiences and living conditions of the service users. They developed a view of service users as actors, as attentive parents, as people with talents and strengths.

Kaszyński and Maciejewska (Chapter 6) stress that a basic objective of their collaborative model is to change the stereotypical perception of mental illness and to create open (non-oppressive) spaces for dialogue that contribute to reducing the stigma associated with mental illness. They deliberately choose to organise the training led by the service user(s) outside the stigmatising institutional context. Instead, they created enabling niches at universities, in galleries or public administration offices. According to the authors, the yardstick for a real dialogue is that it involve all participants in the discussion – not only the service users referring to their experiences – and involve direct contact in order to change the stereotypical view of deep emotional problems.

During the classes, the focus is on the strengths of the service users rather than on analysing their weaknesses, and on health and recovery rather than on illness. The workshops led by recovering individuals not only provide participants with a lived insight into the nature of mental illness but also teach them that respect, patience, dialogue and the ability to listen are important and accessible therapeutic tools.

In research as well, co-working with service users challenges the existing hierarchy and power relations. With critical self-reflection, Natland describes her personal search during a co-writing process, the tensions and dilemmas as well as the opportunities she encountered. Natland's report shows that co-writing with service users is above all a complex balancing act: realising a fruitful and equal collaboration with the co-researchers based on trust and dialogue while at the same time taking the lead and exercising control in a respectful way. Especially in the co-writing of an academic article, the role of the formal researcher is that of a critical friend who provides support and ensures that the users' objectives are included and recognised, but who also takes a more distant and critical stance in order to meet academic expectations and standards. The inclusion of different substantive roles on the basis of equivalence requires extra care and attention.

Face-to-face contacts and real dialogue with service users allow students to experience that we are all human beings, with similar feelings and dreams. What differs are living conditions, accessible rights, resources and opportunities. Most authors write about deep learning, which provides insight into the structural relations of inequality and integrates by awareness raising and critical self-reflection, essential elements of structural social work.

Dialectical analyses: the relationship between human agency and social structures

Structural social work stimulates thinking in terms of relations. It understands the social position, oppression or privilege of individuals as relational, historical and contextual. These processes of oppression are constantly produced, reproduced or transformed by the cumulative choices and actions of individuals within particular social, cultural, political, economical and material conditions. Structural social work challenges the false separation between a person's professional and personal life (Murray and Hick, 2013) and pays attention to a multitude of perspectives, realities, positions and experiences. It enhances the recognition of the legitimacy of each person's voice within analyses of social issues and focuses on the discourse and social construction of knowledge (Mullaly, 2007). Structural social work stimulates mutual learning and opts for radical co-production because it believes that diverse knowledge and experiences contribute to a more complete understanding.

Many of these characteristics can also be found in the collaborative models presented in this book. In Chapter 3, Helen Casey and Peter Beresford report on equal participation and transformative learning in gap-mending projects in social work education in the UK. Co-produced learning influences change and generates new knowledge in order to involve young people in mending the gaps they have identified. By refraining from evident power relations, there is a different dialogue in which young people are put in charge of a mutual learning process by combining different kinds of knowledge.

When service users take on the role of supervisors, the reflection notes from the students show that the input of the supervisors allows the students to look at the situation from a new perspective. It encourages self-reflection and generates new knowledge. The students describe an open dialogue within the group that challenges them to discuss difficult topics based on their practical placement experiences. This open dialogue also seems possible in tandem cooperation and in the actual meetings that allow for a deeper conversation. The service user shows themself as a human being, and in doing so, invites the professional in education to do the same. Professional masks can be put aside, leading to a deeper, mutual learning.

At the University of Krakow, meetings give students an insight into the needs and capabilities of service users, as well as the suffering they can endure, not so much as 'clients', 'patients' or 'invalids' but as people. Service users are seen as people worth discovering and learning from. The training participants also point out the strengths of people with illnesses, including their reflectivity, critical faculties and wisdom. Participants declare that the experience of meeting and dialogue has changed their one-dimensional perspective on people with illnesses.

The Living Library also generates a mutual learning experience for both the user-books and the student-readers. For students, the stories narrated by the Living Books are often their first encounter with experiential knowledge. By being touched and experiencing involvement in and affection for a unique personal story, students feel encouraged and motivated to look for more experiential knowledge. The same happens with co-teaching in tandem in educational programmes: the organised conversations between experts by experience and students, when framed in reciprocal, trusting and engaging relationships, are stimulating and impactful for all involved.

Commitment to social transformation

Structural social work leads also to action based on the conviction that social and political change begins within the social relations of people's everyday lives. Change is constant, gradual, incremental and cumulative and is the result of unity and the struggle of opposites. Tensions or contradictions can become the basis for social change. Social workers can give oppressed groups access to knowledge and state power, thereby using conflicting relations to contribute to social change. Such an awareness can become an empowering basis for transformed, non oppressive relationships and solidarity in search of social justice (Carniol, 2005). In the words of Freire, 'Individuals learn together how to build the future – which is not something given to be received by people but is rather something to be created by them' (Freire, 1970, in Thompson, 2006, p 105). These collective approaches and responses to social issues are also often the result of cooperation with services users in education, research or practice. We can distinguish four types of social change in the cooperation models presented in this book: the increasing power of the service user in the relationship with the lecturer/student or social worker; the defence of the service user; their empowerment through personal change; and social activism leading to political change.

Specific to the models of cooperation is the quest for more egalitarian and democratic relations, leading to an increase in the power of the service users vis-à-vis the other actors involved. In the cooperation in tandem model, lecturers and EBE work together as colleagues in an equal relationship. These tandems are a model for the students. They work together in a position of solidarity, make agreements transparent and share the rationale and responsibilities.

The initiators of the Mobilisation course indicate that the prejudices between groups can be reduced if the groups can interact on an equal footing, that is, if they:

- have an equal status during the interaction;
- have common goals;
- can cooperate in a collaborative or co-productive way; and
- if the interaction between the groups receives sufficient institutional support.

Creating an enabling niche, a situation of equal opportunities for people who meet in an activity aimed at achieving gap-mending, is essential to success. Trust seems to be the basis for cooperation between social workers and service users and for creating solutions together. The participants in the forum theatre described in Chapter 16 also have strong decision-making power. They decide for themselves what they bring to the stage and how they want to shape it. In the supervision model, the role of service users is transformed from being that of objects to that of active agents by providing them with a base of knowledge and institutional recognition so that they can speak and act from a position acknowledged by other agents within social work education. In order to achieve such institutional recognition and anchoring of the knowledge and experiences of the service user, the educational programme in which the service users are involved should be part of the regular curriculum.

In line with radical humanism, a defence of service users is also a type of social action. Some models resolutely choose to give the most vulnerable groups (people in poverty, people without legal residence status, homeless people and so on) the opportunity to participate. In other models they fight for equal status or compensation for the involvement of service users. In the Mobilisation course, the service users become commission students, and as students they have a completely different agency and different expectations. All students have access to university facilities and those who complete the course receive 7,5 university credits.

This automatically results in empowerment through personal change. In critical social work, Fook and Dominelli argue for critical reflection on the unconscious maintenance of power relations through the language we use, and for a critical deconstruction of the social worker's discourse. It is precisely by speaking in a different way that possibilities for change arise.

Many users of services involved in the attributed models make the process for the empowerment of the reports possible. A number of the Living Books report that the project has strengthened their own identity. The organised discussions at the universities in Italy and Scotland showed that involvement can lead to an increase in the self-confidence of the experts through the experience of living independently, creating a new support network and developing new competencies. These results are achieved through involvement that highlights the strengths and capacities of the experts and by respecting and appreciating their contribution to the students' learning. At the University of Krakow, the users of services leading the lessons stressed the importance of contact with the participants in the training. When the feeling of uncertainty as to how they will be received gives way to satisfaction, with deep interest and openness, this helps them to recover and strengthen their sense of influence on reality.

The 'mend the gap' projects developed in the UK clearly support the empowerment of marginalised and discriminated groups in society. An empowering experience that put those parents in a leading role, prioritising their views, changed the way professionals learn from those they want to support. Students who participated in these programmes expressed much greater confidence in their practice and built positive relationships with parents. Recent research on the impact of the Mobilisation course showed that participation in the course strengthens both social work students and service-user students. Many of the service-user students continue on to study or work opportunities. Some of them are hired as guest teachers in other courses in the School of Social Work. Some continue to develop the project ideas they started with during their course. All students indicated that they have developed on a personal and professional level and that they have learned what they did not learn before or did not understand or imagine possible.

The radical social work approach states that social workers are best placed to stand beside clients and fight with them against the social institutions in which they are employed. These organisations must also be democratised for the benefit of both social workers and users. This means that structural social work develops practices of individual and collective resistance within the organisations in which it operates and within the broader social context. Radical humanism also states that social transformation is only possible through the personal transformation of users and social workers. Through this personal transformation, excluded groups break through the 'culture of silence', the learned attitude that vulnerable citizens do not dare to express their own opinions. The identification of common concerns and the linking of seemingly separate struggles through analysis and collective action can lead to a broader struggle for justice within interrelated personal, interpersonal, community-based, political and institutional spaces through a reflexive, collaborative and context-specific approach.

The models described also provide some illustrations of this kind of social activism and political change. In Poland, a group of students, social therapists and academic staff decided to form a civic organisation called the Institute of Social Therapy and Education – Association, which took care of a substantial amount of the training course content in Krakow's universities and prepared a support model that would significantly increase the opportunities for students with mental disorders to obtain university degrees and also to find and keep jobs.

In Finland, the Human Library event was planned and carried out by students, in collaboration with service users, teachers, staff members, volunteers and professionals from various organisations in Helsinki. One of the aims of the students was to develop tools with which to teach anti-oppressive working methods in social work and raise awareness of people with experience of services from different backgrounds. The Living Library at Diak was undertaken through a participatory approach involving the human books at every stage of its implementation.

At the University of Applied Sciences in Amsterdam and the University of Suffolk, students and service users organised a conference together. In Suffolk, the service-user forum, a group of service users interested in public sector education who meet at the university, is in charge. Besides planning the conference, they are also involved in other activities within the university, such as recruiting and selecting students, designing courses and curricula, attending meetings and talking to students about their experiences. Service users involved in the forum do this because they find it important that students hear their stories and understand how they feel. It also gives them a positive sense of self-esteem. This co-creation with service users requires lecturers who are not afraid of uncertain working conditions. A similar group is the Social Work Inclusion Group (SWIG) at the University of Portsmouth. Service-user/carer involvement in the social work programmes has the central aim of developing creative educational artefacts with which to engage with students in a critical and empowering way. The key elements of co-production are the promotion of people's strengths, reciprocity and the idea of people as change agents. Based on the critical theoretical work of Foucault and Giddens on power and the work of Freire, the initiators wanted to create a radical practice based on a contribution to fight discrimination and oppression and the development of new cooperative social relationships. They were inspired by Freire's idea of 'conscientisation', the notion that when a person becomes aware of how their oppression is determined, they develop the ability to take action to change their situation (Freire, 1972). It is a process by which people not only become aware but also act on the basis of that awareness with a focus on creativity.

In the 'user as supervisor' model, the goals are more modest. The authors, Mette Fløystad Kvammen and Tabitha Wright Nielsen, indicate that, due to the inequality of power, which structures positions and relations in the field of social work, some dilemmas of power relations cannot be resolved, but that by recognising them it is possible to work with them and change some of the conditions that affect them. At the School of Social work of Lund University and the University of Agder, the initiators of the cooperation model focused on organisational frameworks, equal working conditions and the inclusion of service users' knowledge in the curriculum. In doing so, they contributed to the recognition of service users' knowledge as equivalent to the academic knowledge presented by teachers in social work education or by the professional social workers who supervise the students.

Wilken and colleagues presented the model of a community of development (CoD), a model that combines learning, research and development. It is a learning community in which service users participate as co-researchers and co-designers. As students often take part in this group, it is also a way to learn from the experiences of service users. In this way it provides a rich learning environment in which to share and develop professional knowledge and improve professional practice. Beresford and Degerickx conclude in their analyses of historical cases that the transition to a more participatory approach in policymaking is and remains a work in progress rather than an easily achievable goal and an everyday reality. In the ongoing struggle, the democratic potential is encapsulated but not guaranteed at all.

Conclusion

Cooperation with service users in education, research and policymaking always has the intention of working according to a structural social work approach, but it is not self-evident how to put this into practice. Continuous alertness and reflection on structurally embedded power relations is necessary. But with strongly committed researchers and lecturers, supporting institutions that want to put solidarity, equality and participation into practice, and with creative service users, much is possible. Service-user involvement can focus on critical analyses and the problematisation of unjust social, political and economic relations, on power and multiple intersecting forms of oppression produced and reinforced by structures. It can provide dialectical analyses, with a focus on the relationship between human agency and social structures and on deep mutual learning in practice. And it can develop a commitment to social transformation. The contributors to this book have described many inspiring examples of collaborative models in education, research and practice that illustrate this.

In the recently developed *Global Standards of Social Work Education and Training* (1 August 2020), the International Federation of Social Workers

(IFSW) and the International Association of Schools of Social Work (IASSW) state with regard to service-user involvement that

> 'schools *must*:
>
> a. incorporate the rights, views and interests of Service Users and broader communities served in its operations, including curriculum development, implementation and delivery.
> b. develop a proactive strategy towards facilitating Service User involvement in all aspects of design, planning and delivery of study programmes.
> c. ensure reasonable adjustments are made in order to support the involvement of Service Users.'

These schools also have to aspire to create opportunities for the personal and professional development of service users involved in study programmes. These global guidelines can structurally support the meaningful models of cooperation with service users presented in this book. We hope that this book can inspire many universities and colleges of applied sciences to implement more of these models in their practice, and that we can make a small contribution to the dissemination of these practices of structural social work.

References

Carniol, B. (2005) *Case Critical: Social Services and Social Justice in Canada*, Toronto: Between the Lines.

Dominelli, L. (2002) *Anti-Oppressive Social Work: Theory and Practice*, Houndsmill: Palgrave Macmillan.

Fook, J. (2003) *Social Work: A Critical Approach to Practice*, London: Sage.

Freire, P. (1980 1972?) *Pedagogiek van de onderdrukten* (Pedadogy of the oppressed), Baarn: In den Toren, Anthos-boeken.

IFSW and IASSW (2020) 'Global standards for social work education and training', IFSW, [online] 1 August. Available from: https://www.ifsw.org/global-standards-for-social-work-education-and-training/

McLaughlin, H., Beresford, P., Cameron, C., Casey, H. and Duffy, J. (2021) *The Routledge Handbook of Service User Involvement in Human Services Research and Education*, Abingdon: Routledge.

Moreau, M.J. (1990) 'Empowerment through advocacy and consciousness-raising: implications of a structural approach to social work', *Journal of Sociology and Social Welfare*, 17(2): 53–67.

Mullaly, R. (2007) *The New Structural Social Work*, Ontario: Oxford University Press.

Murray, K. and Hick, S.F. (2013) 'Structural social work', in M. Gray and S.A. Webb (eds), *Social Work Theories and Methods*, London: Sage, p 110.

Thompson, A.K. (2006) 'Direct action, pedagogy of the oppressed', in C. Frampton, G. Kinsman, A.K. Thompson and K. Tilleczak (eds), *Sociology for Changing the World: Social Movements/Social Research*, Halifax: Fernwood Publishing, pp 99–118.

Index

A

Abma, T.A. 133, 134, 136, 137, 138
abuse 31, 81, 183, 184, 187
access, barriers to 173, 225, 226
accommodation 28, 29, 32, 88
acting ethically 215
action research 147
active partners 121
Adams, R. 40, 170
addictions background 11, 110
advocacy 100, 152, 178, 201
African American men 210
Afzal, Nazir 89–90
agency 15, 58, 83, 117, 125, 224
 and structures 122, 230–1
Ahmed, S. 201
Alder Hey Hospital 210
Allianssi 76
Allport, G. 12, 15, 16, 74
Amsterdam University of Applied Science 40–1, 87–8, 92–3, 184, 187, 234
Andreassen, T.A. 51, 57, 58
Andrieessen, D. 147
Anghel, R. 2, 118
anorexia 65
anti-oppressive practices 49, 75, 80, 100, 226, 231
anti-poverty policies 170, 175, 179, 205
Antwerp 184, 190, 191, 199
Archer, A. 160, 166
Arendt, Hannah 65
Arnstein, S.R. 74, 75, 104
Askheim, O.P. 12, 26, 55, 97, 110, 135, 145
Asperger syndrome 65
asylum seekers 28, 30, 32, 77, 81
 and education 31
ATD Fourth World 175
austerity 93, 120, 205
Austin, M. 162
authorship of research 219–20
autonomy 210
Ayerbe, L. 211

B

Baby P 89
Baines, D. 74
Baistow, K. 179
BAME service users 23
Banks, S. 136, 139, 210, 211, 212
barriers 26, 70, 74, 118, 173, 217, 225, 228

Bartosch, U. 109
Bates, P. 201
BBC 89
Beauchamp, T.L. 210
Belgium 145, 170, 174–5, 191, 194, 199
 anti-poverty policies 35–6
 BZN Atlas 184, 188
 General Report on Poverty 178, 179
belief systems 74, 81
Bell, J. 97
belonging, sense of 37
beneficence 210
Benoit, C. 134, 136
Beresford, P. 2, 38, 49, 124, 205, 230
 on 'mending the gaps' 23, 25, 26, 27
 on poverty 36
 on remuneration 51, 217
 on service users 57, 120, 147, 200
 on tokenism 170
Biene, M. 154
Biesta, G. 169
Bilge, S. 117
Bind-Kracht 39, 224
biographical narratives 65, 86
Birmingham University 33
birthdays 29
Blackhall, A. 86
Bliksvaer, T. 161
Boal, Augusto 188
Boddy, J. 123
Boer, M. 154
Boler, M. 98
Boote, J. 134
boundaries 19, 89, 118, 185, 205, 218
 boundary-setting 15
Bourdieu, P. 50, 55
Bouwes, T. 35
Boxall, K. 25, 26, 38
Bradbury, H. 147
Brady, L.-M. 209
brain damage 148
Brandsen, T. 17
Branfield, F. 23, 24
Breeze, J. 93
Brett, J. 133
Brewer, M.B. 19
Brock, K. 170
Broerse, J.E.W. 133
Brouwer, H. 148
Brown, R. 19
Brussels 184
budgets *see* funding
Burke, B. 216
Butler, I. 210, 219

C

Cabiati, E. 97, 98, 99, 100, 105, 228
Cameron, H. 224
Campbell, J. 174
Canvin, K. 134, 136, 140
carers *see* service users
Carey, M. 211, 214
Carniol, B. 231
Carr, S. 49, 170, 200
Case, A.D. 134, 135
Casey, H. 230
Casman, M.T. 37
Cassell, P. 122
categorisation 12, 19
Catholic University of Leuven 191
Catholic University of Milan, Italy 98, 99, 228
Central Council for Education and Training in Social Work (CCSTSW) 24
challenges 2, 5, 18, 67, 86, 99, 226
  ethical issues 218, 220
  life 1, 114, 115
  of time and economy 135–6
change 121, 123, 229, 231
  agents 118, 234
  drivers of 183, 194
  meaningful 122, 123
  social 194, 231
Chávez, V. 139
Chiapparini, E. 1, 27
Child Poverty Action Group, UK 175
children 24, 26, 28, 29, 31
  child abuse 183, 184, 187
  childcare 28, 225
  child sexual exploitation 89
  deaths of 89
  and education 31
  separated from 27, 30
Children Act 1989 31
Childress, J.E. 210
choice, lack of 77
Citizenne Vormingplus 184, 190
citizen participation 74
Clews, J. 202, 204, 205
Client Speaks, The 23
Clifford, D. 211
Clifford, E. 179
Climbié, Victoria 89
co-creation 94, 213–14, 234
coercion 70
collaboration 148, 152, 160, 163, 225, 229
  collaborative models 3, 38–9, 226, 230
  collaborative relationships 136–7, 139
  collaborative research 158–9, 166, 216
  and structural social work 224
collective learning 149
commission students 13, 15, 17, 228, 232
common goals 12, 15, 16, 232
common interests 124
communication 27, 32, 39, 67, 88, 147, 215
  as a dialogue 158
  effective 105
  skills 45, 98, 165
'communicative action' 159
community 12, 18, 24, 30, 226
  community care 24
  community of development 145–50, 235
    better practice 148–9
    challenges and opportunities 152–4
    involvement 149–50
    value of 151–2
  community of practice 146
compassion 212
conferences 234
  organised with service users 85–90
  speaking at 90–1
confidence 204
confidentiality 210, 218
conflicts, managing 139
confrontation and participation 177
consciousness 123
  conscientisation 227, 234
  dominated 123–4
consent 209, 210, 216
consultation and participation 177
consumerist approach 205
continuity 44
conversations, inspiring 97–8
Cooper, H. 93
cooperation 15, 67, 70, 122, 192, 235
  with service users 61–5
  in tandem 44, 226–30
co-production 17–18, 118, 133, 167, 213–14, 230
  co-produced learning 26
  of creative educational activities 117, 119
  and established research 134
  of knowledge 158–9, 161–3
  of research 140
Corage Baden, A. 135, 136
co-research 133–40, 229, 235
  building relationships 136, 139–40
  challenges 134
  consultative model of co-research 135
  and ethical issues 209, 215–18
  expectations from research 136, 139
  training and support 137–8
Cornwall, A. 135, 170
Corrigan, P.W. 105
Cossar, J. 136
Costello, J. 86
co-teaching 35, 41, 231
Council of Europe 73, 76
Couture, S.M. 61
COVID-19 95

co-writing 159–60, 229
  for a science journal 163–7
creativity, role of 123, 124–5, 185, 234
  artefacts 234
  creative educational activities 117, 119–20
  creative techniques 194
  in the Netherlands 186–92
critical abilities 120
critical pedagogy 227
Croft, S. 2, 23, 57, 206
cross-border cooperation 18
cultural issues
  clashes 29
  culturally acceptable 31
  groups 74
  traditions 29, 80
Curtis, D. 26
cuts 24
  in funding 45, 179, 205

D

Dalen, H. 162, 165
dance 119
Dankers, T. 150
data 6, 27, 39, 67, 134, 158, 213
Davidio J. 19
Dean, H. 175, 178
debate day 120
debriefing 94
decategorisation 19
decision-making 232
deconstruction / reconstruction 19–20
Degerickx, H. 175, 178, 235
De Link 35, 37
democracy 49, 170, 177, 231
Den Hollander, D. 146
Denmark 73
deontological approach 210–11, 212
Department of Health (UK) 24
dependency 171, 172
depression 64
deprivation 171
Desain, L. 202
design research 147
Diaconia University of Applied Sciences 79–81
Diak 73, 234
dialogue 66, 68, 75, 149, 205
  and co-writing 165
  dialogical work 62
  open 230
Dierckx, D. 35, 36
dilemmas 19, 67
  and structural inequality 55–8
Dill, K. 1
disabilities 28, 41, 97, 118
  disability, fundamental principles of 171–4, 228

disabled people's movement 170, 171–4, 179, 205
Disability Alliance 171–2
Disability Discrimination Act 1995 118
discrimination 11, 122, 145, 171, 173, 233
disempowered groups 171
diversity 19, 25, 26, 28, 81, 145, 150, 228
  diverse students 80, 184
  of experts 45
  respecting 32
Dix, H. 93
doctors 70
domestic violence 183, 189–90
Dominelli, L. 232
Drakeford, M. 120, 123
drama *see* theatre
Driessen, E. 41
Driessens, K. 35, 37, 39, 98, 105, 145
drug abuse 11, 110
Duffy, J. 97, 98, 106
Dundee University 33, 98
Duran, B. 136
Dutch government policy 35–6
duty of care 212, 216
dyad working 64

E

economy 203–4
  economic inequality 225
  see also funding
education 30–1, 225, 227
  educational artefacts 234
  of service users 109–10
  systems 13
embodied knowledge 147
  embodied otherness 74, 76
empathy 6, 38, 62, 70, 123, 211
employment 11, 32, 171, 234
empowerment 1, 36–8, 115, 120, 161
  and co-producing knowledge 158
  of service users 61, 71, 109, 122, 231
enabling niches 11, 15–18, 174, 229, 232
England 26, 28, 76, 90
  learning English 31
Ens, A.H. 160
equality 4, 19, 33, 118, 173, 179, 235
  equal status 16–17, 149
  for Eritrean women 29
  and gap-mending 12
  gender inequality 190
  structural inequality 49–50, 55–8, 225–6
  unequal society 211–12
Equality Act 1995 118
Eriksson, L. 123
Eritrea 31
  Eritrean women 29
Esslingen University of Applied Sciences 110, 112, 115
ethical issues 2, 93, 100, 110, 220, 228

ethics of care 212, 213
  and research 209–10, 213–18, 218–20
  and service users 209, 215–18
  and social workers 32
Ethiopia 29
ethnicity 13, 23, 80, 227
Europe 73, 76
  European Anti-Poverty Network (EAPN) 175
  European Social Fund (ESF) 2, 39, 63, 224
  European Union 21
Everitt, A. 211
everyday lives 64, 139, 231
exclusion 18, 175, 190, 194, 213, 226
  definition of 36–40
  experience of 1, 145
experiential knowledge 36, 37–8, 97
  of disability 173
  as a driver of change 183–5, 194
experts by experience 36–8, 40–5, 88, 199, 228
  and CoD 152
  courage 105
  employment of 40
  long-term approach 206
  in Scotland and Italy 97–100, 104–6
  see also service users
expert speakers 117
eye level 110, 115

F

Facebook 115
facilitator of CoD 147–8, 154
fairy tales 161–2
families 27, 29
  family carers 97
  low-income 45
far-right party 175
Faulkner, A. 81, 134
Female Genital Mutilation Act 2003 30
feminist research 212
Ferguson, I. 125
fieldwork, preparation for 147, 200
films and videos 118, 120, 183, 186, 192, 193
finance *see* funding
Finkelstein, Vic 172
Finland 73, 80, 234
Fleming, J. 133, 139, 140
Folgheraiter, F. 100
Fook, J. 19, 122–3, 227, 232
Forbat, L. 137
foster care adolescents 110, 187
Foucault, M. 120–3, 234
Foulger, T.S. 166
fourth world movement, Belgium 170
Fox, J. 97
frame of reference 45

France, poverty report in 175
Francq, B. 35
Frankham, J. 133, 136, 139
freedom 224
  freeing the creative imagination 124
Freire, P. 122, 123, 188, 227, 231, 234
Fricker, M. 167
Frisby, R. 86, 90
frustration with research 136
Fundamental Principles of Disability 171, 179
funding 18, 24, 138, 185, 203–4
  conferences 92, 94
  cuts in funding 24, 45, 179, 205
  and mandatory involvement 135
  in Norway 160
  for research 167
  sponsorship 91
Furedi, F. 214

G

Gaertner, S. 19
Gallacher, A. 211
Gambrill, E. 105
gangs 90
gap-mending 37, 110, 145, 233
  concept 11–20
  power relations 49–52
  principles 12–14
  in social work education 23–8, 230
Gee, M. 99
Geelhoed, S. 153
General Report on Poverty 175–8
genuine involvement 202
Germany 109, 112
Ghent University 193
Gibbons, J. 220
Giddens, A. 122, 234
Gillam, I. 214
Gilligan, Carol 212
girls 30
Gjernes, T. 161
Goldstein, S. 133
good researcher 211
Goris, J. 35, 37
Goscha, R.J. 15
government policy *see* policy and policymaking
Gray, M. 219
Grech, S. 174
Green, L. 51, 53, 55, 211
Greenhalgh, T. 139
group work 17, 19, 99, 148
guest teachers 11–20, 117, 227, 233
Guillemin, M. 214
guilt 183
Gutman, C. 1

H

Haigh, C. 217

Hamalainen, J. 123
Hamburger, F. 109
Hancock, N. 133, 134, 137
harm, preventing 31
Harrison, K. 88, 93
Hatton, K. 117, 122, 123, 124, 125
Hayward, A. 227
healthcare 225
Healy, K. 11
Heaton, J. 133
Heidenreich, T. 109, 113, 228
Heizmann, H. 159
Helsingborg, Sweden 20
Helsinki 79, 234
Heron, J. 169
Herr, K. 139
Heule, C. 12, 20, 23, 43, 50, 51, 145, 226
Hewstone, M. 19
Hick, S.F. 225, 230
Hill, M. 26
Hill Collin, P. 117
Hoban, M. 124
Hodgson, P. 133, 134, 136, 140
holistic understanding 117, 201
homelessness 11, 20
Home Office 29, 32
homes, broken 86
Horne, M. 86
House of Lords 89
housing 29–30, 32, 88
Hubbard, G. 137
Hugman, R. 212, 213
human agency *see* agency
Human Library 227, 234
  see also Living library
human rights 28, 74, 76, 81, 170, 209, 213, 228
human tissue 210
Humphreys, C. 118
Husband, C. 213

I

identities 50, 76, 146, 233
  identity politics 178, 179
  multiple 117
immigration 23, 30
impacts from EBE encounters 104–5
In Care, Out of Trouble 89
inclusion 19, 71, 122, 124, 125, 145
  and participation 178
income, low 171–2, 179
independent living 70, 88, 98
  support for 173–4
independent support 218
individualisation of experience 55–6, 58
indoctrination 123
inequalities 19, 74, 211–12, 225, 226, 235
  see also equality
informal conversations 29, 32

informed consent 209, 210, 216
inspiring conversations 226
institutions 122, 125
  institutional support 12, 15, 18–19, 232
integration 31
integrative model 135
intellectual disabilities 41, 145, 150, 152
internalised oppression 226
International Association of Schools of Social Work (IASSW) 49, 145, 235, 236
International Federation of Social Workers (IFSW) 38, 145, 213, 235, 236
internships 54, 110
interpersonal skills 110, 228
interventions 52, 148
Investing in People and Culture (IPC) 28
involvement of service users 23–8, 49–52, 104–6
  conceptualising 120–2
  in conferences 85–90
  development in the UK 117–18
  key principles 99–100
  with mental illness experience 67–9
  Norway 138
Irvine, J. 98, 105, 118
Italian students 97–8
Italy 98, 199, 233

J

Jagiellonian University 61–70
Jahnke, B. 112
Janik, J. 63
Japanese imprisonment 183
Jeffrey 105
Johannessen, A. 162
Johnson, K. 160, 165
joint activities 146
  joint seminars 110–13, 115, 228
  joint workshops 109–15
Jones, D. 90, 94
Jordan, B. 120, 123
'journey' through services 88
judges 31
  juvenile 192–3
Jungk, R. 14

K

Kaila, M. 227
Kant, Immanuel 210
Karbouniaris, K. 145
Karel de Grote University of Applied Sciences 2, 35, 38–9, 193, 199, 229
Kaszyński, H. 61, 64, 229
Keele University 33
Kendall-Raynor, P. 75
Kepiński, Antoni 62
key cards 17

Kinderpostzegels (Children's Stamps) 184, 186
King Baudouin Foundation (KBF) 175
Kloppenburg, R. 151, 153
Knevel, J. 150, 153
knife crime 90
knowledge 110, 183, 225, 235
  about 3–5, 19, 29–30, 37–8, 183
  and CoD 147, 154
  construction of 230–1
  co-production of 158, 159, 167–8
  production of 49–55, 133
  sharing 200–1
  types of 51, 52, 140–1, 183
  see also experiential knowledge
Knutagård, M. 23, 226
Kowalk, H. 37, 41, 44
Krakow 61
Kreber, C. 98
Kristiansen, A. 23, 43, 51, 226
Krumer-Nevo, M. 170
Kruse, E. 109
Kurdistan 29
Kvammen, F. 227, 235

L

Laging, M. 109, 113, 228
Laming, Lord 89–90
language 140, 147, 153, 199, 214
  and power 232
  of service users 67, 113, 136
Lave, J. 146
learning 128, 146, 230
  collective learning 149
  deep 76, 98, 105, 228
  empathetic 70–1
  experiential learning 33
  inclusive 145, 146
  rich CoD environment 151
  transformative learning 26
lecturers and experts 44
lectures 14
legal challenges 2
Le Var, R.M.H. 90
Levinas, E. 74
Levy, S. 97, 98, 99, 100, 228
LGTBQIA communities 77, 80, 81
librarians 79
life, loss of 179
life experiences 45, 114, 115
  differing 82
life stories 73, 227
'lifeworld' 74
Lillehammer University, Norway 26
listening 90–1, 93
  to service users 23
Lister, R. 170
literature study 13
lived experiences 1, 74, 88, 173

importance of 206
lives, control over own 37
Living Library 226, 231, 234
  Diaconia University of Applied Sciences 79–81
  Living Books 228, 233
  in social work education 73–9
  University of Sheffield 76–9
living situation 225, 226
Loeffen, T. 153
London Road 89
London Southbank University 26
London Underground 12
Louvain-Limburg 39–40
Lovell-Norton, J. 209
Lowry, P.B. 159, 165
Lund University 2, 20, 24, 49, 51–3, 235
  gap-mending 11, 12
  see also Mobilisation course
Lymbery, M. 88

M

Macauley, A.C. 133
Maciejewska, O. 66, 229
management model 18, 120, 205
marginalised people 11, 206, 233
Markstrom, A.M. 123
Marton, F. 76
'matching' service users 113
material circumstances 225
Mayer, J.E. 23
McIntyre, A. 210
McKeever, B. 1, 13
McKeown, M. 87
McLaughlin, H. 117, 133, 135, 140, 149, 158
  on ethical issues 215, 216
  on terminology 3, 14, 37, 49, 50, 98
McPhail, M. 97
media 183, 192, 193
medical education 1
medicalised model 203
meeting places 69
men 210
men and FGM 30
mental health 1, 110, 229, 234
  problems 11, 28, 81
  and social work education 61–9
mental illness 61
Merleau-Ponty, M. 74
methodology 113
migrants, working with 28
Miller, N. 19
Minkler, M. 135, 136
minorities 73, 80
Mjøsund, N. 137
mobilisation and participation 176
Mobilisation course 11, 224, 228, 232
model of social theory 124–5

morals 209, 211
  morally active practitioner 213, 220
  moral pluralism 212–13
Moreau, M. 226
Morgan, A. 90
Morgan, R. 26
Morris, K. 1, 118
Moulam, L. 209, 213
Mullaly, R. 226
  processes of 230
Müllert, N. 14
Murray, K. 225, 230
Murray, R. 148
music 124, 192

N

National Action Plan for Social Inclusion (NAPIncl) 36
Natland, S. 137, 162, 169, 209, 217, 229
Nazi doctors 209
Needham, C. 158
negative experiences 27
neighbourhood teams 36
Neil, E. 136
neoliberalism 205, 211
Netherlands 35, 36, 86, 184, 186, 194, 199, 227
Newman, A. 216
Nielsen, W. 227
Nolan, M. 135, 136, 140
non-judgemental 32
non-maleficence 210, 219
Northumbria University 33
Norway 26, 49, 54, 138
  social welfare system 160
Nowotny, H. 159, 168
Nowotny, O. 133
Nuremberg Code (1947) 209
Nyirenda, J.E. 100
Nylund, M. 227

O

object of research 51
older people 124
Oliver, M. 171, 173, 174
Olsson, M.R. 159
Omeni, E. 1
online platforms 95
Open Mind weeks 192–4
oppression 1, 122, 172, 174, 194, 203, 234
  forms of 183, 225, 226–30
  and forum theatre 188
  and the Living Library 74
organisational conditions 44–5, 203
Orosz, G. 75
Østensjø, S. 135
Ostrom, E. 18
'otherness', problems of 55–6

outcomes 26, 28, 32, 98, 119–20, 206, 232
  from CoD 151–2
  from EBE encounters 104–5
Owen, J. 140

P

Pardasani, R. 73, 80, 81, 227
parents 26–7, 110
participation 36, 176–8, 225
  participation paradigm 170
  participatory epistemology 167
  participatory society 36
  symbolic 134
paternalistic approach 171, 206
patients' resistance 70
pedagogical background 75–6
'pedagogy of discomfort' 98
peer review 118
Penn, D.L. 61, 105
people with lived experience (PWLE) 117
personal development 104, 225, 226
personal experiences 1, 37, 201, 225
personalisation 118
personal presentations 17, 228
personal transformation 233
Pettigrew, T. 12, 15, 16, 18, 19
Philips, A. 35
Phillips, L. 133, 139, 158, 159, 169
Phone Call, The 89
physical disabilities 11, 81
Pinar, M.P. 211
Platt, Dame Denise 24
play 124
Poland 61, 63, 199, 234
police 29, 32, 87
policy and policymaking 2, 6, 23, 170
  disability campaigns 171–4
  and *General Report on Poverty* 174–8
  in the Netherlands 35–7
politics
  political parties 175
  political power 121
  political sciences 120
  politics and welfare 160
Portsmouth Experience 119–20
Postle, K. 88
poverty 152
  anti-poverty policies 35, 36–7
  in Belgium 36–7, 175–8
  living in 171
  people in 170
  in Scotland 175
power 88, 110, 113, 121, 128, 225, 235
  and EBE 204–7
  and oppression 226–30
  power and change 120–3
  powerlessness 138
  power relations 159

in social work 49–50
and status 16–17
PowerUs network 11, 19, 20, 25, 26, 145
prejudices 12, 38, 98
Prison Reform Trust 89
problems 183
  personal 11, 28, 61, 149, 203
  problem-solving actions 147
  social 20, 49–52, 224, 226
professional development 28, 227
  professionals collaborating 89, 151–2
  professional strengths 228
professionalisation of service users 57–8
prostitution 89
psychiatric experiences 112
public funds, no recourse to 28
public sector 87
public services model 18
Putnam, R. 18

R

radical humanism 227, 233
radical Islamic groups 190
Rae, R.T. 49
Raineri, M.L. 98, 99, 105
Ramon, S. 2, 118
Rapp, C.A. 15
Reason, P. 147, 169
recategorisation 19
recovery 66, 70, 86, 112, 229
recruitment 38, 77, 87, 99, 112, 152–3, 215
redefining ourselves 171
Redfern, M. 210
reductionism 50, 58, 211
  emotional 68
reflection 201, 226
refugees 28, 77
relationships 98, 113, 148, 190, 205, 212, 220
  building 17, 27, 28–9, 32, 46, 136, 139–40
  building empathetic 62
  collaborative 162
  reciprocal 11, 19, 203
  relationship-based practice 93
  and research 217
  unequal 51
religious backgrounds 80
Repper, J. 93
research 2, 20–1, 136
  and CoD 145–7
  collaborative 158–67
  co-research 133–40
  and ethical issues 213–20
  governance 214–15
  historic ethical scandals 209–10
  researcher as outsider 161–3
respectful attitude, building a 45, 201

Rhodes, C. 1
Rigano, D.L. 159, 165
rights 32, 33, 37, 74, 184, 225, 235
  loss of 179
risk, avoidance of 209, 214
Ritchie, S.M. 159, 165
Riveria, W. 73, 80, 81, 227
Robinson, K. 2, 26, 97, 121
Robson, P. 25
Rochdale inquiry 89
Roets, G. 179
roles 12, 14–15, 16, 18
  intersecting 117
  role model 148
  role playing 41
Rooney, J.M. 86, 98, 105
Routledge Handbook of Service User Involvement in Human Services Research and Education 224
Ruch, G. 88, 93
Ryke, E. 15
Rynda, M. 64

S

Sackett, D.L. 51
safeguarding 27, 31–2
safe spaces 31, 68, 105, 149, 185
Säljö, R. 76
Scammell, J. 90
scholarships 30
Schön, U.-K. 1, 57, 202
school dropouts 184
Schütz, A. 74
scientific terminology 136
Scotland 24, 175, 233
  Scottish experts 97–8
Sedney, P. 37, 44, 199, 202, 205
self-advocacy 175, 176, 177, 179
self-awareness 100, 105
self-esteem 234
self-reflection 229, 230
self-reliance 36
Sen, R. 74, 75, 81, 82, 227
service users 2, 3, 14, 23, 27, 54, 57, 69, 235
  benefits of involvement 200–1
  and conferences 85–90
  co-operating with 61–5
  co-production with 117, 119–20
  as co-researchers 133–4
  and education and research 145
  and ethical issues 209, 215–18
  and joint workshops 109–15
  obstacles to involvement 202–5
  organisations 54, 56, 112
  pay of 51, 53, 77, 114, 134, 204, 217
  and policy making 171
  speaking at conferences 90–1
  as supervisors 49–58, 53

as tandem partners 35–46
sexual abuse 31
sexual preferences 227
Shakespeare, T. 118, 173
shame 37, 183, 194
Shaping Our Lives 23
Sheeran, Ed 89
Sheffield University 76–9, 82
single parents 110
Skilton, C.J. 97, 201
Skoura-Kirk, E. 118
Smith, M. 105
social, political and economic issues 225–6
social action 123
Social Care Institute for Excellence (SCIE) 25, 118
social education 61, 62, 64, 67
social forces, impact of 211
social innovation 148–9, 154
social justice 104, 145, 170, 206, 209, 213, 224
social pedagogy 123, 124–5
social policymaking and participation 170, 176–80, 224
social psychological theory 74
social services 23
   Norway 160
social stratification 76
social transformation 225
   commitment to 231–5
social work education 20, 24
   in Belgium and the Netherlands 36
   benefits of service user involvement 200–1
   and creativity 124–5
   gap-mending in the UK 23–8
   gap mending power relations 49–52
   and inspiring conversations 97–8
   and Living Libraries 73–9
   with mentally ill people 65–7
   obstacles to service user involvement 202–5
   service user involvement 2, 97–100, 104–6
   service users as tandem partners 35–46
Social Work Inclusion Group (SWIG) 119, 125–8, 234
social work students, voices of 102–4
soft skills 166
Soldatic, K. 174
speaking at conferences 90–1
Spencer-Dawe, E. 93
Spiesschaert, F. 35
sponsorship 91
Staffordshire University 33
Statham, J. 123
status 50, 68, 76, 150
Steel, R. 217
stereotyping 80, 81, 134, 229

stigmatisation 38, 68, 98, 145
   of mentally ill 62, 63, 66
Stoecker, R. 134, 140–1
strength-based social work 11, 38
Strier, R. 136
structural social work 224–5
structures
   and human agency 230–1
   and oppression 226–30
Stuart, P.H. 200
students 30
   with mental health experience 61–9, 65
Sudan 29
Suffolk murders 89
suicides 179
Sullivan, M. 139
supervisors 230, 235
   in social work education 49–58, 53
support for independent living 174
surviving 184
   survival techniques 194
   'survivors' 24
Sweden 11, 20, 49, 145, 199
   government funding 24
syphilis 210

T

taboos 183
tandem model 38–42, 145, 152, 226, 229, 232
Tanner, D. 1, 97
teaching 19, 42–4, 113, 118
Teeside University 29
tensions 5, 29, 134
tensions and dilemmas of research 136, 138
terminology 199
Tew, J. 120
theatre 120, 184, 188, 192
   forum theatre 183, 191, 232
Thomas, C. 173
Thompson, P. 231
Three Girls 90
Tilly, C. 19
Timms, N. 23
tokenism 104, 121, 125, 133, 170
   avoiding 93, 94, 138
   forms of 75, 202–3
Tortike, Har 183, 184, 186, 190, 194
Townsend, Peter 171–2
Tracy, F. 133
training 24, 49, 57, 63, 69, 112, 203
   for co-researchers 137–8
   transformative learning 26
trauma 81, 183
Tronto, J. 212
Tropp, L. 12, 15, 16, 18
trust 149, 228, 232
   and co-writing 158, 168

establishing 15, 17, 18, 25, 68, 136, 165
trusting relationships 98, 139
tuition fees 30
Turner, M. 51, 217
Tuskegee Syphilis Study 210

U

unconscious biases 75, 227
UN Convention on the Rights of Persons with Disabilities (UNCRPD) 174
Union of Physically Impaired Against Segregation (UPIAS) 171–3
United Kingdom 11, 73, 85, 89, 117, 210, 233
 CPAG 175
 Department of Health 24
 gap-mending in social work education 23–8
 and service user involvement 2
university credits 11, 13, 32
University of Agder 49, 235
 supervision at the 53–4
University of Applied Sciences Louvain-Limburg 39–40
University of Dundee, Scotland 98, 99
University of Groningen 187
University of Krakow 233, 234
 service users as people 231
University of Portsmouth 119–20, 125–8, 234
University of Sheffield 73
University of Suffolk 85–91, 93–4, 234
university research and social services 160–1
user involvement *see* involvement of service users
utilitarianism 211, 212
Utrecht University of Applied Sciences 41–2, 145, 187
Utschakowski, J. 112

V

Valentine, G. 76
values 37, 105, 224
 competing values 212–13
 values-driven culture 2, 36, 74, 80
Van Aken, J. 147
Van Bakel, M 154
Van Biene, M. 150
van Erp, N. 205
Van Gijzel, S. 151
Van Regenmortel, T. 39, 145
Vansevenant, K. 145
Van Slagmaat, C. 145
Vanspauwen, N. 37
Videmšek, P. 199, 202

videos and films 118, 119, 120, 183, 186, 192, 193
violation of rights 175, 176, 183, 184, 194, 201
violence 183, 189–90
virtual environments 95
virtue ethics 211–12
Vlaams Blok 175
voices 25, 28, 153, 234
 from Italy 102–4
 of poor people 170, 175, 176
 from Scotland 100–2
 of service users 2, 85, 125
 from SWIG 125–8
volunteers 40, 45, 78
vouchers 114
Vranken, Jan 36
vulnerability 17, 35, 110, 227, 232, 233
 of knowledge 203
Vygotsky, L. 123, 124

W

Wallcroft, J. 26
Wallerstein, B. 136
Walmsley, J. 160, 165
Waterson, J. 1, 118
Webber, M. 2, 26, 97, 121
welfare benefits 204, 217
welfare state 36, 171
Wenger, E. 17, 146
wilful deceit 210
Wilken, J.P. 98, 145, 146, 148, 150, 151
Wilks, T. 51, 53, 55
Witteveen, E. 148, 150, 151
Wolverhampton University 33
women 29, 30, 32, 168, 184, 190, 194
 violence against 183
Woodhill, J. 148
Woodward, R. 125
workshops 41, 64, 109, 113, 115, 183, 187
 and mental illness 65, 66, 68
 Netherlands Kinderpostzegels 186
 and young people 88
World Day Against Poverty 178
World War II 183, 209
Wright Nielsen, T. 4, 227, 235
Wroński, K. 63

Y

young people 81, 114, 183, 230
 in care 26, 28, 110, 186, 187, 188
 and forum theatre 191, 192, 194
 homeless 86
 and the Living Library 77
 school dropouts 184

www.ingramcontent.com/pod-product-compliance
Lightning Source LLC
Chambersburg PA
CBHW070916030426
42336CB00014BA/2440